“What do Men and Women really need from each other?”

by Brother Marcus

What is the true nature of a man and a woman?

From the Author who brought you,
"The Wise Men and Women Have Sent Me to Tell You"

To Sister Fonda,
"Love you and Appreciate you..."

This Book is dedicated to my faithful and loving life companion,
Sister Cecelia...
I love you and I thank Almighty God for your tremendous sacrifice
these last 20 years of my life to help me grow and to evolve into the
man that I am becoming. You are the wind beneath my wings....

Acknowledgements

I would like to sincerely thank Almighty God Allah, who came in the Person of Master Fard Muhammad to whom praise is due forever and His Christ, the Most Honorable Elijah Muhammad for their anointed servant in this day and time, the Honorable Minister Louis Farrakhan. I would truly like to also thank my beloved wife, Sister Cecelia and each of my children, Qurban Saleem, Qadeera Naasira, Qiyamah Sakeen, Qahir Kasib, Qamara Zaafira and Qaani Anwar. You have all sacrificed the most to help me to accomplish everything in my life that I am striving to do. I love all of you very much and thank you for loving me and putting up with me all of these many years!
I would also like to thank all of the brothers and sisters of the Nation of Islam who have guided my spiritual growth and development. I especially want to thank all of the believers in the Muhammad Study Group of Albany, Georgia, and Muhammad Mosque #15 with a very special thank you to
Brother Abdul Sharrieff Muhammad.
I have so many friends who have loved me and supported me from the first day that I met them. You know well who you are and I love you so much for being my extended family! Of course I would like to also give a very special thank you to my family in Brooklyn, New York and Jacksonville, Florida. I love you all and I am sincerely striving to be your servant.

Preface

Peace and Love and welcome to another Motivational Book from Brother Marcus and the Youth and Adult Intervention Services and Training Institute, Inc. I call myself **"Brother Marcus"** not that I am some kind of perfect brother. I have made many mistakes and errors in the past and I am still coming up out of the same mud that many other men and woman are coming up out of. In writing this book I don't believe I am better than anyone else is. I'm just trying to clean myself up. The light of the truth that I have accepted is gradually reforming me into a man of character and honor.

It is such an honor to sit down and pen this book, **"What do men and women really need from each other"**, to you my dear brothers and sisters. I wrote this book because I love you and I am striving to share with you what is yours by birthright. **None** of the knowledge, wisdom and understanding that I will strive to share and impart to you is from me. I honestly wouldn't know where to begin. I feel very, very blessed to tell you that I have been striving to be a student of the Honorable Minister Louis Farrakhan for the last 20 years of my life. I am totally unworthy to try and represent this man to you. But I thought that rather than trying to concoct something and put in a book like I came up with it, I would just share his wisdom directly with you, the reader. This book is just a piece of fruit from such a magnificent tree. It may be controversial but I don't mind that at all. The word **"contra"** only means **"against,"** and **"verse"** means **"your version of the truth."** I want you to see the wisdom of God that my teacher has been sharing with humanity all of these years as clearly as I am able to express it at this time.

We have never looked at ourselves as **"belonging to"** God; we only see ourselves in the light of what The Enemy, Satan and his devils, has made us to see ourselves: As **"ex-slaves"** or **"Black people of no worth or value or purpose in life."** The Enemy never taught us the true knowledge of who we are. We don't blame him because he was given power to rule us. He is just doing what he was made to do. My teacher shared that their time is now up and our time has come! God has come to bring us back to ourselves! We must now be introduced to our intrinsic nature; the essence that determines our character, which is God Himself. The meaning of **"character"** is **"the mental and moral qualities distinctive to an individual (human being)."** If our moral character and our mental character is of God, then we have to ask ourselves: **"What happened to us as human beings that our morals are not where God wants them to be? What happened to us that our mental qualities have been curtailed, brought down—or even killed? What happened to women and men that we are so far down and away from the essence of our own being where we, now, are not even a caricature of what God intended?"** All of us who are educated by our former slave masters and their children are trained in the educational system to conform to this world. We are trained theologically to conform to this world, and, those who find it difficult to conform are classified as social misfits who end up on drugs, in prison, or suffering an untimely death, but those who conform are the ones that society accepts and puts upon them a stamp of approval. How can there ever be a renewing of our minds except that something comes to our eyes and ears that does not come from the architects of this world?

It is written in the scriptures, **"Behold I make all things new. There will be a new heaven, a new earth and the former things shall pass away."**

This book will cut to the heart of the needs that both men and women have and the demand that nature has put in us both towards the other. **My teacher shares that we can't be a man without a woman and that a woman can't be a woman without a man. He further shared that it takes a good man to bring out the best in a woman and it takes a good woman to bring out the best in a man and that Almighty God has fixed it that way.** There is no getting around that. This is why this a principle based book and the principles are applicable to whatever religion we are claiming or lifestyle we might have chosen. I don't care if we profess to be Muslim, Christian, Jewish, Atheist, Catholic, Mormon, or believe in anything else, this book can help us if we would accept the truth upon which it is based. **My teacher shared from the Honorable Elijah Muhammad that we don't judge the commonness of religion by their names. We judge the commonness of religion by examining the principles that undergird them. If we can put the names of religion aside for a moment and look at the principles, we will find a common thread running through all the great religious expression.**

My teacher shared that the best yard stick to judge any action, plan, program or thought is to ask the question, does it strengthen the male and the female in their growth? Does it strengthen the bond of marriage and the integrity of family? The information contained in this book is meant to inspire self-analysis, self-examination and then self-correction. It will encourage, inspire and enlighten every man and woman who reads it and help you with your efforts to be a better husband and wife in this day and time.

Table of Contents

Chapter – 1 Our Greatest First Need

This particular book is an inspired work that we have prepared for with so much love and compassion for who we really are as a people. The purpose of this book is to motivate, uplift and inspire you to think more carefully about the things you are saying and are not saying and the things you are doing and are not doing concerning your spouse / partner. This book was inspired after forty years of research and observations and also working with men and women in workshops and hearing their heartfelt sentiment over the way they have been treated in their respective relationships. We ask that you read this book with an open mind. In this book are powerful observations and insights that may help you to look into your personal relationship situation and consider whether or not you are also having these same issues. There are many different things that influence the success or failure of Male / Female Relationships in this day and time. If you think for a minute that the success of your relationship is all about how you and your spouse or partner feel about each other then you may need to revise your thinking. This book will attempt to show how everything in this society impacts the relationship you are attempting to have with your spouse / partner. To help this book along I will be also be sharing many wise and powerful insights from many wise men and women on the various topics we address in this book. The information contained in this book is not meant to negate anything you have done, are doing or will do in the future in support of your spouse or companion. If you will adopt these ideas into your personal life and philosophy we guarantee that you will be more successful and happier in your marriage or relationship in the coming days, weeks, months and years of your life. We must all accept that family is the most important unit in the structure of civilized people and that family is the basis of Nations. When we have no real strong family we cannot have a strong community or a strong nation and the bedrock of family is marriage. There never was a time that so many of us have killed and abused one another as we are doing today. There never was a time when Black women were so abused and misused as they are today. There never was a time when Black children have been so abused and misused as we find them today. The violence and abuse in the home is so great that every teacher or leader of any consequence should begin to look at the destruction of the Black home, the Black family and the Black community and address these concerns with truth. Black male and female relationships are at an all time low. The Black female can hardly find her equal in the Black male to form a successful marriage and partnership. Therefore, the Black female may be more attracted to the white male and the male members of other races because of the inferior condition of the Black male.

If we do not know who God is in this day and time our relationships are doomed to failure. The Honorable Elijah Muhammad, for 44 years, taught us that God is not a mystery. He is not a spirit, He is not a spook, God is real. He is a real live human being, differing from you and me only in that he is Supreme in Knowledge, Wisdom, Understanding and Power. This is what The Honorable Elijah Muhammad taught us. Domestic Violence is once again on the rise in the black community. My teacher asked, **"Why are Black men beating women as women are being beaten today?"** Many wives who are married suffer because their husband beats you. There are many men in the various religious communities in this world who think that it is okay to beat their wives. My teacher also shared that this is not the conduct of a true man of Almighty God — beating women. A true man of God knows how to handle a woman without beating and abusing her. When you know then you have the advantage. The Honorable Elijah Muhammad said to my teacher, **"If you have to beat her, you should not possess her."** The problem today is that we, as men, have lost the knowledge of how to handle ourselves, so it becomes exceedingly difficult for us to handle our mate. Nature forces us to come together, but we don't know what to do with each other after we come together. We make each other's lives miserable, thus, wife beating is on the increase. We don't even want to say **"wife-beating,"** because men aren't marrying women that much today. Marriage is a dying institution. What is the cause of this? Not only is this happening in the Black community, it is happening on an increasing scale in the White community and in the community of so-called civilized peoples of the earth. Female abuse and child abuse are not only violent in terms of physical punishment, but sexual assault in the home is on the increase. Men are sneaking up on their own biological daughters and having sex with them in every community. Fathers are abusing their stepdaughters or beating and brutalizing their stepchildren who are male. Most often the males who are abusive to the children are not biologically related to the children but are in a relationship with the female head of the household. If the male lives there, it is usually temporary. His presence is then followed by a period of time when there is no male present; then a different male is brought into the home. This cycle creates confusion among the children as to the authority in the home and it creates resentment as well.

My teacher shared that when we open the Bible we see that Almighty God gave Adam all the trees to eat from except one. There is something in nature that, when we are told that we can do all of this but don't do that, then our curiosity is aroused. And because of his curious nature, Adam looked at all the trees that God gave him but his fascination was with that one that God told him to leave alone. Adam's disobedience led to his being cast out of the garden. And from that moment to this, the human being has really had problems in the family; problems in the tribe; and problems in the nation. If we march through the Bible, God becomes displeased with our conduct because we are following the lower self. My teacher shares that mastery of self is the key to mastery of all disciplines, because in some way every discipline is present within us. We have neglected the higher values, the higher calling. God says to us in the Bible, **"My ways are not your ways. My thoughts are not your thoughts. I am from above while you are from beneath."** God is showing us how far the gap is between Him and us. If we can draw our strength from God then we have an eternal source of strength. Satan and his devils intervention has caused us to live on a plane that is so far beneath God's thoughts and God's ways, and we are so deceived in our lifestyle. My teacher shares that in the past, we have been looking at Satan as a spirit. But spirits can't deceive us. Every spirit is in something of material. If we've ever been deceived, we've been deceived by somebody with a bad spirit. Our so called 'lifestyle' is actually a 'death style' because it was given to us by Satan and his devils. The Bible says that there is a way that seemeth right unto the man but the ends thereof are the ways of death. In God's love of Himself and respect for Himself and respect for the higher ideals that He created us to live in accordance with, He challenges us in our wickedness to change.

We do not know enough about each other. As a man, just because you grew up with a mother, some aunties and some sisters doesn't mean that you know all there is to know about women. As a woman, just because you grew up with a father, some brothers and some uncles doesn't mean that you know all there is to know about men. We still have a great deal to learn about the opposite sex. Please do not arrogantly approach this book thinking that you will not learn anything. One of the reasons our relationships may not be working out so well is because we have approached our spouses / partners with the **"I already know"** attitude. We may have given them the **"you can't tell me nothing"** spirit. We have to learn the value of humility in dealing with each other. There are still many wonderful lessons that your spouse or partner has yet to teach you.

My teacher, the Honorable Minister Louis Farrakhan, has shared many profound truths with us from his teacher, the Honorable Elijah Muhammad. One day he shared that unless God is real in your life then you and your spouse will soon tire of one another. One of the signs of the decline of a civilization is its divorce rate. When you look at the divorce rates and statistics in America, you will find that over 50 percent of those who marry get divorced and many times the divorce happens within the first three years of their marriage. This is not a healthy sign for the American family as a whole. *The family is the basic unit of civilization. A strong family makes a strong nation. A weak family weakens the nation.* It's easy to find grounds for divorce but for some it's hard to find grounds to stay in the process of becoming married. In the marriage process, being the right person is as important as finding the right person. My teacher has shared that, **"Self Improvement is the Basis of Community Development."** It is the improvement of each of us as human beings that is lacking in the world and in our marriages, and instead of human beings and our marriages improving, they are degenerating. The Great Roman Empire did not collapse from without, it collapsed from within. Moral degeneracy means that people are being made to believe that they have the right to do whatever they want to do in disrespect of self and others, in the name of freedom of speech and the freedom to be and do as they please. Many times in relationships we are looking for perfection and there is no perfection to be found outside of God.

A few years ago, there was much discussion about the nuclear family. A nuclear family is one where there is a first time husband and wife and from their union they produced three children. Generally the husband is the breadwinner and the wife is the homemaker in the nuclear family scenario. Did you know that in America today, there are less than 10% of families like this left? It has been estimated that seventy percent of all black households are headed by a single black female. In fact, the fastest growing family unit in the United States is the single parent family. Family life in America has to be reconstructed. Over the last five decades there has been a disintegration of the American family and most definitely the black family. The disrespect of marriage as a basic institution instituted by the Creator, cannot lead to the respect of women, the respect of children, and the respect of family life.

What are husbands and wives really arguing about in such a terrible time on our planet as this? Why can't we get along and make each other's lives as peaceful as we can? It is so very, very simple. We have allowed this world to pervert every natural, pure and beautiful relationship and turn it into something unnatural, unwholesome and so unfulfilling. The first need that every human being has is for his / her Creator. You and I need the active and immediate presence of our God in our lives like we need air. The only way to gain a true perspective on oneself is through a proper relationship with God. We should never confuse our great need for our God with our need for our husbands or our wives. My teacher once shared with us that, **"If there was no God then men would worship women."** Isn't that profound! One of the first things I would like to share with you, if you don't already know, is that there is a Mighty and Magnificent God for us as men and husbands to give our sincere worship and praise to. He is not a God! He is the one true and Living God that is known to us by many different names and all of the names of God are good. As handsome and beautiful as men and women are today, none of us are worthy of worship. Only the true and Living God, the sovereign Lord, Ruler and Sustainer of the Universe is who we should find in our lives and offer Him our sincere and complete obedience in this terrible day and time that we live in. Because we have neglected this first, foundational relationship with our Creator, which is our greatest need, this is why our relationships with His other creatures have not worked out to well.

My teacher shared with us what Almighty God shared in the Bible, **"For my thoughts are not your thoughts, neither are your ways my ways, saith the Lord. For as heavens are higher than the earth, so are my ways higher than your ways, and my thoughts than your thoughts." Isaiah Chapter 55, Verses 8-9** These words being addressed to the people of God manifest how far off the mark the people are from that which God intended the human being to be. In the Holy Qur'an, the 113th Chapter, Verses 1-2 reads, **"Say: I seek refuge with the Lord of the Dawn, from the mischief of created things." My teacher shared that** this verse teaches us that natural things created by Allah (God) are used by Satan to create mischief. The male and the female are far beneath God's intentions for us. The institution of marriage and the resultant family are far beneath what God's intentions are for us. As hell is beneath heaven, and, Satan is beneath God, this being the world of Satan, these scriptures are teaching us that Satan has been and is the director of the lives of most human beings, and, has taken the natural order and creation of Allah (God) and has made mischief with God's creation. Therefore, we are far beneath the high thought and purpose of our creation; and our marriages, for the most part, represent hell. Therefore, our communities and nations universally have a hellish existence. What are Allah's (God's) thoughts and ways for human beings, for the institution of marriage, and, for the development of family? His thoughts and His ways are found in the nature of what He created. Let us then look into the Bible and Qur'an to find Allah's (God's) purpose for the male and the female and His purpose for marriage, and His purpose for family.

This book is going to ask you to confront some things you may not be willing to confront. I believe that many of us love God but I do have a couple of questions. **"Why don't we love God more? Why don't we love God enough to obey Him more? Why don't we love Him enough to follow His will and His ways?"** My teacher shared with us that our problem is that we have not fully known God's will. We are in the House of an alien or enemy of God's will that has taught, shaped and molded us in rebellion against God. So even though we praise God with our lips, our hearts are far removed from Him, not because we want to be removed from Him, but our ignorance does not allow us to know His will clear enough that we may do that will. Why have so many of us allowed this so – called society to reduce God and our expression of love for Him to a mere Sunday morning Church / Temple / or Mosque service manifestation? The Bible says Adam is the first man made by God, and He made him from the dust of the earth. He made him, according to the Bible, in His own image and likeness. Every man and women that we see here on this earth is made in the image and likeness of God. When God made Adam, he gave Adam what? He gave him *the way*. He wouldn't put Adam in The Garden and not give him the way. He didn't give him a religion, he gave him the way. What way did he give Adam? God said to Adam: **"I made all of this that you see in five days, and I said it was all good; and I made you on the sixth day. Later on I said it was not only good, but *very good*. But with you, I'm giving you a chance to choose. I'm not making you like the sun. The sun can't disobey, neither can the moon, nor the stars, nor can the creatures disobey"—they all follow the nature in which God, created them."** Adam was given free will and Adam rebelled against the way. What was and what is the way of God? **"Obey My Will."** Obedience to God is The Way. Not a religion by this name or that name or the other name. Obedience to God is the way and because Adam rebelled, the scripture said, **"Death came on all men because all have sinned."** Sin is rebellion or transgression against the law.

My teacher shared from The Bible that God made the woman and brought her unto the man. In this case, God was the *Perfect Matchmaker,* for, He made the man; He knew what He put in the man; and, He knew what the man would need to complete his make. So, God joined these two in marriage and declared that a man should leave his mother and father and shall cleave unto his wife and they shall be one flesh. This indicates that if man and woman in marriage are to become one flesh, in them shall also be one mind and one spirit. This is what presents the difficulty-making the two of one mind. The Scripture says that what God puts together let not man (the man of sin) put asunder. Satan's world desires to separate a good man from a good woman and vice versa, and, he certainly desires to separate believing Muslims or Christians from their Head which is Muhammad, the Mahdi, the Christ Figure or the Messiah. These are not three or four different persons that the three monotheistic religions are looking for; it is really two human beings under the title of Mahdi and Messiah. These titles tell us of the great work that they are to perform. We are to be called out of this world to be married or wedded to this Messianic Figure. We begin the language of mathematics with the number *one*. We begin our journey into the knowledge of God by declaring that He, Allah (God) is *One*. We begin the real journey of life through the institution of marriage when we declare our desire to become as *one*. Since Allah (God) is *One*, the universe is *one*, the only way that marriage can be successful is for the man and woman to strive to become as *one*. For the man to see the woman only as an object of pleasure or to further him in procreation is only partially seeing the purpose of Allah's (God's) creation for the female. The strengthening of the union of the male and the female in the institution of marriage is the best preparation for the production of family.

In Genesis, the first chapter, the 26th verse it says, **"And God said let us make man in our image and after our likeness."** In the 5th chapter of Genesis it says, **"Male and female created He them, and called their name Adam."** So both men and women are made in the image and the likeness of God. The Holy Qur'an, which is the religious book of Scripture for Muslims, teaches us that both male and female have the same essence or come from the essence or being that is Allah, the All Wise God. He has given both male and female complimentary natures which, if acted on properly help each mate to attain to fulfillment, perfect peace, and full development or perfection. The woman is a part of man: therefore, for a man to mistreat, abuse, disrespect or to be unkind to her is really to be all of that to ourselves. My teacher shared that Almighty God created nothing in His **"image"** or **"likeness"** but the *human being*, so how could we be **"in His image"** and **"after His likeness"** and not have His Divine Nature? To **'make'** and to **'fashion'** is the same thing. When we are fashioning something, it means it's already here, we're just putting our idea on it and to make something, we didn't create the essence, the essence is already here. What we did was use our wisdom to make it into what we wanted. What is the *essence* of something? According to the dictionary, the essence of a thing is the **"intrinsic nature,"** or **"indispensable quality"** of that thing; especially something abstract that determines its character. Here's God, now, creating a human—the first human—from a *single essence*; and creating the woman of the same. If God created us from the same essence, then what is that essence that determines our character? The essence of us is God Himself. ***The essence, that which determines our character, is our connection to The Creator of the heavens and the earth, Who is also your and my Creator.*** My teacher shares that if we really want to know what's in the mind of somebody, we should check out what they make. Scholars can read us by what we produce. Well, how do we know God is God? We only have to look at what He created. When we look above our heads, and we see the sun, moon, and stars, the birds, the bees, the fish, the trees, we say, **"Whoa, what a mighty Creator this is."** He forces us, even if we don't know who He is. He forces us to say, **"This is magnificent."**

God is going to make a man. If He's going to make him, He wants to put something in him that makes him greater than the sun. **"What do we mean greater than the sun?"** According to the scriptures of the Bible, man, and this doesn't mean just male, it means female too, is the glory, not a glory, the glory of God. As men, we have to confront the tremendous amount of sexism that is sitting up inside of us as men. How could we be **"the Glory of God,"** and not have within us Gifts from Him that will manifest His Presence? When we walk, God Walks! When we talk, God Talks! When we fight, God Fights if you are connected to God! The aim of The Enemy, Satan and his devils, is to disconnect the people from The Source of their Power, their Strength, their Wisdom, their Knowledge, and their Life. So we need a Teacher, we need somebody to give us Guidance. I am offering you all of these things from my teacher. In the Qur'an which is the book of Scripture revealed to Prophet Muhammad, Peace be Upon Him, for the guidance of the human community, God calls man the crown of Creation. Man is not man without woman. Male and female, man and woman, have the power of God. No matter what a woman's race, color or ethnicity, they have unfortunately never looked at themselves as a part of The Divine. Human beings start as animals and then we rise to humans. The highest level of human development is the reflection of Divine. When everything is lost, the degenerative process begins. Once you are deprived of what it takes to be human to reflect the Divine, then the animal in the human manifests itself. Man and woman is the crown of God's creation. Man and woman is the supreme existence but since God created man first and woman from man. The Holy Qur'an teaches that Allah (God) created the male a degree above the female. A degree is a stage in a scale of rank or station. My teacher shared that God was not trying to show off supremacy, but somebody has got to be the boss and somebody has got to be the head. Some men reading this might say that, **"My wife is the head in my house."** Well if your wife is the head in your house, you need to work on your head a little bit more as a man. God intended for the man to be in authority over the female. This is why He created him a degree above the female. **Otherwise the woman would not be able to look up to us.** Anytime a husband has a wife that does not look up to him he's in real trouble! Satan and his devils have created so much mischief with the nature of the male and the female that there is a prophecy in the Bible that says, **"The younger shall rule the elder and the weaker shall rule the stronger ... women shall rule over them."** In this sick, twisted society, the Black female in today's society literally is several degrees above the male. She is manifesting superiority in education and in the work force. Whereas the Black male for the most part is unemployed, most of our educated females are working and generally making more money than the male, and, in many instances is providing for the man that lives with her. So, we can say that Satan and his devils have reversed the roles that Allah (God) intended for the Black man and woman demonstrated in our relationship to each other.

We may not want to believe this in this modern day and time but God made women to look to us as men. It's a hell of a thing that some women have never found one man in this whole world to whom they could look to and depend on. One of the lines the great and beautiful Mariah Carey sang in her song, **"We Belong to Together"** was **"Who am I going to lean on when times get rough..."** After putting the last 20 years of my life into the process of marriage I can bear witness that times can get pretty rough. There are so many times when you are not sure what to do. Bills are constantly due and the pressure is always on a man to produce and to provide for his family. Many men have felt during those times that they have had no one to turn to even as everyone in the household is looking to them. As men, we have to know that Almighty God made the female to look up to us, to respect us and to honor us, as men. But this wicked and evil world that we live in has made the female to look down on us because the world has taken from us our crown as men. So we are not the crown of creation in reality, we are nothing to what we once were or what we were created to be. We as men have taken our crown and cast it away and now in a Universe filled with knowledge, wisdom and understanding all some want to be taught as grown men is, **"Can you teach me how to 'dougie'!"** I am so pleased to share with you that our God has come and He wants to put our Crown back on our heads and return we, the despised and the rejected, to true power!

Now let's get back to this sun! The sun is bad, but it's not the glory. The moon is great, but it's not the glory. The stars and mountains are magnificent, but they're not the glory. The greatest of God's creation is the human being, male and female. We are the best of what God has ever produced! So we are called **'the glory.'** So what He put in us, if we let it come forward, it makes the sunlight diminish in its brightness. And you know there's no light out there the equal of the sun, but what He put in us as His **"special creation"**, to reflect Him, will make the sun look like darkness, if we only understood who we really are. If we knew who we were we wouldn't want to be anything but who we are. If we understood the true value of a man and a woman then we wouldn't try to be other than ourselves. If we understood the value of who we are then we would look for the tools that would enable us to be what we are. And since this world has not provided us with the tools to be real men and women of God then God is justified in saying again to us in this modern day and time, **"Let us make man. Let us make him again, but this time let us make him in the image and likeness of God"** because this world has made nothing out of us of good! Let's agree on truth. We don't have to resist God re-making us over.

Very few of us believe that there is really anything spectacular or even special about us. We probably feel this way because we have had such a small amount of personal cultivation of the divine essence of God, our mutual Creator. Because of this lack of cultivation there are so many black men out here that are psychologically immature when it comes to conducting a healthy relationship with a woman. Some men have been brought up to believe and see women as **'things'** to be manipulated rather than the Creatures of God to be cherished. This is also very true of black women today. Some women could care less about a man in this day and time and view him as nothing but a tool to be used and discarded. We are going to have to confront this mistaken belief system. God is real brother and sister! We don't have to say to Him, **"Don't make me over."** I have very unfortunate news to share with you. *We are going to be made over in this day in time one way or another, willingly or unwillingly.*

Every man who has been made in the image and likeness of God has the potential to be a God. God didn't just make Adam in His image and likeness, but my teacher pointed out that God gave him power and dominion. No man was made by God to be powerless. So why do we, as men, refer to ourselves as powerless? If we are creatures of God then we have power. What's happening is in the way we think, our power is so confused and misused, it's like there's a short in a wire. We get a burst of light, but it's not hooked up right so it can't do its job. The power is there, but there's a short in the wire. The power is there, but the thinking is not right. We have the power, but we don't know that we have it. The first thing God gave man was power, and the second thing He gave him was dominion. Every man, in order to be what God wanted us to be, has to be given power, then dominion. Dominion means rulership. A man that has been given power by God is not given that power to lie down and do nothing. No man can be happy being non-productive. My teacher has observed that our women are hurting. They're hurting, really because we're hurting, and we're hurting and don't even know why we're hurting, because we're not producing. God is a ruler, and God uses power to create, and to rule, and master what He creates. So the question then is, **"What does God want man to rule? What does God want man to have power and dominion over?"** It's simple. It's written in the Scriptures. God wants to give man power and dominion over the fowl of the air, the fish of the sea, and every creeping thing that crawls upon the earth. Man is supposed to be the ruler. Man is not only supposed to rule fowl, and fish, and creeping and crawling things, man is supposed to rule his own house, man is supposed to rule his own community, his own nation, and master the earth. This beautiful life that God has fashioned is capable of not only coming from the womb of our mothers' weak and helpless, but is capable of coming from a weak, helpless state that once was nothing to speak of, to become a master. Not only of the environment but a master of the earth, and a master of the heavens above and a master of the laws that govern creation. Every man has the potential to become master of his environment, master of the earth, master of the laws that govern universe. All of us as men and women have that potential. In every man is the innate desire to rule in his own domain. Each and every man is to be a ruler. **Not some men but all men!**

The reason I share this with you is unless we know, totally accept and believe these kinds of powerful, magnificent governing truths from the core of our beings then we won't even attempt to reflect our Creator. A man **can't** be made in the image and likeness of God and then remain a demon. No, that's so contrary. God's actions are godly. When human beings act godly that means that human being are thinking on a higher level. This is not mind boggling information. Mind boggling means mentally or emotionally exciting or overwhelming. Once we know who we are as men then we will know what we should expect from ourselves, then we have to make up our minds to be who we are which is little gods on the planet. Not the big God, but a god with a little **"g"**. I sincerely hope that by the time you finish this book that you will see that both the man and the woman are wonderful creatures and that both are from Almighty God.

My teacher shared that the reason this great knowledge from God that we have been talking about is placed in the Bible in a chapter called Genesis is because in the word Genesis is the word genes. God wants us to know that these instructions are written in our genetic coding. We were born with power. We were born to rule. The command of God to us as men is also, **"Multiply, replenish the earth, subdue it."** These are commands that are right in our nature. When God created man and woman, He gave them assignments. He didn't tell us **"go to the nightclub," "hang out in the bar," "get drunk and fornicate."** He gave us instructions that come out of the very nature of our creation: *"Be fruitful and multiply."* What do you think that means? If He created the cattle, and they reproduce cattle; the birds reproduce birds, the fowl reproduce fowl, the beasts of the field reproduce beasts of the field, what did He create "man and woman" to do? Well, as with everything else that He created, He created the human being to reproduce themselves! But if we are in the image and the likeness of God, then He, too, is being reproduced every time we properly reproduce! Multiply doesn't just mean use for us as men to go out here and make a whole lot of babies. Multiply also means whenever we have a multiplicand and a multiplier we produce a product, and every man, by nature, is born to be a producer. If we are not productive, our life is going against the nature in which we were created by our God. Some men don't even know why they get angry and are upset and filled with stress. Maybe it is because God is commanding us in our nature to multiply and we are only obeying the commandment in the basest way. Just look at all the children in our communities! They are a witness that at some point we were present in the lives of their mothers. We certainly have been multiplying in the basest sense of the word. The police may have taken one gun away from us, but we have another gun that we have been firing at will! We're multiplying so fast, those students of demography or the study of population growth say that by the year 2056, Black people in America will be either equal to or greater in number than white people. And our Mexican family are working very hard to out-do us!

When we have a community full of black men who don't have jobs and are possessed of undeveloped minds to create job for ourselves, it's very difficult for them to stay in homes that constantly remind us of our impotence. So we flee the home. Many black men have been married, had children. Many men not only get divorced from their wife but they also divorce their innocent children. When we act like that as men our children suffer because now they have no stable relationship with a man. In this day and time men are just abandoning and neglecting their children. My teacher has shared that abandonment is a form of abuse. Because we make babies we have a responsibility. But if we don't have a job and no way to make a dollar, then men don't want to stay there and face that fact. So we leave the woman. We are out of the picture, but the sex drive doesn't diminish because we don't have a job. In fact, the sex drive may increase because every avenue of pleasure is closed to us except the avenue of sex. This is terrible. Today, most black men live in their dreams. Look at the way we dream. How many of men have had dreams and in the dream we were doing very great things? Our dreams are manifestations of our hopes and desires, and if our desires are frustrated and we cannot fulfill our personal dream, then something inside of us makes us very upset, angry and stressed, because we're not doing what we are born to do. Our dreams are indications that we can achieve, but reality has not allowed us to achieve. So we're frustrated. How do we take off our frustrations? Some of us go right back out into the community to work off the stress of being non-productive men.

"Hey Mama, come here baby." All some of us can do is talk about our sexual exploits. And five minutes after it's done, and we're done, and our dreams are still there, unfulfilled. So we run from one woman to the next. **"I'll try this cookie and take a bite out of it— damn that tastes good! Let me try this one!"** Like a dog in a meat house, biting off of every damn piece, spoiling it and none of it satisfies our taste, because a woman was not created to satisfy our appetite for greatness. She was created to help us to achieve it. My teacher shared that God gave us sex. As men and women, we find so much pleasure in the underworld, from the navel down, in our pleasure centers. Sex has become the instrument of pleasure, so our enemies, Satan and his devils can feed us AIDS through our instruments of pleasure. They have also crafted drugs that are so diabolical that when they touch the pleasure centers of our brains, we do not even want food or sex as pleasure. The drug is a higher pleasure. We are a people in pain in a world where there is no justice, no equality under the law and no freedom to become what God has put within us. This is our pain trying to fit into a system that is diametrically opposed to the very nature in which you were created. Yet, they call this a democracy. He didn't give us sex as a means of destruction of ourselves; he gave us sex as a means of procreation of self because we are not made in this body to live forever. So he created everything according to the Holy Qur'an in pairs. We may not know this but *the grass is male and female.* The tiniest of atoms are male and female. The scientists are discovering particles of matter that they call a quark, but they too are in pairs. We are male and female because each of us must die but the human species must live. Sex was given to us so that when man and woman sees each other and finds each other attractive and they come close to each other and they love each other and feel a need for each other they begin to repeat the Genesis. They ultimately say, **"Let Us Make Man in our image and after our likeness".** My teacher shares that as men from this day forward we should not make merchandise of our women and girls. We should treat them with respect and honor even if they don't deserve it because underneath all of their foolishness, they are God's child. Even after the sex act is completed Almighty God keeps saying over and over in the Holy Qur'an for men and women to, **"Keep your duty!"** Keep your duty not to your wife or your husband first, but **"keep your duty to your Lord."** Greatness comes from bowing down in complete submission to the will of God. And that's why our women and our wives don't satisfy us as men.

Men who have a purpose in their lives have to be producers. My teacher shares that the time is now to do for self. We must unite, pool our resources and become producers. We need to be disabused of the thought that our president can create enough jobs for our millions of unemployed. Satan and his devils still have control over Black people, and they do not intend to let us go. They are holding Black people in their grip even though they do not have anything for us to do. We are unemployed, without any outlook for a job. They have closed their society to Black people. We suffer from a lack of health care, bad education, the worst quality of food, drugs and guns. The Honorable Elijah Muhammad said, **"As long as we are consumers and employees, our future is in the hand of somebody else."** Think about this: If 40 million of us could put $1/month in a National Treasury, we could buy land and produce our own jobs and not have to beg Satan and his devils to do for us what we could get up and do for ourselves! That's the only way our souls can be satisfied. I'm very sorry to tell you this but the woman can't make you happy like that. My teacher has shared that productive work will make us happy; when we can see our visions and our dreams come alive!

We can't call God our Father and don't grow up one day to be like our Father. In the Bible, David the Psalmist said, **"Ye are all Gods; children of the Most High God."** My teacher shared that we all talk about God, certainly we love Him and we bear witness that He is the Greatest. We live in His Universe. There is nothing to compare with it, so there is nothing to compare with Him. But Who is He? We want to know our Creator, we want to know God. Whatever our religious persuasion may be we have to know today Who God is that we will not make a mistake and serve other than Him. The Bible teaches us that God breathes, sorrows, sees and hears, and loves and hates. The Bible teaches us that the stench of wickedness reaches His nostrils. The Bible teaches us that Abraham met God in the plains of Mamre. Three men came to Abraham and the Bible declares that one of them was the Lord. Sarah came out of her tent and said, **"Lord, if I found favour, pass not away. Lord, if you are hungry, I will feed you. Sit down, Lord, it you are tired."** How can you feed a spirit? How can you sit down if you have nothing to sit down on? It says that Enoch walked with God. Moses walked with Him and spoke with Him face to face as a man speaketh to his friend. All throughout the Bible, we are taught of a man, not some spook or formless spirit. My teacher asks, **"What about the Holy Qur'an?"** The Holy Qur'an uses the personal pronoun **"I"**. The **"I"** belongs to whom? It uses the soft pronoun **"We"**. Does God have associates? Does He have partners? Why say **"We"**? God Himself revealed the book and knows best the language. Why did He use the language of a human being? Who is God? The Attributes in the Holy Qur'an are not the Attributes of a Spirit, they are the Attributes of man in whom the Spirit dwells. Allah is the Beneficent, the Merciful, the Powerful, the Life-Giver, the Sustainer, the Securer, the Destroyer.

My teacher shares that we can't compare with the divine Supreme Being, but in our sphere, each of us is a god, having force and power. That's what makes us greater than the sun, because the sun can't think, it can't plan, it can't vision and bring into existence what it visions, but we have that potential. We have power, but our power is all screwed up because of the way we think. We are the original people of God, and we are created from a single essence, and our mate is from the same essence. So we are not just family from the same mother, but we are family from the same God. Because I have been taught and now believe this, I refer to myself as Brother Marcus. To me, you are truly my brother or sister and I am truly yours. **My teacher has guided my thinking to make a pact with you that I will give my life for you, because my life is not more important than yours. You are greater, I am lesser.** I must become your servant, and we must grow and mature to see our people like that. When your brother or sister is down, that's you. Help pick him or her up. *We should never allow different colors, or religion, or creed or belief systems to make us feel that we are different people.* My teacher has shared that when he looks at us, he doesn't have to wait to see the Father…that he sees the Father in us. We don't have to wait until we see the Lord of the worlds! If we treat each other right, then we are treating each other the way we would respect God. When we look at each at our wives and husbands we are really looking at God. I remember when I first met my teacher in person and I was trying to tell him how honored I was to meet him. And he smiled so beautifully at me and said, **"It's my honor, brother, to meet you."** And I looked at him and said, **"How are you honored to meet me?"** And he said, **"Because when I meet you, I'm meeting a person that has never been on the earth before, and there will never be one quite like you ever, ever again. So when I see you, I have to treat you like I would honor God. I have to respect each human being. I have to respect you, brother. Even though you don't know who you are, I know, and because I know, my duty is to honor and respect you."**

My teacher went on later to share with us that we should have that spirit and frame of mind even with our little children. Yes, they are little babies but soon they will hopefully grow to be mighty men and women so we should start respecting them when they're in the cradle. We should start respecting them when we see the woman forming the child in the womb. Almighty God created everything out of the Dark Womb of Space—*everything*; and He gives a woman a womb that resembles the Darkness of Space out of which everything is created. Man doesn't have a womb—it's *given to the* woman. And what is her womb for? Her womb is the Workshop of God. Every king, every ruler, every prophet, every wise man or woman, every scientist, every general, every person of value came through The Womb of a Woman. The Most

Precious Womb was the Womb of Mary. Her womb was the Worship of God because God from her womb produced that one which would reconcile the whole of humanity back to Himself. The womb is a special place. My teacher shares that we should not wait until the child gets here in the world. No man, who's a real man, will beat a woman. No man, who's a real man, will disrespect a woman, because it's through woman that we live. If we live to be the age of Methuselah, which is nine hundred sixty nine years, we're still going to die. So how do we continue in this world as men? We continue through a woman. So when she says, **"I love you,"** if she means it from the depth of her heart she's saying, **"I want to give life to you. I want to extend your life by my love."** So you and she enter into a contractual arrangement that is from divine, and after nine months, she suffers the pain of death to give birth to you all over again. So as a man who has a child, if you love God, and love yourself, when you see yourself growing again, you have a chance to make that life better than you were made. **As men we have to overcome this sick, ego driven crap that we have in our hearts and minds about women. The ignorant, immature and juvenile way we have handled our women has affected them greatly.** In the Bible it says, "God is Love". The very creative force behind all that you see is Love. We as men as well as our women are possessed with the power to love. My teacher shared that where there is no love in a woman for what she is producing within her then she cannot produce a child in the image and likeness of God. So it behooves a man to work the field and the field here is the woman's mind. A man has to cultivate her natural ability to love. We should never even think of planting our seed into her before we do that. The worse thing a man can do is try to find his way to the secret part of his woman before he finds a way to cultivate that woman's natural love for him. That's why sex is not first; it is last. It is the culmination of a love developing. And it is not a base expression; it is the highest expression of two people who genuinely love one another. And when we genuinely love each other and when God and your woman bless you as a man and that new life comes, it's like a potter's clay. We can shape it, we can mold it and we can make it something of great value and worth.

This is why we need to understand Jesus so bad in this modern day and time! Man has fallen way down. In the Book of John it is written, **"God is a spirit, and those that worship Him must worship Him in spirit and in truth, for such the Father seeketh."** Jesus didn't say, **"I'm seeking worshippers."** He said, **"The Father is seeking."** So when the disciples said, **"Master, teach us how to pray."** He didn't say, **"My father which art in heaven."** He told them say it like this, **"Our father..."** What do we mean **'Our Father'?** Didn't you have an immaculate birth? Didn't God come down from heaven and get into

Mary? How could He be 'Our Father,' when my father lay down with my mother, and my mother gave birth to me from the sperm of a man? How could God be your father and my father? Well, Paul gives answers to this question in the Book of Romans. Paul says, **"Jesus was the seed of David according to the flesh, but he was declared to be the Son of God according to the spirit of holiness."** Now let's reason with this. David was a natural man, who gave conception to children in a natural way. Since we have a body from the earth, and Jesus had a body from the earth, he had to have a father from the earth to father his earthly body. But Jesus was more than earth.

I have learned so much more about Jesus from my teacher. Before I met my teacher I thought I knew and really loved Jesus. I did, I loved his name. My mother made me love Jesus! She played Gospel music so much and we went to Church so much that I hungered for Jesus even as a young boy. The way the Gospel Artists sang about Jesus formed grooves on my mind. They described Jesus to me through their songs as a friend to the friendless, a home for the homeless and water for the thirsty. I had an expectancy that if I lived righteously that I would be with Him one day. But I only knew his name, I didn't know his face and I didn't know who the person of Jesus was but I was looking for him. In church I mostly listening to what the preacher said. I wasn't reading for myself and I certainly didn't understand too much back then. His sweet, Holy Spirit was enough for me. I attended a Holiness Church where people would get the **"Holy Ghost"**. Sometimes I would be in Church and the Pastor would say that the Holy Ghost was in the building. Folks would start falling out everywhere in the Church. This Holy Ghost was something else. He jumped into this person and that person and their body just went to running and jumping up around the Church. Everyone seemed to be able to **"catch"** the Holy Ghost but me! I was happy that others could catch him but why didn't the Ghost want to come inside of me I wondered as a little boy? When I met the Honorable Minister Louis Farrakhan, I met my father. No he didn't physically father me, that honor belonged to my blood father, Joseph Arthur Girard. But I can say to the world that my teacher fathered me into knowledge, wisdom and understanding. He brought out of me what The Creator had put in me for the service of my people. If I am anything of value today, it is because I have a good father, a good example and a good teacher. **He shared that the secret to our rise as a people is the unveiling of the Jesus that is on the scene today.** He taught me to read the Bible for myself and look at all of the text and not just some parts. Once I began to read for myself I now know a whole lot more about this most important man, Jesus and I now love him enough to try and follow him. My teacher shares that the Four Gospels tell us about Jesus - *not* the Jesus of today, but the historical Jesus who spoke in parables. This

Jesus spoke in parables so that the people would get a picture of The Future through the parable. The Honorable Elijah Muhammad said 75 percent of what we read in the scripture for Jesus is about a Future Man that comes at The End of The World of Satan and his devils! When I understood that my teacher was not some **"appointed"** man by Satan and his devils to lead black people **but in fact was the man that Almighty God has** *anointed* **to preach the Gospel to our people and to the ends of the Earth. When I met my teacher I had finally met the man I was looking for all the days of my life!**

My teacher shares that the word **"Messiah"** is well-known to Christians and Jews. The word **"Mahdi"** is well-known to Muslims. The world is looking for the return of Jesus Christ. The Jews are looking for the **"Messiah"** and the Muslim world awaits the appearance of the **"Mahdi"**. They are all looking for a man. If the **"Messiah"** comes, are we looking for a spirit to come out of a closet? We are looking for a man. If Jesus Christ is to return, we are looking for the return of a man in flesh and blood. If we are looking for the **"Mahdi"**, we are looking for the coming of a man. What kind of man is He? He is an extraordinary man, but he is a man. Why should **"Mahdi"** and **"Messiah"** come in the form of a man? It is because man and woman have been degraded. Man and woman have become beasts in human form. Man and woman have degenerated. Man and woman have fallen. We don't know the resurrected man, the elevated man, the man made in the likeness of God, the Original man. We do not know ourselves, therefore, we have to become acquainted with ourselves. God sends One to us in your own form, but Mighty in Power and Wisdom; One who not only carries Light, but is the Light. My teacher taught me how to truly follow Jesus, the Christ. My teacher shared with us that Jesus Christ is the Supreme Example. He said, **"Jesus is the Supreme Example because he is** not a **"prophet"**, in the classical sense of that name; he is the Master of prophets. He comes, not as "a" star of God, but 'the Star" of God - for in Jesus is a witness, not that God is coming, but that God is Present."** My teacher continued, **"Jesus becomes the Supreme Example because he is not moonlight, but he is actually sunlight, or, "the Light of the World".** So, Jesus gives man a glimpse of his potential. Jesus is not here for you to worship him; he is here for you to follow his example, that where he is, you may be. Meaning that what he has become you also can become if you follow that path." Christ is not Jesus' last name! Christ is his title. Christ is man in his perfectly developed state. Therefore, Christ, fully developed, is man in whom God dwells. Christ is the expressed likeness, image of God. Christ is so important because he allows men to see the realm of possibility. We can be more than the prophets. My teacher said that we should not go around saying, **"I'm the child of God,"** and never grow up to be like our

Father. **Jesus was the only man in the Bible, or scripture, that had such a unique relationship to God, to where he referred to God, not as 'Elohim,' 'Yahweh,' or 'Allah,' he referred to Him as his Father.** When the disciples wanted to learn how to pray they said, **"Master, could you teach us how to pray?"** He said to them to pray on this wise, **"Our father!"** If the Father made Jesus so special, what's wrong with us? Are we saying that we're not special? Do we mean the Father didn't make anything out of us? We're nothing, but our elder brother Jesus is something? Muhammad is something, but you're nothing? Moses is something, but you're nothing? This is how many of us who claim this Prophet or that Prophet of God talk, feel and act. Everyone is special and we're nothing. This is totally false.

Every one of us is as whatever Prophet that God used to bring us His light is. The only issue is we have to choose to submit to the source that they submitted to. We should worship the Creator and not the created. All of God's servants and prophets submitted to God. Even the great and beloved Jesus submitted so well to God that he said in Scripture, **"I, and my Father, are one."** Jesus is the Prime Example, and he said in Scripture, **"I of myself can do nothing, but whatsoever the Father Wills, that I do"**, he is telling us that he is dependent. He is not Sovereign Lord. He is dependent upon a Power bigger than himself. Jesus is your brother and servant. His disciples asked him in Scripture, **"Master, when were you hungry and I fed you not? When were you naked, and I clothed you not? When were you out of doors, and I gave you not shelter? When were you sick and imprisoned and I ministered not unto you?"** Read his beautiful response to them for yourself. **"Inasmuch as you have not done this to the least of these, my brethren, you have not done it also unto me."** My teacher shared, **"If Jesus is the most, and then he takes the least, and calls them 'my brother,' then if you're the brother of Jesus, then whatever is in Jesus is in the brother of Jesus, because they all come from the same source. So the least little man or woman in our community is the brother or sister of Christ."** Just imagine if we all had that thought in our minds as we dealt with each other as we worked with each other in our marriages and male / female relationships today! Just imagine if we really believed that each and every one of us was flesh of each other's flesh, and blood of each other's blood, and bone of each other's bone! Imagine in the black community if we really believed that we should never, ever spill the blood, the sacred, precious blood of each other. My teacher shares that this is why the world awaits the Messiah, who brings in the Kingdom of God on Earth.

My teacher shared with us from the Scriptures that we must never have a picture of God, because the body will only last so long, but

God is forever. Don't make any images or statues and don't bow down to any image, because no image or likeness of God is worthy to be worshipped-- not the flesh, because the flesh is finite. The flesh is not God, but it is of God. God can dwell in this house in this body. The Ka'bah at Mecca is made of stone and it is called the House of God, but God doesn't live there. We have many churches in America that call themselves the Universal Temple or the House of God, but God doesn't live in any of them. The human body is God's House. God can dwell in you, if we will open up and let Him come in. If we will let His Wisdom come in, then act on that Wisdom and grow into Knowledge, Wisdom and Understanding until we are able to exercise Power in His Name. When we get to that level of development then that is God walking in us, God talking through us, God living in us; then there is nothing in existence but God. We have to accept that we are created in the image and likeness of God. That is all true. We have to accept that we are also created with the capacity to be like and to think like God. The Honorable Elijah Muhammad taught us that we are born of the Righteous. And if we can think like God we can act like God. My teacher shared with us that when we submit to God, He actually comes into us. He travels into us through the word and the word contacts the essence of our nature, which is the same as His nature, and turns on the divine essence of us, and we start growing spiritually, just like we grew physically.

Brothers and Sisters we have to pray to God to get His help in this so called **"modern"** day and time in which we live. Even the great MC Hammer had a song that shared with us, **"We've got to pray just to make it today!"** There are many unfortunate husbands and wives out here who know little or nothing about prayer, or the nature and power of prayer. It has been said that, **"The family that prays together stays together!"** Prayer helps to build a family and brotherhood and sisterhood among the family members! My teacher shares that we have to pray for strength in this hour to do that which is pleasing in the sight of God! Being close to God and His magnificent way of doing things will give us that nearness we want from Him and will produce the blessing of God. It is written in the Holy Qur'an that Allah is closer to us than our own jugular vein. There is no one closer to God in our lives than us but we must recognize it. Husbands and Wives must continually pray for one another because sometimes we get so down that we may not even be able to do it ourselves. My teacher shares that prayer gives us the security and peace of mind that will relieve our irritations. If we see faults in one another, we must pray for one another.

We just have to accept ourselves and be ourselves and we will manifest the righteousness of God. We must pray specifically for each and every one of our children. Prayer and love heals an open heart. Who have you prayed for today? Do you still pray for your mother? Do you still pray for your father? What about your sisters and brothers? Many of us are estranged from one another because we won't offer up one prayer for our own flesh and blood family members. Let someone know that you took the time out to think of them during such a special time. It does wonders and builds bonds! Prayer is talking to God, communing with God (versus simply acknowledging God). There is a lot of difference between saying prayers and praying. When you talk to God, you can praise him, thank him, ask him for your needs, seek his will, and ask him to intervene in our lives as well as the lives of others. Most of us should know that our most powerful tool is prayer. Prayer is consciously being with God and I should add it is being with God in a very deliberate way. Faith and prayer are the vitamins of the soul; man and woman cannot live in health without them. My teacher shares that faith is the bedrock of all works. The stronger our faith, the greater our works will be. Prayer is our bridge between Earth and Heaven, our way of opening our hearts to the Lord. Through this intimate relationship we find peace and guidance. But we have to constantly check our attitudes towards prayer. When a person won't pray they most likely have some serious aberrations and engrams about prayer that they haven't dealt with. When a person won't pray they most likely have foolishly tried to replace the true and the living God with materialism. So many couples today have a room in their home for their Big Screen or their Plasma Screen televisions but they don't have a prayer room in their house. We have eating rooms or dining rooms but we haven't made any provision for a prayer room. We have a **"Sex Room"** or a Bedroom but we don't have a prayer room in our homes or in our apartments. Some of us act like we are embarrassed to make prayer in front of our children although we came out of homes where prayer was very present and said all of the time.

Nowadays so many men and women don't pray. Husbands and Wives and Fathers and Mothers are not praying like they used to either. When a mother stops praying and ceases to seek the assistance of Almighty God to help her then who will come behind her and teach the children to pray. A motherless child will see a hard time in their lives. Throughout the ages no nation has ever had a better friend than the mother who taught her children to pray. Many people are professional prayers and indeed pray all the time yet we do nothing after the prayer. The Scriptures remind us that Faith without works is dead. We have to pray as if everything depended upon God but work as if everything depended upon ourselves. We should ponder; consider the words of God found in the Holy Qur'an, **"Pray to Me, *I will answer* you."** God will not answer us if we don't pray. One man said that occasionally he'll do a little prayer here and there if he felt the need to. For so many prayer is something we can do if we feel like it or if we don't feel like it. But Almighty God is offering man and woman specific guidance to us in this day and time regarding our prayer life. Again in the Holy Quran we read, *"O you, who believe, seek assistance through patience and prayer; surely Allah is with the patient."* Don't we have to be patient in marriage and in male / female relationships? God can help us to be patient if we would call on Him more. But why won't we call on Him?

Now my teacher shared with us that both the Holy Qur'an and the Bible teach us that God has no need for any of His creatures. He is above need of His creatures. He is independent of His creation, but all creation depends upon Him. According to the Holy Qur'an man thinks himself to be self-sufficient and doesn't need any God meddling in **"his business."** For some reason man doesn't recognize his incompleteness. Man is created in need and he or she goes about his whole life in pursuit of the fulfillment of needs; yet we don't even recognize our need of God until trouble afflicts us. At some point in our lives, we have all called on Him, oft-times when we were in great trouble. Every one of us, when you get in deep trouble, we fall down on our knees and call out to God. At that moment, our prayer is sincere. We pray, **"Lord, Lord! If you just get me out of this, this one time, I promise I'll serve you for the rest of my days."** This tells us that in nature our duty is to serve our Creator. The more trouble afflicts us, and there is no one around to help us, then we call on God, making our prayer sincere. The word sincere is derived from a Latin expression meaning **"without wax."** This word is used to translate a Greek word meaning **"suntested."** We are told that there was a time when sellers had very fine porcelain which was greatly valued. Often when it was being fired it would crack, and dishonest dealers would fill in the cracks with a pearly white wax which concealed the crack. However, if it was held to the sunlight the wax would melt and the crack would be revealed. Today, we want to show God that we too want to be sincere and without wax. My teacher shared one day that he went into the sweat lodge with our Native American Brothers and Sisters. And he said that if you have never had that experience---it is an experience. In there with fire; heat like you have never felt; darkness that resembles the darkness of the womb out of which birth comes. He told us that he was outside of the 'inipi', listening to those who went into the inipi in front of him and He said that he listened to how they called on God when they were praying. When that heat got hot, he heard them say **'Oh, Grandfather!'** And there was no insincerity in it. He said that you could tell they were reaching for somewhere deep down within. He was traveling with other Muslims and he shared that he heard them in the **'inipi'**, saying **'Oh Allah!'** I mean, they cried His Name out with such fervor, such sincerity. He concluded this story by sharing this,

"God has to keep us in total trouble in order to get a sincere prayer from our lips." Isn't that true? When things are going just fine in our lives and in our marriages we don't really have a great need, we feel, for God. We may pray a little bit just to placate God. But when we are in trouble in our lives or in the marriage relationship we know how to find God by whatever name we call Him and sincerely beg our God for the help that we know only He can provide.

My teacher further shared with us that even those who think they don't believe in God may soon find themselves reaching out for Him. Just travel on these airplanes and wait until it hits a severe (air) pocket and bumps. You see the Christian grab for his cross. You see the Jewish person get the Star of David or the Talmud; a Muslim gets the Qur'an or something divine. They don't ask for the navigator, because he cannot see where he is going. They reach outside the plane to somebody that they know, or believe, has power over this wind, over the forces that are tearing this plane apart. And the Qur'an says: **"And lo! (When I get you safely to port), you set up other gods besides Me. Surely man is ungrateful."** Look at how we get on the plane and the man says, **"This is Flight 242, American Airlines. We will be landing in Los Angeles in 3 hours and 40 minutes. We will be flying at speed of 450 knots, at an altitude of 36,000 feet and we are looking for an on time arrival."** He does not say, **"God Willing."** He doesn't recognize that there is another Power here. He (thinks he) is the power.

Read these words carefully. My teacher shared with us that word, **'I'**, that personal pronoun **'I'**, represents **'independence.' 'I' will do this. 'I' will say that...Don't worry, just as good as done. I will take care of it.'** It's the ninth letter of the alphabet. The number nine (9) represents completion. Man is complete, yet he is incomplete, but he does not want to recognize his incompleteness. He is not sufficient, but he wants to think that he is self-sufficient, so his thinking of his self-sufficiency and his completeness damages his perception of reality. So he says, **"I will see you tomorrow. Oh, yes, the money I owe you. I will pay you on the weekend."** Brothers and Sisters, we cannot speak independently of God. We have no control of tomorrow. We must always recognize God and remember our need of Him and our complete dependence upon Him, lest we abort our development. My teacher shared that the moment we say **'I'** and we don't think there is another Power and we don't recognize that there is another Power, we are setting up a state of mind, an attitude, that will abort our own meeting (with God) and start us on a degenerative road. The Bible says, when we speak, we should say **'I will do thus and so, if it be the Will of God.'** The Qur'an says, when we speak, say, **"I will do thus and so, Inshallah (if it be the Will of God)."** Because between today and tomorrow, there are forces that we know nothing of, that can interfere with all of our plans. So our plans must be contingent upon whether God will permit it, or whether Allah will permit it, or Grandfather will permit it, so we must acknowledge Him, lest we make a serious mistake and abort our own progressive development and improvement in character. Look at us in our Marriages today! Look at how independently we speak to one another. Look at how we as a couple speak. **"We're going here tomorrow and there the next week"**. Many of us have our planners and have plans months and perhaps years in advance carefully laid out – but without even the thought that maybe God has another plan for us. Please look at this tendency in you as a husband or a wife to speak like this. All of us are guilty of doing this but perhaps after knowledge has come to us, we will do a lot better.

If we as parents don't pray, our children won't pray. The way we handle the struggles of life our children will handle their struggles in life the same way and perhaps even worse. One of the most important functions of a parent is to unite their children with the source of their own lives. My teacher shared that the greatest gift that any parent can give a child is to give that child is the knowledge of God. To turn our lives over to Him, and, to feed on the perfection of His Word is to begin the process of rectifying all of the mistakes and errors that have been made by those who have stewarded our lives and have been the guardians of our rights. No matter what failure, we as parents have made in the rearing of our children, if, or when our children learn to seek refuge in the **"God of men,"** they will be freed from the whispering of a slinking devil that whispers into their hearts from the emotion of our anger, pain, envy, jealousy, fear, grief and, from the whispering of others who try to comfort us in our negativity against our parents, teachers, and leaders, by encouraging us in our condemnation of them. When our children see errors or mistakes in their parents, politicians, leaders; when our children see weakness in leaders, when we seek refuge in Allah (God), the God of men, we will cease to blame others for any failures in our life, but, we will take the responsibility that God gave us when He gave us life, and, that is, to take charge of our lives and to live our lives in accord with the Will and the Way of God.

In our marriage we have not just taught our children how to pray but we have made it our parenting policy that the children must come to know Almighty God for themselves. There comes that unfortunate day in the life of each and every child when their parents will leave them. How many children can't move on with their lives after the death of a mother or a father whom the child could not see past because that's all that child or the children know? All they know is **"Big Momma"** or **"Big Poppa"** will handle this or that and now he or she is gone. And they stay stuck at the funeral not really sure on what the next step is after their loved ones are gone because we didn't untie their little hands with the Big God from whom we drew our strength and sustenance all of those years! Never be ashamed to tell your children from whence cometh your strength! Never be bashful about telling them, **"How I got over!"** in today's times. Our children need strong, resilient, spirit filled, God loving and God fearing parents in this day and time! Parents who are not timid to talk about the Way maker! Good parents will never make their children to look to them as the source of their lives when they know in their hearts they are passing away. They will go out of their way to show their children their total love and complete submission to their God and only true friend and deliver! Good parents don't believe they have done their job until they are absolutely sure that their children thoroughly know God for themselves. My teacher shared with us that the greatest gift that any parent can give a child is to give that child the knowledge of God. However, to turn our lives over to Him, and, to feed on the perfection of His Word is to begin the process of rectifying all of the mistakes and errors that have been made by those who have stewarded our lives and have been the guardians of our rights.

It's important to know that our God today will not accept praying as a substitute for obeying. Have you found nothing to thank God for lately in your life? One very great pastor was famous for his pulpit prayers. He always found something to thank God for, even in bad times. One stormy morning a member of his congregation thought to himself, **"The preacher will have nothing to thank God on a wretched morning like this."** But the wise pastor began his prayer, saying, **"We thank Thee, O God that it is not always like this."** Do you even experience grateful thoughts about God anymore? One man felt that a single grateful thought toward heaven is the most perfect prayer. Are you appreciative of the goodness of God's blessings to you and your family during these difficult times for us all? Have you told God about it? Will we taken the children and just express to God in front of them our appreciation for Him delivering us from bills, bad health, accidents and from death and destruction as we have labored out here in the hells of North America? We live in the valley of the shadow of death! Appreciation is the highest form of prayer, for it acknowledges the presence of good wherever we shine the light of our thankful thoughts. What have you taken to God recently in prayer? Do you not think that God would care? Have you become too big for God? Have you become too pompous for God? Any concern too small to be turned into a prayer is too small to be made into a burden. Prayer must mean something to us if it is to mean anything to God. A problem not worth praying about is not worth worrying about. Anything large enough for a wish to light upon is large enough to hang a prayer upon. If your prayer isn't of sufficient importance for you to try to pray it, why expect the Lord or God to answer it? Many people fervently pray, **"Oh, God, guide me"** then they grab the steering wheel. Is prayer your steering wheel or your spare tire?

Does God have to bring us to our knees and force us to acknowledge Him? He is so able to do that and for some He is doing just that. God can reach us wherever we are on His planet and one of His attributes is, **"The Abaser"**. It reminds me of a story. An old farmer was invited to dinner by a man who was well learned and cultured. As was his custom at home, he simply bowed his head and asked God's blessing on the meal and expressed his gratitude for it. When he had finished, his host told him that asking the blessing was old fashioned and that it was not customary any more for well-educated people to pray at the table. The farmer answered that with him it was customary, but that some of his household never prayed over their food. **"Ah, then,"** said the gentleman, **"They are sensible and enlightened. Who are they?"** The farmer answered, **"They are my pigs."** What God wants is a sincere prayer from us the prayers that we send up to Him from our heart's deep core. Experience teaches us that we do not always receive the blessings we ask for in prayer. In this day and time, God is looking for people to use, and if we can get usable, he will wear us out. The wise men and women have shared with me that the most dangerous prayer we can pray is this, **"Use me God."** Too many of us are like the old deacon who prayed, **"Use me, O Lord, in Thy Work -- especially in an advisory capacity."**

God is waiting eagerly to respond with new strength to each little act of self-control, small disciplines of prayer, feeble searching after him. Most of us would be in more trouble than we are if all our prayers had been answered. I believe that more of us would be filled if we would only hunger and thirst after what God is offering us today to help us save and strengthen our marriages and relationships. God has stored within our minds and personalities, great potential strength and ability. Prayer helps us tap and develop these powers. God's way of answering our prayers for more patience, experience, hope and love is often to put us into the furnace of affliction. That's why I love Him so because Almighty God is not satisfied to make the road easy for us. One of the most unfortunate things about the way many of us believe is that our road or our path is supposed to be easy. Many of us have put these thoughts into our own children. I work with young people every day. Many of them don't believe that they should have to struggle or work hard for anything that they want. They sincerely believe that it ought to be handed to them. And maybe they are so **"weak willed"** because they have not had to exercise their will much in their lives. Many of us as parents are so busy giving our children what we never had but we have forgotten to give them what we did have and received from our parents, the great blessing of struggle.

We have started this book speaking about our relationship with our Creator because we wanted to give you, the reader, the best foundation we are capable of giving you in order to enhance your marriage or male – female relationship. Root your marriage in God. Make Him your foundation and your strength. We need more humility to approach God and to repair our relationship with Him. We can't repair the damage that has occurred in our marriages until we repair the damage to our relationship with Almighty God. When that first and primary relationship is secure, firm and right then all other relationships will get into order. If we are arrogant and suffer from other assorted spiritual diseases how do we expect success in our marriages today? You may not know this but humility is definitely one of the most universally attractive and desirable qualities. Humility is a decision, an attitude, and a philosophy. It is a way of living, being, and communicating. It's attractive. *Humility is a characteristic that oftentimes is taken as weakness but it is one of the greatest characteristics a husband or wife could ever possess. It is humility that allows us the ability to see our own mistakes and errors. When we are humble we don't think more of ourselves than we should. A humble person is not too proud or loud.* Humility is missing in our marriages. Husbands need more humble wives and our Wives definitely need more humble husbands!

Your spouse needs you to admit your mistakes especially when we've hurt the other person's feelings by what we said or did. Continuous arguing right now is wrecking many Muslim, Christian and Jewish homes in America and throughout the world. When everyone is arguing, who is listening? You can't both be angry at the same time and any good come out of it. Sometimes your partner may try to bring up everything you have ever done wrong in the relationship. Smile at them and say that you are striving very hard to learn from all of those experiences. Take the humble road. Take the road less traveled. This is how you teach your children about being a True Christian, a true Jew or a true Muslim. We model the life for them. **We have to redeem each other.** My teacher shared with us that the human being has powers yet untapped because human beings are so deviant in our behavior that our deviate behavior has crippled the power of our minds and our ability to regulate the affairs of nature. God did not create us in His image and likeness for us to be subject to the forces of nature. He created us to be the master of the forces of nature and this is why Jesus Christ was told that God had given Him power over all things. Then when Jesus calmed the storm, he turned to his disciples and said, **"Oh ye of little faith."** Why did He say that? Because in words, what the disciples woke him up to do, they could have done if they would have awakened. Doesn't our nature need to be awakened in our homes and marriages? Our home is where we practice our Christianity, our Judaism and our Islam. If we claim any of those faiths to our children yet we can't work out our marriage differences then we may have undermined the faith to your children and to others who may have been secretly and silently depending on you and your spouse to keep it together.

Sometimes you have to approach a situation in a very unorthodox manner. You have to develop a Poker Face. The Poker Face is the face you put on when you don't want the other player to know what kind of cards you are holding. It's a blank look that does not display any emotion at all. It's not sad, it's not happy, it's just a look. This bit of information is very useful to you because your partner has most likely studied you very carefully. They can read your non – verbal signals so you have to learn to control the ones that you are sending out. As you listen to your partner be conscious of folding your arms, raising your eyebrows in skepticism, and mean and disgusted looks that appear on your face. Acknowledge the truth of what they are saying to you by nodding your head in agreement and leaning forward on your chair. The idea here is to convey that you respect who they are as a person and they are worth listening to even if they are acting out to get their message across. It takes courage to say, **"I'm sorry… I was wrong… I made a mistake and I apologize."** This sort of humbleness does not degrade or humiliate you. In fact, just the opposite is true. Your spouse may end up admiring you for your decency and courtesy and it will pay you dividends to admit you were wrong and apologize to the other spouse. To promptly admit your mistake when you are wrong and apologize to your person when you've hurt them can immediately turn their anger into a lasting friendship. But you can go even further than that for even better results. All you need to do is say you're sorry when you're not at fault. When you're not in the wrong, you can afford to be big about it. If just saying you're sorry will restore peace in your family, and mend the broken relationships between two people, then say it so you can get on with the more important business of enjoying each other's companionship, rather than stewing and fretting about who's right or who's wrong.

We've all seen a great chastisement going on all over the Planet right now. It is evident that God is not pleased. People are dying like flies. God is angry, and-the only way we can turn it aside is remembering and practicing what the Scripture teaches us: *"If My people which are called by my name will humble themselves and pray and seek my face and turn from their wicked ways, then will I hear from heaven, forgive their sins and heal their land."*

"What do Men and Women really need from each Other?" - 30

Chapter 2 - The true Nature of a Man and Woman and the great struggle to unite

My teacher pointed out that in the Holy Qur'an in Chapter 4, titled **Al - Nisa** – The Women Chapter I verse I reads, **"O people, keep your duty to your Lord, Who created you from a single being and created its mate of the same (kind), and spread from these two many men and women. And keep your duty to Allah, by Whom you demand one of another (your rights), and (to) the ties of relationship. Surely Allah is ever a Watcher over you."** My teacher shared that the name and the number of every chapter of the Qur'an is significant. The chapter from which this verse is quoted is titled, *"Al-Nisa –The Women"* It is the fourth chapter of the Qur'an. The Honorable Elijah Muhammad taught us that the number four (4) represents foundation and preparation. The people and nations of the world must understand that women are the foundation of civilization, and the preparedness of the woman is the basis out of which a good family and a good civilization comes into existence. No female can be prepared to be the foundation of a great society if that female is disallowed the fullness of education, the cultivation of the nature in which she is created, and the cultivation of her God-given gifts and talents.

This verse of the Holy Qur'an opens by teaching us that our first duty is to our Lord, our Nourisher, and our Sustainer who evolves us from a tiny life germ and makes us attain stage after stage until we reach our eventual perfection. Duty to God is the prerequisite for all other duties. Life without duty or obligation is a meaningless life and a life of vanity. Life without duty to Allah (God) first and foremost is a life that will fail in its duty to self and others. Why? If we cannot be dutiful to Him who created us and gave us a creation out of which we sustain our lives from which we create livelihoods then, that dereliction of duty to Him will cause us to be derelict in our duty to self, parents, wives, children and society. So, keeping our duty to our God, regardless to whatever name we know him by, is the foremost duty for human life. **We are obligated to serve Allah (God). We are obligated to worship Him and to set up no rival or partner with Him. We are obligated to pray to Him and to ask His assistance in all things through *patience* and *prayer*.** This verse of the Qur'an under discussion is teaching us that Allah (God) created us from a single being and created our mates of the same essence and from these two He spread many men and women, then, we are reminded again, *"And keep your duty to Allah, by Whom you demand one of another (your rights), and to the ties of relationship."* Recognition of Allah (God) the Supreme, the Sovereign of the universe, is a must because He is the One who created in the male and the female our nature. This nature of male and female causes us to demand of each other our rights. Every human need is a human right. The male has needs that his nature demands to be fulfilled or sufficed by the female, and the female has needs that her nature demands to be fulfilled or sufficed by the male. **It is these unspoken demands of our nature that is the basis of our duty to Allah (God) and to each other.** We will get to the demands of nature in just a moment.

My teacher shared that the role of every male is to do the work of God. In the Holy Qur'an, the man is made to stand in the place of Allah (God). This means that the work of the man is really the work of God. That work entails the building of a world that manifests the characteristics or attributes of God. This world includes a nation, a government, and systems of education, economics, judicial, trade, commerce, research, development, science, industry, agriculture and agribusiness. This is the work of Allah (God) to supply the needs of the human being as He has supplied the needs for all of His creatures. When man assumes the posture of Vicegerent or Khalifah, or one who stands in the place of God acting on the Will of Allah (God), then the scripture in the Book of Psalms is fulfilled, wherein it reads **"Ye are all gods, children of the Most High God."** In all of the work that man is to do in the place of God, the woman is his helper in forming the nation, the government, the systems; exploiting the gifts, skills and talents of the people in their service to God. Each gifted man needs a gifted woman to help him to fulfill the objective of standing in the place of God.

My teacher asked us one day in the most authoritative black newspaper on earth, the Final Call Newspaper, **"What is God's view of the female?"** Then he proceeded to thoroughly answer the question. He shared that the woman is the manifestation of His attribute of mercy to the world. She is undeserved kindness to us, for; through her we are extended through the generations. It is only through her that we live again, and again, and again. It is only through her that we continue to move toward the true perfection that Allah (God) desires for His creation. She is the cornerstone of the family and therefore is critical in the whole process of nation and world building. Allah (God) speaks to us in the Holy Qur'an saying that, **"We should reverence the womb that bore us."** According to Random House Dictionary, *reverence* is **"a feeling or attitude of deep respect tinged with awe, veneration; a gesture indicative of deep respect; an obeisance, a bow, or curtsy."** As men, we must reverence the womb that bore us. Since the womb of our mother is sacred, then, this teaches us that the womb of every female is also sacred, for it is from her womb that all the Scientists, Prophets, Sages, Messengers, Kings, Rulers and Gods have come and will come. According to Random House Dictionary, *sacred* is, **"devoted to some** deity or to some religious purpose; consecrated; entitled to veneration or religious respect by association with divinity or divine things: holy; regarded with reverence; secured against violation, infringement, etc; properly immune from violence, interference, etc." How many men or women see the womb of a female as sacred? If the womb is sacred, then the passageway through which the seed of life enters the womb is also sacred. The male and the female should be of one mind in doing the work of God. All of this can and will be done when we adopt Allah's (God's) view and purpose for the sacred institution of marriage.

My teacher shared that in the Bible Adam was told to dress the garden. Dress means to trim; ornament, adorn, prepare for use and to cultivate. This word dress implies that Allah (God) intended for man to adorn, beautify, prepare and cultivate the earth for his use. This tells us that we have to master the sciences that would allow us to dress the garden or cultivate the earth and prepare it in such a way that it would be a heaven for ourselves. Education must teach us to master the sciences. If education does not prepare the human being to do what God intended for us to do, then, it is not the proper education for us. This improper education is called training; training us to fit into a world order that is controlled and dominated by Satan and his devils who are the enemies of Allah (God). The more the human being has grown into the knowledge of the sciences, the more we have been able to cultivate the earth, develop it, and mine out of it what is in it that it may serve our purpose.

In court a person may be found guilty of a crime even though they did not know they were breaking the law. But the judge will say to that person, **"Ignorance of the law is no excuse."** If you don't know, that's your fault. Why don't you know? You may say from the Bible, **"My people are destroyed for the lack of knowledge."** That doesn't mean that knowledge is not available. In the face of all of the knowledge on relationships that is in available in countless books and tapes not to mention the tremendous amount of information on the Internet, do we really have an excuse? We all have to do a better job of availing ourselves to the knowledge that is attainable to us. Every person should take the time to understand the nature of himself and the nature of his partner. The nature of our partner is always active whether we are aware of it or not. We often hear heated discussions about our relationships based more on fiction than fact. The appalling lack of good information that is mutually shared between us determines much of the way we interact toward each other, and creates misunderstanding and faulty generalizations about what we mean to each other. Men need to hear the perspective that a woman brings to every situation. The more a man encourages a woman to take a very active and definitive role in the rebuilding and in the shaping of the destiny of their family, the better his family will become. The more a man desires a woman to be in the background and for her not to raise her voice to help shape his family then his family loses the balance that they should have. This is true for the destiny of a man's personal family and the same is true for the destiny of a people. Most men do not understand that it doesn't matter how many times they switch women up as their wives. Almighty God has given all women the same basic nature to operate from. The same is true for women. Some of my sisters mistakenly think that they need to leave this man over here to run into the arms of that man over there. They have to also understand that men have been given the same basic nature to operate from. Hopefully we have already established that both men and women are from Almighty God.

My teacher shares that Allah (God) lays on everything of His creation, an obligation. Therefore everything in creation has a duty. If all things have a duty, Sun, Moon, and Stars... and duty implies a prescribed function, from the furthest planet to the hugest planet to the tiniest atom, everything that God creates has a function and a duty. Well that doesn't let you and me, out of it. We are also under an obligation and a duty that was given to us from our Creator. Allah is under an obligation to make clear to us our duty. Every father is under obligation to make clear to his children their duty. Once you make clear to a person their duty, then you expect from that person a response to that duty. My teacher often shares how powerful a book the Holy Qur'an is. This is why you can hardly go anywhere in the city, the county or the State in which you now live and find yourself a copy. Yet, there are millions of Bibles out here in America and you can find them everywhere. Many people I know go by their Bible everyday! Right by as they go out to do their thing! In truth, maybe we don't read the Bible or the Holy Qur'an enough. My teacher shared that the Bible and the Holy Qur'an are not books that should be in our houses as if they are something that we put up to **"keep devils away."** They are books to be read! They are books to be studied! They are books to be acted upon! So my teacher shared that the Holy Qur'an teaches us it's not our positions that makes us great as men and women. Some are called Minister, some are called President, some are called Emperor, some are called King, but that doesn't make us great. Only in the eyes of a fool does position make us great. But in the eyes of the All Wise, true and living God, he says, **"It is he who is most careful of His duty. That is the one that is most exalted in the sight of the Creator."** At the end of the day who really cares how many diamonds we have, how much money we have, how many degrees we have, how many cars we drive, or what kind of fancy home we live in? My teacher shares that **it is our observance of duty that makes us** great in the sight of God and then He exalts us in the presence of men.

A man and a woman, a husband and a wife have a duty by one another. It is the lack of spirit and will to carry out that duty to each other that leads to so many divorces in our community. Man is created of Free Will so He can abide by His duty, carry out His obligation, or He can go contrary. When a husband or a wife continues to go contrary to our duty to one another this causes us to end up in divorce court. It is written in the Holy Qur'an that Allah lays not on any soul a burden or a duty beyond its scope. A burden is *a load being carried; a difficult or worrying responsibility or duty; to give somebody a task that is difficult to deal with or something worrying to think about.* It is also written in the Qur'an that Allah (God) has ordained *struggle* for each of us. My teacher reminds us that Almighty God is not satisfied to make it easy for us. What is struggle? We are struggling when we are trying very *hard to deal with a challenge, problem, or difficulty. We are struggling when we are making a great physical effort to achieve or obtain something.* This Divinely ordained struggle is to manifest the dormant qualities and characteristics which when manifested cause us to glorify Allah (God), our Creator. Whenever there is struggle, there is a degree of pain. Wherever there is a burden being carried, there is stress that demands great *endurance.* Endurance demands that we continually expand our threshold of pain so that we might endure to the end. Pain is necessary for growth, development and for the manifestation of character. Endurance is about *bearing anything; lasting quality; duration.* Pain, though not welcomed, along with work and endurance are necessary for success. This is the reason why Allah (God) puts in our bodies centers which gives us *pleasure.* Pleasure is a feeling of *happiness, delight or satisfaction; gratification of the senses, especially sexual gratification, recreation, relaxation, or amusement, especially as distinct from work or everyday routine.* My teacher shared that the pleasure aspect of life is the reward for going through the pain of struggle. This is why Allah (God) says, *"After difficulty comes ease."* In the ease that comes after difficulty, is the joy or pleasure of relief from difficulty and momentarily relief from struggle and the heaviness of the burden. There are many things in life that give the human being rest, ease, comfort, consolation, and pleasure. Sometimes, there is the comfort of a touch or a massage; the comfort of a hot bath; the pleasure of good company; the pleasure of a good musical or cultural experience; the pleasure of seeing ones creative mind manifested into concrete reality as the created object gains for its creator recognition, honor and praise. Along with these things, there is the great pleasure that comes from a sexual relationship or sexual intercourse. We will talk more about that later on in the book. Before we get to the pleasure part though let us get more understanding.

My teacher shares that Almighty God has given us a duty and it is not beyond our ability to perform that duty. The duty that we are to perform comes out of our unique and powerful natures. There's no such thing as failure written for our marriages if we will lay hold to new and useful information. God did not create any of us to fail in marriage. We were created to succeed, but our success is directly relative to our performance of duty in the marriage. My teacher shares that ultimately we have to answer to Him who gives us our duty. If we are on a job and our boss gives us a duty, that boss has an obligation to require of us the duty that he imposed. And we have an obligation to that boss to carry out that duty. *Any failure to carry out duty puts a strain on the relationship. Failure to fulfill obligation, failure to carry out duty leads to consequences. Conversely fulfilling obligations, carrying out duty brings a reward.* For instance, black people seek freedom in America. God desires that as well so He imposes on us a duty and an obligation which will bring freedom. If we don't carry out the duty then we don't have a right to be free. Freedom is a right and it's based on a law and it encompasses duty and function. How can a non - functioning, non dutiful, non obligated people who refuse to obligate themselves to the function that brings freedom, demand freedom? **Out of duty comes rights and privileges which we forfeit on failure to live up to duty.** People cry out, **"I want my rights."** Have you done your duty? We have to understand that it is duty before rights. Duty justifies us having rights. **Without any duty we forfeit our rights and we give up our privileges.** Whether it is the citizen of a Nation, a member of an organization or society, or a marriage; when we refuse to carry out our duty we give up our rights and our privileges. Any failure to live up to perceived duty leads to a strain or a break in relationships. This strain in relationships by default in duty is seen in Nations as well as in the affairs of individuals. A man marries a woman a woman marries a man they say, **"I do." They say "I do" to duty. They say I do to obligation.** We cannot say, "Oh this is going to be a swell thing! Oh boy everything is going to be peaches and cream!" Just because our mouth said, **"I do".** Is **"I do"** in our hearts? Will **"I do"** be seen by our actions? My teacher shared that our mouth is only supposed to speak the will of both the husband and the wife to carry out the duty and obligation. Any failure to carry out our obligations as a man, a father, a husband, a woman, a mother, and a wife puts a strain on the relationship.

We may not yet be able to recognize that one of the greatest problems we have as a people is that we are still suffering from the residual effects of slavery! The United States was settled by persons who claimed the love of Jesus Christ, yet, our fathers were sold, bought, transported, sold again, and bought again mostly by so-called Christians and Jews. We can never forget that slavery successfully placed black men and women in America a degree below nothing. Many of our people still do not comprehend nor do they even desire to know what happened to us as a people that reduced us to become such a low, cheap people that live on such a miserable and despicable level. Many of only know a little something about how we were brought out of Africa on a westerly course to a north country and brought into slavery. Some of us don't know much at all about the system of slavery and how we were robbed of the knowledge of self, and made blind, deaf and dumb so thoroughly that in today's modern times many of us have eyes, but we cannot see; we have ears, but we cannot hear; and we have tongues, but we cannot speak. the anti-slavery movement, the sharecropper system, discrimination, segregation, *the terrors of the Ku Klux Klan, the lies of carpetbaggers (from the North), the disorganization of industry* and even much information about what is happening to black people even in contemporary America. The genocidal practices of slavery, lynching, colonization, etc. are easy to identify, but the most recent institutionalized and covert forms of genocide produced by legal systems, educational systems, public health systems, etc. are difficult to distinguish. Most of the time there is no public outcry over these latter forms of genocide for two primary reasons: I) active propaganda disseminated throughout the media keeps the mass of people ignorant of, and agents in, their own genocide; and 2) lack of media access slows those who are knowledgeable about genocidal practices from sharing that knowledge with and empowering others. Legal slavery continues in the form of modern day incarceration and in the mentality of Black male youths who feel it's an honor and a badge of courage to **"do time."** Slavery was big business yesterday and the warehousing of Black bodies usually for crimes against other Black bodies' fuel the prison industrial complex today. You may not know this but nearly 150 years after Emancipation some blacks are still trapped by extreme poverty, isolation, fear and shame, are still remain victims of neo-slavery in rural areas of the South, locked into work in fields, factories and assorted industries. While not bought and sold at auction blocks, these poor Blacks are forced to work, live in shacks, often have no indoor plumbing and are often trapped in peonage, tied to land where they owe owners debts that are never repaid, according to activists and researchers. Most American people haven't made a sufficient inquiry into the effects of the institution of slavery on black people who still live in this society in the United States. Why should they if we don't appear interested and are afraid of learning our own history?

Some of us are frightening to death to even learn any real knowledge about how slavery and its powerful aftershocks led to and caused the great breakdown of black male female relationships in this modern day and time. I was the same way until God strengthened my heart to learn the truth that I am now generously striving to share with you. Right now I am practicing the best religion for my teacher shared with us that the best religion is to do unto others what we want done unto ourselves. He taught us that a brother is not a brother until he wants for his brother what he wants for himself. I want you to know what causes us to be at odds in male female relationships so much. This is not about blaming somebody. Certainly the present-day government and Whites are not guilty of the institution of slavery, the present-day Africans are not guilty of selling their brothers to Europeans, but each of us has to accept the responsibility to repair the damage that has been passed on to this generation. No one should disagree that America should take the appropriate steps to help in the repair of the damage done from 300 years of slavery, 100 years of segregation, and 50 years of the misuse and abuse of governmental power to destroy Black organizations and leaders. We, as Blacks, have to accept the responsibility of doing something for ourselves in the way of repairing the damage. All whose fathers have been party to the destruction must accept the responsibility to help to repair the damage. My teacher shared with us one of the greatest perspectives on slavery that I have ever considered. He said, *"Our great beginning as a people has started from the tragedy of slavery. Where we think that our slavery; and our suffering; and our total destruction as a people is a cursing, underneath what appears to be a cursing, is a great blessing; for a new history begins on the basis of a tragedy...That in our darkest hour, an hour when we think we should give up because the forces arrayed against us are so mighty; so powerful; and they look as though they have totally overwhelmed us, it is in that hour that we have our greatest opportunity for triumph..."* Today, the legacy of slavery remains etched in our souls. Understanding the role our past plays in our present attitudes, outlooks, mindsets and circumstances is important if we are to free ourselves from the spiritual, mental and emotional shackles that bind us today. **The only way we are ever going to be free is to separate completely from Satan and his devils.**

So with that being said and understood we can move forward in our understanding. Yes, in slavery, the slavemaster did all they could to prevent us from using our minds for our benefit. Yes it is traditional in America for the power establishment to work against anyone who tries to uplift Black people. Yes, it was the desire of our former slavemasters that the power of their Black slaves to think constructively for themselves be forever destroyed. They did everything that they could think of to eliminate the very root of the power of our enslaved ancestors to reason for themselves; to form rational judgments for their benefit and for their descendants; us. Yes, it is true that Black people in America were made into an altogether new people by reason of - the manner and method used to bring us to this country and then the impact of slavery on us. And yes it is also true that there is not another people who ever lived or who exist now, like the Black man and woman of America. We are a new people who have been produced through the furnace of the profoundest kind of affliction. Now what does any of this have to do with, **"What do men and women really need from each other?"** My teacher shared with us that if we don't know what was then we won't know what is and if we don't know what is then we are ill prepared for what is to come tomorrow.

Many of the problems that occur in our relationships in our lives are because we don't listen to one another because we already have our minds made up about where each other is coming from. We are a very, very emotional people and our emotions often cloud our reason and rationality. Men are becoming more emotional today because of all the soy that is in the food nowadays. Today many black women are too tired, aggravated and stressed out to even try to imagine what black men are feeling, thinking and doing. Unfortunately, we are allowing the same no good rebellious devil to come between us and interpret black men to black women and black women to black men through radio, television and movies. It's like we can't have a civilized and rational discussion in our homes anymore about us. One of the only real ways a man is going to know what's going on with his woman is when he beings to talk to her. One of the only real ways a woman is going to know what's going on with her man is when she begins to talk to him. The sad part about this is we don't always know why we are behaving the way we are behaving.

One of the things that black men and women really need from each other is to know more about each other. Brothers we should not assume that our women know enough about us. Sisters you should also not assume that black men know enough about you either. Somewhere along the line I was reading where one sister compared learning about black men with learning to swim: you can read all the books in the world about it but you really won't learn anything unless you jump in the water. Her metaphor ended by saying that there was no pool, no water and no bathing suits for many women simply wanting to know things about black men. *"We are left to guess what black men want, feel, think and know and simply have no place to practice these things."*

Both men and women have to always be willing to have the proverbial check up from the neck up in this day and time. None of us are all the way sane because we have grown up in an insane world. Did you grow up in this world? How could you be all the way sane then?

You probably already know that you are crazy or at the very least, a little bit off. One of the main things that we are looking for in our partners is a person who can put up with our uncultivated state of being. We have to be honest. Many of our people are uncultivated, immature and puerile in our emotional development, our financial development our social development and even in our sexual development as men and women. There is one thing that we have to accept as true. The Black Man is going nowhere without the Black Woman, and the Black Woman is going nowhere without the Black Man. So since we need each other, my teacher shared with us that we need to learn how to get along in peace with each other and stop fighting each other for supremacy and learn our role and play our role -- then we can find peace and happiness in our role. To do that effectively we need to learn our nature.

I have to bear witness that we have been blessed to thoroughly learn the nature of both the man and the woman in this day and time. Compare what you have read from all the scientists and scholars that have written books on Male Female Relationships and you will find nothing they have said or are saying can compare to the truth of what you are about to read. What is the true nature of the black man and the black woman in today's times? My teacher offered us this powerful knowledge us to consider as we try to stay in the process of marriage. In the Holy Qur'an in the 30th Chapter it reads in one of the verses, I believe, gives us this verse: **"So set thy face for religion, being upright, the nature made by Allah (God) in which He has created men. There is no altering Allah's (God's) creation. That is the right religion but most people know not..."** Now what does that mean? It means that the nature of a thing - the very essence of it -- can never be altered. It remains unalterably the same. You can alter the characteristics of a thing but you cannot change its basic nature.

My teacher pointed out that an ant can't take off its nature; it's created to be an ant. A bee will always be a bee; a spider will always be a spider. We can take a lion; we can take a tiger; we can take a dog --we may train the dog to sit up; we may train the lion to do tricks; we may train the tiger to roll over -- we have given it certain characteristics that are not characteristically of that particular cat family but we haven't changed its basic nature. We may have altered its characteristics coming out from that nature, but it's still a lion; it's still a cat; it's still of that family. Now, even though we take that lion and rear it from a cub and make it afraid of the whip, the lash, or the gun we must be careful to keep that lion away from an old lion, less that old lion reacquaints this trained lion with its true nature. Then when we come back in there with the gun and with the stick, the lion is not by nature made to fear anything. The only way we can make it afraid is to rear it from a cub in fear! But if it gets next to that old lion it will be its lion self --then when we come back into the cage again with our little self, that lion will wipe us out because that lions nature has been revived!

What about the nature of the Original Black Man and Woman? Somebody has to come along and teach us all about our magnificent, beautiful black selves. Someone has to revive our Original nature! Someone has to share with us who we really are from the inside out and show us how to be our own self. And this is why I am sharing with you what I learned from my teacher. He shared with us that by nature we are made to act in accord with the Truth. When we hear truth and are too weak to accept it and begin to fight against the truth, we are fighting against the very nature of ourselves. By nature, my teacher has shared, the black man and woman is of God, meaning by nature, we are created to submit to God. As the Holy Qur'an teaches, Allah (God) made everything to submit to His will, except, the rebellious devil. By nature the devil was made to oppose God's law, so he's created or made with the nature to rebel, while we as black men and women were created by God with the beautiful nature to submit. If we would just notice, everything that God says that we should not do -- the ruler of this world, Satan says: Just do it! Satan and his devils has been our teacher and guide for the last 400 years of our lives here in the hells of North America. That's whose hands God allowed us to be in during that time in order for us to fulfill the Scriptures of the Bible. Satan is a total rebel against the will and law of God. So what happened to us was that Satan and his devils captured us as Black people and became our teacher and after he had mastered us he taught us to practice wickedness and devilishment on each other and in this society. Every time we see a no good, ignorant acting and sounding black man and woman in America they were made in America. **We should be able to see this clearly but just in case we don't know, Satan and his devils have absolutely no future! My teacher is in the world to bring all the Satan's of the world and all of their devils to their well bought doom, damnation and total destruction!** He is backed by the two most powerful beings in the world to accomplish this task and I stand with him 100% to help him. We should be happy to know that my teacher has shared that those whom Satan and his devils taught were subhuman are to become the rulers of that which believes itself to be human.

Even in this modern day and time, Black men and women have developed so many rebellious characteristics. But my teacher is quick to remind us all that Satan and his devils haven't altered our Original nature. Our nature is still of God, so therefore, we are a righteous people, still by nature. Thank God for the nature He gave us. I thank

God for my teacher helping me as I strive to cultivate that righteous nature. I thank God for what I have learned of Christianity as well as Islam. I love the Lord. He heard my cry. He pitied every groan. So as long as I live and troubles rise I will be found hastening to his throne! Many of us do not know much the knowledge of Islam at all. Islam is an Arabic word meaning **"to submit to the will of Allah (God)."** We need a thorough understanding of both religions in order to undo the effects of Satan and to struggle harder to manifest our true nature. We have to understand that any creature that is deprived of its nature is deprived of the power of its own being. This renders that creature powerless in the face of others because his nature is not active.

My teacher pointed out from the Holy Qur'an a verse that both plainly and boldly states, **"Men are the maintainers of women with what Allah has made some of them to excel others and with what they spend out of their wealth."** It does not say women are the maintainers of men it said men are the maintainers of women. That is a very weighty statement. Women today say, **"I don't need a man to maintain me. I'll maintain myself."** These are very independent sisters today. My teacher shared with us that in some respects that's bad, but in other respects it's good. But, when we start getting away from the nature in which Almighty God has created us, we start getting into problems. **The nature of the female demands maintenance from the male.** When anything is demanded it means that something is being asked for urgently or firmly leaving no chance for refusal or denial. To demand means to claim as just or due. To demand is to ask to be informed of. To demand means to need or require as useful, just, proper, or necessary. To demand is to summon to court and to claim formally; lay legal claim to. A demand is also an urgent requirement, need, or claim. A man must be a provider not only in the economic sense, but, in the moral and spiritual sense of the meaning of this word. Every man, therefore, must be taught and trained to be prepared for marriage and for the demands, that the wife will make upon him by nature. These demands that are in the nature of the female become the basis of her satisfaction or dissatisfaction with her mate. No matter how handsome or well formed the male may be, or how unattractive or malformed he may be, this demand never changes, it is constant. When we fail in the obligation to suffice the natural demand of the nature of the female, dissatisfaction begins to grow and arguments start on the basis of this dissatisfaction because of dereliction of duty. If we examine the arguments that come from the lips of the female which take place in our homes, most of these arguments revolve around some failure on the part of the man to fulfill a duty.

When something is demanded of us, there is something that we are required to do or we receive some penalty. Whenever there is a demand notice to pay the light bill, gas bill or phone bill and we do not pay attention to that demand, there is a cut off of lights, gas or a disconnection of the phone. This is the penalty for the failure to pay what is demanded. In marriage, when the demands of our nature are not met, there is a cut off of service that the female is required by nature to give to the male. The Qur'an teaches us that her nature is one of consolation and that she is to give the male peace and quiet of mind; but, when we are derelict in the duty that is demanded of us by her nature, then, out of her mouth and in her expression comes the notice that we are being cut off. It is the same in the demand of the nature of the man. He has the right to expect peace and quiet of mind and the consolation that Allah (God) put in the nature of the female for him. When he is a dutiful man, providing for his wife, children, and being a maintainer of her spiritually, morally and financially and he does not receive from her what his nature demands as his right, there is a cut off and slacking up of the desire to be the provider or the maintainer. Arguments then arise increasing the dissatisfaction and soon the love between the two vanishes for there is nothing to hold the marriage together. The mortar for marriage is love and that which produces the mortar is duty.

Most of us as men in this system have not been prepared to be what the nature of the female demands. Since we are in a society where Black males are unemployed, unqualified, and untrained to work in a service oriented economy, how then can we be basic providers for that which nature calls on us to do? (Being Maintainers). Nature causes us to be attracted to each other. Nature causes us to cohabit with each other. Nature drives the procreation of the human being, but, education and preparation is what will allow us to be dutiful. My teacher shares after slavery the family was more complete. There was a man, a woman, and children in our meager homes in the south or our apartments in the north. The men worked in the fields or in the factories to provide for their wives and children, and even though we were unlearned, there was more peace in those homes than there is now with all of the educational opportunities that are afforded to us. The arguments that rage between the male and female are because we do not understand our natures and how our natures are made to complement each other.

Now what does that word 'maintenance' mean? Maintenance means to keep in existence or continuance. It is man's job to keep the woman in existence and in continuance. It is his duty to preserve her. It is his duty to keep her in due condition. This is not dealing with money; it's dealing with her head, essence and nature. As black men we always want to deal with our women from their navels down. We don't want to deal with her from the neck up and she resents that. A woman resents a man only looking at her as an object of pleasure when God created her as a very serious manifestation of His own Will. To maintain means to keep unimpaired. As men, we are to keep our wives and our women in the nature in which God created her. We are to keep her in a specified state. Who specified the state that she should be kept in? Who but her Creator? And what is that state that she should be kept in? A man's duty is to keep or hold her against attack; and the last thing in maintenance is to provide for her upkeep and to carry the expenses of the woman. The money part has to be there. We should never think that we are going to have a good relationship with a woman if we can't keep up some expenses. There are many couples today that are trying to solve budget problems. The basic problem is always the same. People spend more than they take in as income. What all of us have to do is to constantly infuse our minds with how to make more money to solve our budget problems and create financial independence! We have to figure out ways to increase our money flow, our revenue, our paper, our cheddar, our bread, and our stacks so that our home budgets will not only be balanced but that a profit will result. We should be concentrating on earning more and not on stretching our income to the point that we are denying ourselves what we want. So many couples spend hours trying to figure out ways to cut back, to skimp, and somehow get by on their current income. They sit in bed losing two and three hours of sleep every night worrying about how financially bad off they are and what would happen to them and their families. At the same time my teacher shared with us that in today's world where the man has to struggle so much for what little he gets, women have to keep their desires in line with what this man is able to afford, lest your desires drive him to do the wrong things just to please you. If that is our duty as man then are we doing that? I believe that we would have kept our women if we would have been left alone but Satan and his devils have been trying hard to alter our nature. Now we have to take control again. It is not that we as men are guilty. My teacher shared that if we are guilty today of anything it is that we have been too lazy to take control after we have been taught better.

I am going to stay on this for a few more paragraphs. Nature makes a real man desire to provide for a real woman. Nature puts within a man to secure a woman, and this is why men are the maintainers of a woman. Please read these next few lines over and over again from my teacher. **"All women by nature look to a man for maintenance. They look to a man for guidance. They look to a man for sustenance. They look to a man for provision, so naturally the man is out front."** We are talking about women who are functioning from the Original nature that God has put in women and not this independent woman that Jamie Foxx and Neyo are singing about. My teacher shared that when a conqueror comes up against a nation and he conquers the men of that nation, he's conquered the vanguard or the wall that keeps the woman protected. The woman, according to the Holy Qur'an, should always be protected. When you have money you try to put it in a safe place. When we have jewelry, we don't leave our jewels out for the thief to steal. My teacher passionately shared with us that women are more valuable than all of the gold that's in the earth. Women are a greater treasure than any treasure that can be found in the depth of the sea. No wise man will leave his woman unprotected. A man's duty to the woman is to preserve, protect and upkeep her and to keep her in the specified state that God has made for her. Men fight over women but we fight over her for the wrong reasons. A man is not worth anything if he will not protect the woman that gives birth to his own nation. When the man is destroyed, the woman is the prize that the conquering army gains. Therefore, she's called in some slang filthy terms, **"booty."** What is booty? Booty is the prize that you win in conflict and in war. I have even heard a song called, **"Shake your Booty". Whenever we turn on BET, MTV, VH1 and other video channels we see Satan and his devils 'shaking their booty' in front of the black man's face.**

Whenever two nations fight and one nation is subdued by another, the manhood of that nation is conquered, is destroyed, therefore the women of that nation is the prize for the conquering army. By nature women look to strength; by nature women lean toward that which is strong and they move away from that which is weak. When the conqueror comes in he automatically has an attracting point with the women of that conquered people. This is exactly why our conqueror has never loved or respected black men in America and he used to move in and out of our community putting his seed into our women and girls. Once Satan and his devils hooked us up to a plow, and made our women to bear us in fear for her life, she brought forth children who were afraid of the oppressor. In the South, the mothers, in order to protect their children, had to teach their children how to say, **"Yassa", "No-suh"**, and bow and do little things to get around Satan and his devils. Fear of the oppressor was bred into our babies, for survival's sake. He sets up education fostered the way of life of the conqueror. Even today it is the same and that's why many of these schools are dropout factories! My teacher shares that if we see ourselves in the process of education, our nature makes us run to it. All the great philosophers of western education said, **"Know Thy Self."** That's the best knowledge and that's what's missing in the educational system: It's the knowledge of self. The knowledge of this world is rooted in a doctrine that creates demons. We have no right to be proud of an educational system like the one we have passed through. We have no right to be proud of what it has made of us. We have no right to be proud of what it is making of our children and if we see it for what it is, then we want no part of it. Either we destroy it, which it must be destroyed, or we must take control of it, redirect it, manage it. But it takes power to do that. My teacher coined a phrase, **"He who gives you the diameter of your knowledge prescribes the circumference of your activities."** Satan and his devils know just where to find us. They don't even worry about us because we are so completely satisfied and happy to remain under their complete control and domination. Because Satan and his devils are our educators it is no wonder that we continue to act just like slaves in this modern day and time. Today we are educated slaves; always busy voting for another **"slave-master"**. We have to admit that we look pretty silly as a people waiting and hoping that President slave-master will change our condition when with the proper knowledge we can change it ourselves and change America in the process. We don't have to ask why we should control our education. The answer is clear. We should control it because if we don't we will always be under somebody else's control. By now we should be able to see that it doesn't matter if that President is black or white, if we don't unite our condition will never change.

The schools bred and continue to breed in to us love of the oppressor. Many churches bred and continue to breed into us worship of the oppressor. One of the main reasons today that Black men cannot control the Black Woman is because we don't have the knowledge of how to control her. In our homes today, wisdom and truth are the controls. Women will readily submit to a man when we are truly possessed of these two things and submit to them ourselves. Most women who refuse to let a man have any type of control are by themselves. Some of us unfortunately don't have the manhood that it takes to command her honor and respect nor the freedom to do so, therefore Satan and his devils would just come get her at will. He changed the education so that the woman now brings forth seeds that admire the conqueror. Through the black woman Satan and his devils have destroyed a whole nation of people because every baby born to that woman is born in love with the conqueror; born to admire the conqueror; born to bow down to the conqueror. Just think of the holidays that we celebrate and practice to this day in the face and in the light of so much truth and information out here. My teacher has shared that until another conqueror comes to conquer that man that conquered the man that woman belongs to, that woman remains in the camp of the conqueror. The only one that black women want to be independent from today is the black man. But where are you going dear sister without us as black men? Where do we think we are going without you? Both black men and women have been in America for now well over 400 years like nothing. We don't even consider that we are very capable of making moves independent of Satan and his devils. Some of us don't see anything wrong with being ruled over by our enemies. Black men today can't say with any real truth that we are the vanguard, the wall of protection around Black Woman. In truth black women have had very little protection from Black Men. Our women have been free-for-all women for any man that wanted her. As men we have not done anything to protect black women from the men of other nations coming in to use her as they have willed. Our women have been the doormat of every people and we as black men for the most part, have allowed them to wipe their feet on the Black Woman.

This is why my teacher shared with us that 75% of his work is with the woman. Any of us who want to help rebuild our people, our marriages and our families must think in terms of re-building and reforming the woman of that people. Any of us who want to help rebuild our people, our marriages and our families must think in terms of re-building and reforming the woman of that people. Black Women are not filthy women and we are not really filthy men. No one ever told us that when Satan and his devils brought our fathers to America and began mating us like dogs, like you mate horses or cattle or pigs, this was to break down our morals as a people. History teaches us that black men were used as stud horses. History teaches us that Satan and his devils used these stud black men to breed black women and fill her with babies that they could rear as slaves on the plantation. Black women had no rights. She couldn't say, **"No."** She couldn't say, **"I don't like you."** She couldn't say, **"There's no love between us."** She was treated an animal; she had no right over her own body. And this went on for centuries. What effect do you honestly think that this kind of activity had on black men and women and do you honestly think we have outgrown the effect of this? Satan and his devils don't have to put his seed in us so much today because they have made black men today just like them. As you look at our condition you would have to conclude that today we are the same women and we are the same men! Yes we are a better dressed, refined, educated and better speaking slave than we were a century ago. But black men are doing the same thing today that was done in slavery. We love to have our women and we love to make them pregnant. But we still in this modern day and time don't love the responsibility of supporting what we have made! And some of our women love to be had by anyone that desires them. With our women properly taught, we will have a beautiful nation and a great hope for a great future, but we don't need any more ignorant, uninformed woman in our community. My teacher shared with us that an ignorant, uninformed woman is really an enemy to the rise of a nation. No woman is born to be ignorant. Women are all smart and crafty in their own ways and now they have to grow to become as wise as they may be smart. There is a big difference. My teacher shares that it is natural for a woman to test a man, because you've got to know what you got. And you devise little things, you know, to test him, to see what you got. And some of you are very, very, very surprised when you find he's not what you thought he was, because you tested him.

Everything women put into their children's heads represents the future. If our women learn how to take good care of themselves they will bring forth children into the world that have a chance to live a longer life because of the way their mothers care for themselves. My teacher shared that a woman must be so careful when she and God are co-creating and fashioning this new life in her womb because that new life is nothing more than what the mother eats and what the mother thinks! The *vaginal tract* of the female is the entry to The Womb, and that is *sacred*. That tract is protected by a thin piece of flesh, and it's not easily accessible. There's pain and there's blood when you enter that sacred chamber. If we look at the *Panama Canal*: It took billions of dollars to create from the Isthmus of Panama a canal that would link the Atlantic Ocean to the Pacific Ocean so that the travelers would not have to go all the way around the tip of South America. So that channel is *so valuable*, that armies protect that channel. *Geopolitically*, gulfs and other strategic waterways are so valuable that people will fight for the advantage to be in those places so they can govern, monitor, control and even keep ships—*that they don't like*—from using those waterways. That's how valuable channels are. The Channel to the Womb is a Sacred Channel that must be *guarded*. My teacher shares from the Holy Qur'an that women are to, **"Guard their chastity"** because when they leave that canal, that channel, "unguarded," they may open themselves up to diseased men; people that don't care or have any value for you! But will just use them as a **"pleasure tool,"** and then throw them away! Some women do not think that they will get a man unless they lay down and open their knees to that man! If a woman has to open her knees to get a man, he is no "man" and he is not worthy of you! When a woman is "easy" for a man to get, she is not the woman that he will want to marry and spend his life with. She is the woman that he will come to when he wants pleasure, but he is not the man that will give her the type of *love, honor* and *respect* that she yearns for. And you will never get it if her channel is like a "free" channel. This is why it requires a great woman to become a superior mother. *Prophet Muhammad said,* **"Heaven lies at the foot of mother."** *Prophet Muhammad was asked,* **"After Allah (God) and His Messenger whom should we honor most?"** *The Prophet answered,* **"Your mother."** *The companion asked who next? The Prophet answered,* **"Your mother."** *The companion asked again, and, the Prophet answered,* **"Your mother."** *The companion asked a fourth time, and, the Prophet answered,* **"Your father."** These two sayings of Prophet Muhammad (Peace Be Unto Him) teach us the importance of the female in building a heavenly society, and, the level of honor that should be accorded to our mothers right after honor to Allah (God) and to His Messenger. In many respects most of the truly great men resemble their mothers in temperament and adaptability. The qualities of a great woman, it's not that she has a lot of force and all this over a man, the quality of a great woman is that she loves deeply and unselfishly. The quality of a great woman is that she serves with joy. The quality of a great woman is that she feels good as a sweetheart, a good wife, a good mother, a good grandmother, a real companion to her husband. Over and above all the other great qualities of a woman, the greatest quality that she has is love. If a mother knows how to mother she can produce a child in the image and likeness of God.

There is a saying, **"The hand that rocks the cradle rules the world."** If Satan's hand is on the female that rocks the cradle, then, through that hand, Satan rules the world. The converse is also true. If God's hand is on the female that rocks the cradle, then, Allah (God) through that female will bring into existence and rule the new world. Once our women learn a higher knowledge they will produce babies who will lie down on their stomachs and lift up their little heads to look around at birth! Women today have to learn the right foods to eat while they are pregnant and while they are not pregnant. In the future once we have accepted knowledge we will produce children that will be bright-eyed and filled with an exceptional capacity! We have to stop killing our children's capacity with the type of thoughts we are thinking and the type of food we are eating. My teacher shared that when a woman is pregnant that's the time when she has to watch her thinking and watch her eating. It is not an old wives' tale that a woman can mark her children by the way she thinks! No husband should allow his pregnant wife to just sit up in front of a television looking at foolishness while she is carrying a child! Pregnant women must be active and she must think the right kind of thoughts. As men we must put the right thing in our wife's brain because what is in her brain is actually going to become a part of this child. What she eats becomes a part of the babies flesh. What she thinks becomes a part of the babies mind. My teacher shared with us that a woman is so powerful that she can bring a child into the world with tendencies towards greatness by the way she thinks! We have to remember that every great man that we love, honor and respect was born of a woman! And every woman had to be prepared for the birth of a great child. Mary brought forth Jesus. We all know in truth and in reality that virgins don't have babies. All women are virgins before they meet a man sexually but after that, they are virgins no more. The point is that Mary was prepared for that new birth. Somebody taught Mary what to eat. Mary knew the foods to eat and the thoughts to think to prepare her to bring forth that child. Every woman could bring forth greatness today if she would get into the process that will help you to reform. My teacher shared that our women could bring forth from themselves the type of people that the community needs to deliver it from the bondage of Satan and his devils if they would reform themselves. Mothers can learn to give their babies strength from birth and they must know what they are doing when they start teaching their children. If all we can offer our children is the latest dance, then none of us will have a future. Too many of our beautiful black children are growing up under our feet as parents without any real care, without consideration, without any thought, as though they are like weeds that don't need cultivation and growth. Too many of us have children and don't know what to do with the child once it gets here into the world.

According to the Scriptures, we are called a foolish nation! That's a heavy burden to carry, but we are said to be the most foolish people on the earth. Satan and his devils has been hard at work to destroy our women and make them foolish women who produce foolish children that don't do anything but become the grapes of wrath! Many mothers have watched the very children they birthed into this wicked and satanic world grow up and then turn on them - cussing their mothers and fathers out and hating their own parents. We've got to break that cycle. Most women don't even consider that it is through their wombs that the answer to every prayer has come into the world. One day my teacher asked us, **"Did we pray and if we did, what did we ask for?"** He shared with us that everybody prays at one time or another and even an atheist prays when we get him cornered. My teacher pointed out that many of us have relatives that have died of cancer or are dying of cancer. Some of us have friends that are dying of AIDS; some of us have loved ones that are dying of tuberculosis and other diseases like Cerebral Palsy. When we see somebody whom we love leaving us because of an illness that there is no cure for, what do we do? Even if it's not a spoken prayer, what happens in our breast is our hope for a cure for the dreaded disease. We hope, *"God, I hope for the day that a cure will be found for this dreaded disease."* My teacher then asked us, **"Where did we think the cure was going to come from?"** He shared with us that some woman is going to produce a child, male or female, that is born to bring the answer to what we hoped for, what we longed for, what we prayed for and that's why the womb of every woman and every woman is sacred. My teacher then reminded us that any man who violates a woman is accursed of God; *for the woman is our link to God and that most men were very abusive to women.*

My teacher has shared that the woman is the most precious gift that God could ever give to a man. There's nothing in creation other than God that is greater than a woman including the Sun, Moon, or Stars! Nothing is greater than woman but God. If that is true, and it most certainly is, have we as men checked our attitudes towards women lately? How do Judaism, Christianity and Islam treat women? We live in a world that has put women down. No religion is free from some blame. Not that God did this, nor did His prophets do this, but misunderstanding, misinterpretation of scripture has caused males in religious positions to put the female down, justifying their mistreatment of the woman by talking about what Eve did. Eve could not do anything more than what Adam permitted. It never was Eve's fault. In the past, in the synagogues, Jewish women could not learn the Torah, like the men. In Islam, the women did not study the Qur'an like the men. And in Christianity also, women could not preach or teach because it was forbidden for a women to do that, up until recent times. Yes, these are the revealed religions of the Western World but we have to honestly look at how women are treated in them. My teacher asked, **"Who are the persons in the Black community who are the seers and will tell you something about your future?"** It's not men, most of the time it's the woman. Why is that? Why is it that most of the time the woman sees better than the preacher can? Yet, some sexist men do not believe that a woman is supposed to preach! How is it that a woman could produce the greatest human being that walked the earth, Jesus, the Messiah, and teach and nurture him? **If a woman could teach Jesus, shape him and mold him,** what other man is there that a woman can't teach, shape and mold?

My teacher has shared that in this society woman are play things and pieces of meat and their clothing is not designed by righteous designers. God took our private parts and put them in a place where they could be hidden between our legs. But the designers design clothes to bring what is hidden into view. There is no natural man that is not stimulated by the sight of certain parts of a female. And that's only if that man is a natural man. It's the same on the other side. The female is stimulated sexually by certain parts of the male anatomy. So the scientists who know and study this make our clothes because evidently the sewing machines don't work in the black community any more. They make them and we wear them. They make them and we buy them. They got jeans so tight that the sisters can measure a man up. Many sisters in our community have jeans on so tight till her crotch becomes an inverted pyramid and we see the point she was trying to make. Some sisters walk the street and their breasts are not tied down. They have on high heels and everything is moving. They say that fish don't like any dead bait and that fish like a **'live bait'** that's moving. So when a woman walks she is just moving and a man's eyes go to dancing in his head. Then his eyes go from the breasts right down to the apex of the pyramid which is now inverted. Then the woman walks by and she watches him and it leads most men to thinking on a lower level. And it makes a woman attract a man at the lowest level. And what the sister sees is just about what she gets! A woman gets a man who doesn't care about her mind. He's more interested in something that rhymes with mind. After the man starts working with that woman's body and discovers it, he moves on to the next one and to the next one, and to the next one. My teacher asks, **"What does Satan and his devils have in mind when they strip you down to make you reveal your form, so that men may see your form and never come to see you as you really are?"** In today's times if a woman thinks she has a good shape, she want to show it because if she shows it she is going to get some attention even if it's the wrong kind of attention! Some women have said that no matter what they wear in public **"that a man ought to be able to control himself."** My teacher shares that he ought to be able to, but it's very difficult for a man to control himself and a woman is disrobed. A man was not made to exercise control in the presence of a naked woman. If a man exercises control in the face of a naked woman, she begins to wonder, **"What's wrong with him?"** You've got to help a man keep control. You've got to help a man keep control. If you don't help him, he will be a dog for the rest of his life!! You've got to help him to become a man!!

Some women end up so disillusioned with men that they have no desire to be hurt by a man again. Many women are out here in the community now trying to imitate this sick posture that some of the men have towards women. Many women are now saying, **"I'm not going to love any man. I'm going to treat men like they have delighted in treating women..."** I can understand why women feel this way but sisters you must never forget that God has not made you to act like a man. Women are not really getting back at men if they do this. We are only further destroying what's left of Male – Female Relationships in the black community. By the way, in Islam, although Prophet Muhammad had respect for women some have taken Eastern Culture and overrode what the Qur'an teaches and the Prophet's example. My dear sisters you must realize that the Enemy, Satan and his devils, wants you dumb! My teacher shares that the Enemy wants you to think nothing of yourself, so The Enemy strips you of your real nature. He has denatured the female—and the male! And anytime somebody de-natures you, they have de-valued you! So right now as a Black woman or as a Black man: We are not valued. And the worst part of that is we don't value ourselves because The Enemy has made us to think so little of who we are.

My teacher shares that when women look at themselves on the screen today in Hollywood, and other places, how does Hollywood portray not only Black women, but White women as well? One Jewish author who described in his book about how "Jews invented Hollywood," they keep the Black woman looking like a **"tart."** Do you know what a **"tart"** is? **It's something sweet and nice; delicious, delectable, delightful, as in an "after-dinner tart."** What they want to make of you, a woman that was created in the image of God, is to make you in such a way that you will come down—way down; and bring your man down with you. And they also want you to teach your children in a way that they, too, will be down. They want you to look at yourself in your nakedness, and *enjoy* seeing yourself in a degraded state. Look at *Rihanna, Beyoncé or Nicki Minaj.* Type them up in a Google image search! It's like they are actually competing for the title of **'Ms. Fine Black Thing' or 'Ms. Bootylicious'!** My teacher shared that the problem is that women today have been made to think that their bosoms and backsides are their **"stock and trade"** and that is what makes them "valuable"! Many men and women flock to strip clubs throughout the country to see women in this degraded state. My teacher shares that in 2008 when President Barack Obama was elected, there was a Black woman in the papers who talked about the First Lady of the nation, Michelle Obama; that, **"She's got back."** What in the world are we thinking about that we measure the Value of a Woman by the shape of her backside? Is this a real example of what a free modern day woman looks like in this day and time? Is this what women want to be? Or do women want something better than what Satan and his devils have made of them? We can see that the present world in which we live is ruled by Satan. All of the efforts to protect the female from Satan's hand have failed. Therefore, through the female, Satan's power is shaping the children of the present world order. This is why a knowledgeable, God-fearing, spirit filled woman is the base of Allah (God's) new world order and the Kingdom of Heaven. For, the Honorable Elijah Muhammad taught us, **"Where there are no decent women, there are no decent women. For, the woman is the mother of civilization."** In so many communities in America there is no peace between male and female because we violate each other because we do not know or appreciate divine laws and natural law. We can never make peace with one another without first making peace with God.

Young and older women are not to be played with because they are so sacred in the sight of God. Our young women are sacred! My teacher shared that sex is so powerful that to abuse a young girl is like killing her. Young girls who are growing up today are so beautiful and so well formed at eight and nine and ten. They put all these hormones in the meats to fatten the animal up to get it to market quicker to make a profit, and when our young men and women eat these kinds of meats they find themselves growing a whole lot faster. Many of the young female children today at 10 and 12 have breasts that are bigger than their mothers! They have Barbie Doll's in one hand and sanitary napkins in another. Some of these young female children are developing so fast that at 8 and 9 years old they are ready to be able to bear children but their minds are not yet prepared. Some of the young men and old men in our community see our young women developing like this and they are now preying on our young girls. Look at the videos on MTV and BET that our young people are watching. Listen to the music on the radio that our youth are listening to. We can't tell these young girls and boys, **"You shouldn't commit fornication."** My teacher shared that you can't tell that to grown men and women today. Satan and his devils have gone under the Law of Moses, Jesus and Muhammad and have tapped the very law of nature itself. The law of God is correct. We shouldn't commit fornication or adultery. These are acts that destroy families and break the brotherhood. But when we live in a society that is constantly feeding the sex drive and there is no monitoring of male-female relations, people fall in love and we leave them alone without chaperone or supervision, then the law of nature subverts the law of **"you shouldn't commit fornication."** Many of us as parents are not watching our children! Many of us are too busy watching soap operas and too busy pursuing a living and we mistakenly think our youngsters are watching themselves.

Some mothers are so desirous of companionship that they bring any kind of man into their homes. Do we know what it does to a male child to hear his mother carrying on in the next room with a strange man that is not his father? Do we know what we are doing? So many of us don't care anymore! We have become so much like animals that we will bring a man into the home knowing that our children are there and we will make the children look at the TV while we go into the next room to perform acts with strangers. Some of these kinds of lowdown, despicable men have one eye on the mother but their other eye is on her own daughter. My teacher shared with me that in the Islamic way, we don't have any free intermingling with the sexes. You really have to be close to the family if Islamic men will allow you to get around their women. If you are around then that means you are very special because in the Islamic way men do not allow any man around their women. You can see her, you can respect her but we will not allow any play thing and if a man comes into their house to play with their daughters they may be eliminated off the planet for that. In the Islamic way, they don't let any man get our daughters on some street corner trying to talk to her. Men should have to come and talk to the girl's father. In my home, any man that will have the desire to talk to my daughters will have to come and talk to me. And he better come correct because I am the door to my daughters! My wife and I reared them both and taught them both. We have treated them their whole life her like righteous girls. I have never played with my daughters or abused them in any way. Their mother has taught her how to be good, decent and respectable girls and she has been their personal example of a how to be a woman. They have value so no man should ever think that he can come and mess in my house! They will see a whole other side of me! Any man that thinks he worthy should come and talk to me and tell me what he has got on his mind. Because when he takes my daughters from me, I want to know that she's got a man that's going to look after her like I looked after them. Because I have never abused my daughters I will not allow any other man to abuse her. This is how my teacher has guided fathers to be.

Again I say to you my readers from my teacher that the woman is sacred and it's the violation of women, it's the disrespect of women that has the world that it is in. **God put women beside a man to give balance to the power that He would give to a man.** When we as men shove a woman out and tell her she doesn't have any voice any place in the home then there is no balance for that man's power. Again, women bring forth the children. My teacher shared with us that men don't know what it's like to go in labor. We don't feel for children like a woman does. All men know how to do is to send them their children off to fight wicked and unjust wars. Women have to be involved in everything in the marriage and the relationship if it is to be successful. They can't just be involved in the making of children but they have to be involved in the governance of the entire society. If they are not then we don't have balance. Even the divine attributes of God are male and female! If a man wears the magnificent attribute of Hakim, which is the male or masculine for wise, then who is his wife? She is Hakima... because she has wisdom also just as a man has you got wisdom. My teacher shared with us that we should never tell a wise woman she can't stand beside a wise man in ruling and governing the affairs of the world. We would be out of our place if we did that. In most societies on the earth women are persecuted, women are oppressed. America is the most enlightened society on earth, but yet women in America are oppressed. As a woman, you may say, **"I'm not oppressed, I'm free."** So many sisters are blind to the level of their own oppression right here in America! Many think they're free, but they're not free to be what God wants to make them. They're free to be what man wants to make them into and what is Satan and his devils interested in making out of women? In this so – called society women have become glorified piece of meat! Women are not encouraged to be a woman with spirit or intelligence to think and plan, and create, and be a balance for a man in government, in politics, in business, and in religion! I know the entertainer, Beyonce, recently sang in her video about girls running the world but she is incorrect and perhaps uniformed. If she is informed then she is outright lying to you! Women and girls run nothing in this world! You wouldn't even want to take credit for the sad state of this world today. My teacher shared that in this society, women are kept out of everything! By locking women out, man's own power has made him unbalanced, and his own power has driven him crazy! Man has made a world that is so wicked and self destructive, that my teacher shared if women don't rise up as mothers and as a woman, to take their place the world will go down and take them down with it! This is the one of the primary reasons that there's so much hell in Islam, in Judaism and in Christianity! There will be hell in any society on the earth where women are oppressed. My teacher shared with us that God is stirring women up today! They are not going to take it anymore! Women have got to have their rightful place in the marriage, in the relationship, the society and in the world!!!

A woman needs a man to cultivate her. Did you ever consider why so many women were around Jesus? It was because Jesus never abused women. And even today when a man displays intelligence and wisdom it is attractive to a woman. When a man displays intelligence and wisdom you may have to look at him in a different light. So Jesus used wisdom and understanding to cultivate women. And whatever way the woman came to Jesus she didn't leave the same way. Mary Magdalene was a prostitute who just happened to meet Jesus. Jesus didn't try to get her in a backroom somewhere, **"Hey.. yo Mary.. you know I uh.."** He accepted her where she was and began to teach her. When a woman meets a man that understands her needs are more than physical, and he understands that she has other needs that include the emotional, the psychological, the spiritual, the economical and financial needs, then that woman has found a true man. And a man is not a true man until he has cultivated and nurtured God's essence in him to its perfected State. That's what every female wants and that's why women in particular love Jesus so much. Because Jesus in his person represents what a real man looks like.

It is because men are not what we are supposed to be that leads so many women to adultery. Men do not meet the demands of a woman's nature. My teacher shares that Adultery marks this generation. Adultery is voluntary sexual intercourse between a married person and a partner other than the lawful spouse. The act of adultery is punished very harshly by God in the Law that He gave to Moses and the Law that He gave to Muhammad (PBUH). Why? Because adultery and infidelity interfere with the activity of love and begins a process of death by destroying the activity or life of the marriage. Adultery is punished by death because adultery brings the death of marriage and family.

Adultery is a termite that undermines the pillars of nationhood. And although with fornication, the person is not married and therefore have not broken any vow, the punishment for fornication under the law of Moses was also death. All of these actions we take for granted are destructive of the process that Allah (God) intended for human beings in our growth to become one with Him.

My teacher shares that in the Bible when God wanted to exalt and make Israel a great nation for His glory, He sent down strong law because, if the Children of Israel would grow under that strong law, they would become the foundational stone for a world that respects the sovereignty and righteousness of God and His law. Similarly, by living the law, we would find greater peace, harmony, love, and brotherhood inside the Nation. Fornication and adultery were punished by death. Why would God, who is the ultimate in forgiveness and compassion, ask for a woman or man to be stoned to death for adultery? Because there are huge consequences! The punishment that Moses gave for adultery was to stone the guilty party to death. Why stone the adulterer and the adulteress? Because the violation of the word or commitment that one has made to the other in the presence of God is a violation of the upward journey toward God. The violation of these vows and its manifestation breaks the family. Whenever a married man allows a strange woman into a relationship with him, he has broken the bond and interfered with the life of his marriage. If it breaks the family, scatters the husband and the wife, it damages and makes insecure the children, and there is a whole consequence of activity that comes when the family is broken apart. If the law is that a person is guilty of fornication, or adultery, and that person should be stoned to death, then in carrying out that law, if we take up a stone and throw it at the person who is guilty of this act, for every action there's an equal and opposite reaction. By our stoning the person that is guilty of that act we are in effect, stoning the thought in ourselves to commit such an act, which then is a preparatory stage for helping us to deal with the origin of sin. The people that followed Moses, some of them loved the law. David said, 'The law is an lamp unto my feet. I delight in that law.' But there are others who don't delight in the law but feared to break it because of the consequences, but their minds are against the law. Jesus was born into the world to take them to a level of spiritual growth-from which they had fallen-by trying to get the people to see that sin starts in the mind. They were in gross darkness and he came with light but they were so in love with the darkness that they hated the light. So that poor man who carried the light had to suffer because of the gross darkness of the peoples' minds. My teacher shares that law is a cover for hypocrisy. It makes us look right when we are wrong. It is hell on the inside. This is why Jesus said that he that lusts after a woman in his heart has already committed the act;

Jesus was not interested in us looking good on the outside, he was interested in purifying man from the inside and the law will never do that. Someone has to grow a man out of this childlike stage. Jesus said, **"He who looks upon a woman with lust in his heart has all ready committed adultery."** Even though the act is not consummated, the thought is so real that the consequence comes from the thought even though the action hasn't been completed.

The enemy, Satan and his devils, loves to find our weakness and expose our weakness before the world so that we can be condemned and laughed at and mocked by those who thought better of us. We have to be so careful how we judge in this day and time. This is why the Scripture says that we should judge not lest we be judged. In the Scriptures, Mary the mother of Jesus, became pregnant and the circumstances surrounding her pregnancy were such that she had to be put away privily because they could not see the father of the child. It was the law at that time, if they found a woman pregnant with no husband, then the woman was charged with committing fornication or adultery and would have to be stoned to death. So, they hid Mary away because the law would have killed her and the baby in her womb would have died. My teacher asked us to imagine the loss for the world that would have been.

My teacher shares that men are so deficient that we create adultery and that the woman is not adulterous by nature. She is adulterous by circumstance. She would be faithful to us if we could complete her desire for a man. We do not care whether she completes our desire as a woman. As men in the nation, we have lost the moral authority in our houses because of adultery. We have to put the blame where the blame belongs. We have violated our contract of marriage and our oaths. We have violated our wives and our families. How can we make a strong family again? There was a woman found in adultery that was brought to Jesus. She should have been stoned to death according to the Law of Moses. Jesus bent down and wrote in the sand, which one of you is without sin may cast the first stone? No one threw a stone, for all were guilty. Jesus was innocent and, therefore, He could have cast stones at her, but, He who was innocent said to the woman who was guilty, woman, where are your accusers? Neither do I accuse you. Go and sin no more. As you read this book, I say to you from my teacher, as Jesus said to the woman who was found in adultery, go and sin no more. If we want a strong people, if we want a strong nation, then we must produce strong men and women with strong commitment to each other through the institution of marriage.

A woman has much to offer a productive man with a vision and some goals. A woman can't help a man do nothing. A woman's soul can't be happy with nothing because she comes from a Creator that does things and is always moving and making progress. A woman who doesn't study herself or her nature may not know why she is frustrated with her partner. She may not know why he angers her so much. A woman likes to see her condition improved. And if a man is in her life and he moves to slowly then she will get up and make the progress that the man didn't make, couldn't make or perhaps didn't know he should make. The Black woman is completely frustrated and hurt by the lack of development in the Black male. We can reverse this trend only if the Black man can be reflective of the characteristics of Allah (God) by submitting to Allah (God) that He may guide the Black man to being himself. When the Black man is himself, reflecting the characteristics of Allah (God), the soul of the female will be satisfied, then, she can be as Allah (God) created her to be, man's consoler; and, man will find peace and quiet of mind in her.

We have tried so very hard to be successful with what Satan and his devils have given us to function from and have been placed in a miserable state and condition all over America and the world. The Bible says that we were born in sin and shaped in iniquity. Ever since we have been down from following them, we've been longing to get back up, so my teacher shared that whatever we desire for ourselves that we are deprived of, soon the Law of Nature will bring forth from the womb of a woman a child born to satisfy a natural need that we have been deprived of. We have to look again at each other as black men and women. By nature, Black men are good and right. Good is in accordance with our nature and does not burden us. My teacher shared that practicing righteousness and doing good is not something we put on as we put on our clothes and take it off at night when we want to go to bed. The doing of righteousness and goodness to our women and children is our nature. We wake up in the morning with it; we go to sleep with it; it is a part of us. We eat it; we sleep it; we drink it; we talk it; we walk it, because it's the very nature of us as black men. Circumstances have made us other than our own self. Even today in this modern day and time, we love right. We love for someone to treat us right. My teacher shared that even though we don't do right ourselves, yet we love right. Especially when it's somebody treating us right. By nature when a person does right and we know they're right we can't help ourselves, we love them and respect them. You may not be what I am. But because you see me trying to practice what I am striving to share with you from my teacher, you love and respect me. This is because by nature we love right and we respect right. Even though we have been following Satan and his devils for well over 450 years we still can't get away from our nature. Even though we have developed some extremely rebellious characteristics they haven't altered our nature. Our nature is still righteous even though we are acting other than self. One nature is horizontal, which allows human beings to walk like the lower animals with their tongue hanging out of their mouths like a dog. These are human beings who act and function from their low desires and the lowest levels of thought. But our true nature is to walk upright or vertical. We come into the world lying down, then we learn how to crawl, but, as soon as we find something strong we pull up and we grow in uprightness. This uprightness is what separates us from the lower forms of life. The true nature of the human being is to be upright. All over the world, humanity as a whole lives on a horizontal plane. Many people actually prey on one another. Many people live like snakes. Their tongues do not speak truth. Many people lie and deceive on a daily basis. Their word means absolutely nothing. As soon as we take the Black Man away from the teachings of Satan and his devils and put him under his own good guide, we will go to our own good guide and we will follow him because, by nature, black men love good.

Our women really need men today to become morally strong and self-disciplined. They desire men of good strong character. When we are like that it makes our woman show respect to us. My teacher shared that women will respect us as men when we don't run after her like a dog after a bone. When we act like that she loses all respect for us you for she loves men that she can't get and not the kind of men that run after her. Women are so precious to us as men. She'll be good if we as men will help her to be good. My teacher shared that when we see a no good woman in our community, she was made that way by a no good man. Most women don't go wrong until some man takes advantage of her. Strong men will make a woman strong. A weak man will prey on the woman and keep her going in weakness. Women often test men to see whether they are strong or not because that is her nature. When she finds a man strong, she'll submit to them. If she finds a man wise, she will not fight us, she will respect us. If we are wise enough to guide her; she will obey us as men because her nature makes her that way. No woman will fight a man as long as he uses wisdom and rules her with justice. When a man does that then a woman is happy to be under his rule. My teacher has shared that the only kind of liberation that today's modern Black Woman needs is to be liberated from foolishness, filth and to be liberated from the image that a woman is only for the pleasure of a man! Black Men need to be liberated from the kind of mind that only allows him to see a woman in some bedroom situation! Men have to be liberated from the mind of a dog in this modern day and time. My teacher shared that a man can never act like a man if he thinks like a dog! A man will only be a man when he starts thinking like a man.

When a man thinks like a man he then will begin to think like God. God knows the purpose for everything He created. And when we know the purpose of a woman we just cannot misuse her or abuse her. When you know the purpose of ourselves we cannot degrade ourselves lying around in the streets of America doing nothing and being totally unproductive when we know who we are. Again I share with us from my teacher with great pride, **"We are the absolute people of the Divine Supreme Being!"** We are the Creator, but we are not showing that Creative mind of the Creator.

We should all clearly see by looking around our community that both black men and women in this day and time are entirely too fat! My teacher shares with us that we weigh other than ourselves whenever we think and act other than our righteous nature; we are overweight, sloppy and slovenly. We should never think because we are thin that we are healthy. Some of us are skinny, sloppy and slovenly. Eating pork and other slave foods helps to keep us unhealthy. My teacher shared that nature did not make the hog and bird with any regularity in eating. Although hogs stop eating when they get enough, the foolish pig will never stop eating until he is sick and all but ready to drop dead. The horse will stop eating and the house cat will stop eating when it has enough, but people will not. It is just as the old saying goes, **"We dig our own graves with our teeth."** We need to learn how to eat the proper foods. Every human being in a relationship is physically involved. All of us must work to keep ourselves up physically. Your health is extremely important. The Human body is not constructed to hold a great deal of weight. My teacher shares that our physical body is the true house of God and we must keep it up. Because the best form of exercise is walking we should strive to walk as much as possible. How can we do good to others if we refuse to be good to our own self? We have to think in terms of our health. We can no longer violate the principles of health in our community! My teacher shared that fast food equal's fast death! We need to let go of the cigarette. They are not good for our health. We should not say that a three inch thing has so much control over us that we can't give it up. Man and woman can do what they will to do! However if our will is weak then we will hold onto the cigarette. How could we still be smoking when we know that of the more than 1.3 billion smokers alive today, about 650 million will eventually be killed by tobacco, according to a UN report? How could we still be smoking when we know that unlike most other causes of death, tobacco kills more people during their most productive years? Satan and his devils have us so hooked on nicotine that they can place the warning right on the box of cigarettes *that smoking this is going to kill you*, and we still are out here smoking like a chimney. Cigarettes are not good for us and we can give them up if we can replace them with a true and sincere love for the God that gave us our magnificent bodies. We also should not smoke reefer. Many things grow out of the earth and we can't eat everything that grows out the earth just 'cause it grows! There are a lot of poison weeds that grow out of the earth -- we would not go and boil up some of that and make a stew because it grows. That's not an intelligent argument. Drugs do not expand our mind to any degree where we can progress. We have to give Satan and his devils their vices that help to keep us slaves back to them in this day and time! We don't need to be hooked on a cigarette, on wine or whiskey, on drugs or hooked on watching a million cable channels filled with sport and play. If liquor or reefer, or watching football and basketball year in and year out could have gotten us out of this condition we would have been out of hell of a long time ago! We just cannot afford to be sitting around just enjoying ourselves. It is good to enjoy ourselves but we have to admit that there is too much enjoying of self and too little preparation of ourselves.

As a people we have to mature to see that no one is trying to take away pleasure from us and we have to put **knowledge, wisdom and understanding** in our heads. If we had more of those three then we would be a whole lot happier in our marriages. If we had more of those three then we would be happy in a manner that was right and conducive to stronger families. Can't we see that we need to be reformed? Reformation takes place in the mind and in the heart. When we are truly reformed others may indeed be able to see it's manifestation on the outside but we will know that the real reform took place on the inside of us. Most of us don't even want to consider that it is us who needs to be reformed because *'we know so many other people who need to be reformed first'*. Women may be thinking that it's the men who need it first. Men may be thinking that it's the women who need reform first. My teacher shared that both Black Men and Black Women have to be reformed if we are going to make it during these dark hours this country is facing.

Many who are reading this probably wish that I wouldn't address these kinds of things but I know my teacher has taught me better than that. Some may be reading this and are upset that I keep referencing for us what my teacher said. But why should we run and duck real wisdom? We have to face these facts if we want to be successful. We have to think of the history that we have suffered here in the hells of North America. We cannot be successful in building our marriages and our families without taking into consideration the roots of slavery and what that slavery has done to twist us! Satan and his devils have not made us wise enough to get around the effect of slavery which is still with us! Just look at the state of Black Male / Female Relationships in our community? Do we know what we're doing? **All the divorces going on in our community is the proof that we don't know what we're doing.** Our condition bears witness that somebody needs to advise us about what we're doing and tell us what to do! The woman is most important in building or re-building a nation. Here I am trying to help my teacher to rebuild broken marriages and really a broken people. How are we going to rebuild our people, except through the black woman? We just can't do it any other way. If our black women aren't reformed then nothing we do as black men means anything. Why do I say this? We all will die, sooner or later because no man lives forever. When we're dead where's the future coming from? The future is coming from the woman. When we look at a female we're looking at the means by which our life is extended. Every time a wife tells her husband she's expecting, an intelligent husband is not sad. Every time a man looks at a woman, he's looking at his future. Every time a man mistreats a woman he's mistreating his future. Every time a man shows respect for a woman he's showing respect for his future. Women bring forth from their loins our children who are made in our image, our likeness, our furtherance to be the next generation of life on the planet. This is how a man lives. He lives through a woman. We didn't fall down in this condition without a design. Satan and his devils knew exactly what they were doing. As we as men were destroyed through our women the only way the Black Men can ever be rebuilt is through the same thing that Satan and his devils used to bring us down. This is why I thank God so much for my teacher! We need a teacher and a teaching that elevates us, reforms us, and makes us to think differently. We need a teacher and a teaching that makes us love our woman, respect her and desire to protect her. We need a teacher and a teaching that shares with us the right foods to eat to keep us looking young and gives us good health. We need a teacher and a teaching that shares with our women how to take care of their own bodies so that when she brings forth a baby into the world, it comes forth strong and prepared for the rigors of life. I am trying my best to help my teacher stand my brothers and sisters up so that we can take our rightful place. Our place is not at the foot; our place, is at the top. We can't go to the top unless we have the right stuff on top. The right stuff is knowledge, wisdom and understanding.

My teacher shares that we must come back to God. We must be knowledgeable of our duty to Him and perform it. We must gain a thorough knowledge of self and Allah (God). This self-knowledge will lead to the attainment of the requisite knowledge that will cultivate our gifts, skills and talents. This will allow us to fulfill the demand of the female and the rights of the female from our nature as men. This will cause us to extract the beauty and the comfort that God has created for us in the nature of the female. My teacher shares that the female is like a vault that is sealed. We can open the vault only if we have the right combination, and the right combination is our preparedness to fulfill the demands that her nature requires of us. The more dutiful we are, the less argument there will be; the more dutiful we are, the less adultery there will be; the more dutiful we are, lesbianism will diminish; the more dutiful we are, the more peace there will be in our homes. My teacher shares that the burden is not on the female. That first duty and burden is on the male. When we are beings that fulfill our obligation, the female at peace becomes the foundation of a good family and high civilization. Her preparedness through the cultivation of her mind, gifts, and talents will be the base of a highly educated, developed, cultivated society. If we desire a great nation, then, we must return to our duty to Allah (God); our duty to ourselves; our duty to our mates and she will make for us the greatest nation ever in the history of the world!

Chapter 3 – Straight Talk to Men regarding Marriage and Male / Female Relationships

The only way I could even attempt to guide my brothers is with the wisdom that I have received from my teacher. Otherwise I wouldn't know anything else to tell you. I have utilized the wisdom my teacher has shared with me my entire adult life and I have observed many other men utilize the wisdom and the council that my teacher has shared over these years with much success. The purpose of this chapter is to motivate, uplift and inspire you to think more carefully about your crucial role to your family and to the overall community. I would like to address some of the little things that many brothers fail to think about on a daily basis but the importance of which can never be taken for granted. These little things may be affecting the quality of your work and your performance as a man and a husband. This chapter will help you to look into your personal relationship situation and consider whether you need a proverbial, **"Check up from the neck up"**. I am blessed to be married to the same woman that I started out with nearly 20 years ago and from whom I am blessed to have six children. I brought a significant amount of baggage with me into my relationship with my wife, Sister Cecelia. I was so very, very, very ignorant, immature and underdeveloped and I needed someone to act like a sponge for me to absorb all of that out of me. Every man needs a woman to help him get his foolishness out of him so he can be a respectable and honorable man. In the initial stages of my relationship, I didn't even want to acknowledge that I had my own personal issues that were silently lying beneath the surface of my transparent exterior. As men, all some of us want to do is point fingers at our women and blame them. Blaming and accusing are attributes and characteristics of the devil. At one point in our relationship, I was very eager to point out what was wrong with Cecelia but yet so unwilling to hear how my own defects were manifesting to her and affecting her. Now, people see me now and some of them say, **"Brother Marcus is one great man!"** I just laugh and I always tell them, **"To God be the glory and that what they are seeing is a reformed me."** I am a long way from being where I need to be but at least I am on the road. My teacher has greatly helped me as a man to come out of the sick, twisted, juvenile and chauvinistic way I was thinking. I am now connected to my Creator in a most powerful way. I strive to act so much better because I now know that I am a part of the people of God and that my nature is to bow down to the will of God.

My dear brothers, there are four important questions in life that you must be able to answer at all times. The first being who Am I? The second being where Am I going? The third being how am I going to get there? The fourth being who will help me get there? Every black man has three identities to deal with: the man he wants others to think he is; the man he thinks he is; and the man he really is. To the degree to which these three identities coincide determines the depth of your reality and the amount of peace we will have in our life. That's a lot of pressure for a man to be under. Do you consciously think about who you want others to think you are? Do you consciously think about the man that you think you are? How conscious are you regarding the man you really are? Have you ever given much thought to the pressure that most of us as black men are constantly under? At home, we have the pressure of spending time with our family, doing our fair share of work at home, and being sensitive to our wives. Once we leave out of the home there are other standards that apply to who we are for instance at work. We are expected to behave aggressively, to make the sale, to create the new project, to win the contract, to be a good negotiator. At work we are expected to compete through any available means. We are expected to be a good son to our parents, a good husband to our wife, a good father to our children, a good employee to our boss, a good boss to our employee, and so on and so on! **Many black men are so busy trying to be good to everyone else that they end up being horrible to themselves.** The question is, **"Can we successfully please everybody?"** Should we even attempt it? Bill Cosby is quoted as saying, **"I don't know the secret of success. But I do know the secret of failure, and the secret of failure is to try to please everybody."** Brother, all of these people and factors are what God uses to make us into God's. If we are overwhelmed by the relatively small amount of people that we have to deal with in our lives, then how on earth will we handle what soon will be coming into the lives of every one of us who have a divine rendezvous with destiny. Jesus said, **"If you are faithful over little, I will make you ruler over much."**

Crisis is normal to life because our crises are the catalyst for our change. If you were to look at your life so far, it was the crises and challenges that you went through that helped you to see yourself in a greater light. One wise man said that, **"Crises don't make the man; it only exposes him for what he is."** Each step of maturity or growth generally occurs through some crisis. The only constant in life is change, and change customarily produces crisis. Now there are some constant things go on in the life of every responsible black man that once he masters these things they bring him closer to becoming a powerful and superior man. We call these things the Science of Manhood. What is *"The Science of Manhood?"* It is the depth of a brother's knowledge, wisdom and understanding of what makes him who he is. My teacher broadened my understanding of who and what I am. When I began trying to follow my teacher I came to him as a Christian but in name only. The life I was leading was hardly Christ like at all. I was doing everything I was big enough to do in Jesus' holy and righteous name. However I wanted to be totally sure that my teacher loved Jesus and respected Jesus before I could submit myself to him. Isn't that something? I wasn't really even following the man Jesus but I wanted to make sure that my teacher was. I am so happy to let you know that today I believe I am a better servant of God today because I have a real, live, flesh and blood example in front of me that is leading me. Today, I am not just a Christian. I have grown in understanding so well that I can also say that I am a Jew. But I can also say with great pride that I am also a Muslim. Am I confused? In no way shape or form. These are all names that we have given to the way of God. Let me make this clear with the help of God of why I am a Muslim also. I am striving to be a Muslim not because Prophet Muhammad (Peace be upon him), or Abraham came. Jesus said in Scripture, **"Before Abraham was, I am"**. As a people we were in existence before there was an Abraham, Moses, Jesus, Muhammad, or even a Bible or *Holy Qur'an! We were* there in our fathers and in our ancestors. We were Muslims from the very beginning, because that is the nature in which we were created. **We say this to all of our Arab Muslim brothers and sisters, meaning no disrespect, but Islam did not begin in Arabia.** Islam begins with Allah (God), Himself. Islam is not 1,400 years old; Islam is as old as Allah (God), Himself. **We say this to all of our** Arab Muslim brothers and sisters, meaning no disrespect, but Islam did not begin in Arabia. Islam begins with Allah (God), Himself. Islam is not 1,400 years old; Islam is as old as Allah (God), Himself. I don't like anyone to try to get on some ego trip and try to convert me. Even though we have grown up in the West as Christians, we are not converts to Islam, for the Qur'an teaches us that Islam is the nature of Allah (God), and it is the nature in which He created man. If it is God's nature, and it is our nature, then we have only accepted to be what our Creator created us to be. So we do not wish to be made in the image of Arabs. We do not wish to be made in the image of any British person. And after over 450 years of evil and mistreatment from Satan and his devils we sure as hell do not wish to be made me in the image of White Americans. My teacher shared that *you cannot convert us to what we already are*! You can just encourage us to be ourselves! Now, the only thing I am interested in doing is converting ignorance to wisdom. We are black and if Satan and his devils would leave us alone we would accept our own and be ourselves. Our nature is to submit to Allah (God). Islam does not come from a book. Islam comes from the nature in which we are created, so the book comes from within ourselves. But, when we have lost the path, then Allah (God) sends a prophet with the guidance and a book to guide us back to our nature that we have violated. If we know better we will do better. I got some further help with my issues when my teacher directed us to get and study a book by L. Ron Hubbard, **"Dianetics – The Modern Science of**

Mental Health". After I read through the book and received what is known as 'Dianetics auditing' I am even further on the road to my true self.

What so many men don't want to do is to open their mouths and ask another man to come and help them to see their problems and their situations from another perspective. The Bible says, **"Men sharpen men like steel sharpens steel."** If we were really brothers we could accept the truth from one another. The brother sitting next to you may have valuable wisdom to share with you that you really need to do better. He's only sharing the information with you and he doesn't benefit at all if you implement what he says or not. As men we have to realize that we don't have to figure this thing out all by ourselves. A man's respect level is one of the things that make a man who and what he is. Respect for What? Respect for the Various Relationships that a man has in his life. Here are some examples of what we are talking about:

One of the main relationships in a man's life is his relationship with God
Another is his relationship with himself
Another is his relationship with his wife
Another is his relationship with his children
Another is his relationship with his parents
Another is relationship with his relatives
Another is his relationships with his co – workers male / female
Another is his relationship with his friends
And yet another is his relationship with the people of his church or mosque

My teacher shares that no man knows who and what he is without marriage. This is why the Qur'an does not condone being a monk. The Qur'an does not condone being a nun. This is something that God has not put on us, this is something that we put on ourselves. God has not instructed, in neither the Bible nor the Holy Qur'an, for a man to be a eunuch. God has not asked the Pope to take a vow that he will not touch a woman. God has not asked the Father or the Cardinal to take a vow that they will not touch a woman even though you ache so to do and do. God has not asked a woman to take a vow not to have a man. The very growth and development of a man or a woman as a person is our struggle to overcome the difficulty factor in uniting the male with the female, and the female with the male. By any man denying himself that joy, that pleasure, and that struggle, and that pain, is denying themselves a part of the journey toward God himself.

Men need to learn how to take charge of all of these relationships. Part of what makes us who we are as men is our ability to take charge? Did you know that it is expected of every man that he take charge as the **"Head of your household"**. You might ask who expects this? Certainly Almighty God expects this along with our wives and children and all the members of the righteous society expects for us to take charge as the true head of the household. This is true my brothers even if they don't lift a finger to help us to do it. Even if they put roadblocks in our way, they still expect for us to do it. You may ask, **"What happens when a man doesn't take charge?"** The answer is that he is looked at as being less than he really is and everyone who depends on him to take charge is disappointed. Brother, we need to look at what it means to truly be the Head of our household and how Almighty God has equipped us as men for such a responsibility.

My teacher shares that no man knows who and what he is without marriage. This is why the Qur'an does not condone being a monk. The Qur'an does not condone being a nun. This is something that God has not put on us, this is something that we put on ourselves. God has not instructed, in neither the Bible nor the Holy Qur'an, for a man to be a eunuch. God has not asked the Pope to take a vow that he will not touch a woman. God has not asked the Father or the Cardinal to take a vow that they will not touch a woman even though you ache so to do and do. God has not asked a woman to take a vow not to have a man. The very growth and development of a man or a woman as a person is our struggle to overcome the difficulty factor in uniting the male with the female, and the female with the male. By any man denying himself that joy, that pleasure, and that struggle, and that pain, is denying themselves a part of the journey toward God himself.

Some brothers don't know this, but men are expected to provide for nearly every aspect of the lives of their family members. This includes spiritually, financially, morally, educationally, psychologically, emotionally and sexually. God wants to build boys into men so that they may bring spiritual maturity into the lives of their wives and family. Today, we want to really know what it means to be a Powerful and Superior man. This world does not want a black man to think constructively about anything at all. This world promotes easy lives and complete devotion to personal desires to men. However, it is only when we, as men, struggle earnestly for the higher values of life that makes us worth remembering. This world does not want a man to even acknowledge the contributions of men who have preceded him to the final destination. This is because this world wants every black man to have to start off fresh from the bottom without ever having the benefit of the knowing his fallen brothers mistakes and successes. This world never wants a man to reflect on his own life and what he has devoted his life to. This world produces men that think too small and can only think about their little house or apartment, their little job and their little car. This world produces men that seem to lack the capacity of worldview thinking. Powerful and Superior men understand how to interpret and evaluate issues across the spectrum of politics, economics, morality, entertainment, education and a seemingly endless list of other fields. They are able to break these things all the way down in ways that interest their wives and their children.

What is a man's spiritual responsibility? The Bible is clear about a man's responsibility to exercise spiritual maturity and spiritual leadership. Of course, this spiritual maturity takes time to develop. This spiritual leadership is central to God's vision of marriage and family life. A man's spiritual leadership is not a matter of dictatorial power, but of firm and credible spiritual leadership and influence. A man must be ready to lead his wife and his children in a way that will honor God, demonstrate Godliness, inculcate righteous character and lead his family to desire righteousness and goodness. Spiritual maturity is a mark of true manhood, and a spiritually immature man is, in at least this crucial sense, spiritually just a boy. Did you know that in all the major religions, it is expected of a man that he will help lead his family to God? A man has to read and study the Scriptures of God for himself that he may be a guide and a living example of the Scriptures to his family and community. It is the duty of every man to study the word of God. You must study for yourself. It is the inferior and lazy thinking man that doesn't want to study for himself and is waiting on a Minister, Pastor or Imam to study for him. A good shepherd of the flock loves for the men and women under his spiritual charge to be well studied. Prophet Muhammad (PBUH) said that one learned man is harder on the devil than a thousand ignorant worshippers. A man should crack open the Bible and the Holy Qur'an as often as possible. A powerful and superior man makes sure that every member of his family has a Bible and a Holy Qur'an to review for themselves. Too many brothers only have one Bible and one Qur'an in their household as if they are rationed out or something. As a man you should go and buy a few more as soon as possible. Did you know brother that you are expected to lead your family in all daily and meal time prayers?

A man should know how to pray. As a man you should invite the presence of God into your life at all times. We should pray that in all of our endeavors as men that we be guided on the right or straight path. You should make sure that you are aware of what you are saying when you pray. In my home we pray together all the time. When we are at home we pray throughout the day. When we leave out of the home we pray as we get into our car to head towards our destination. When we are on the way back home again we pray some more. God will not care for us if we don't pray. Prayer and constant communication with God is everything to people who want to be right. Your family should wait for you to sit down at the table. The children and even the invited guests should wait for you as a sign of respect for you and your leadership. You should always sit at the head of your table and because you are the man of the house wherever you sit is the head of the table! No one should eat at your home until you have set down if you are there. If you are there at your home you should be there on time for dinner and you should establish some regularity of eating dinner with the family. It is especially important to develop the habit of cheerful and pleasant conversation when the family is all together if we want to have friendly and harmonious relationships in our home. We have to mature to always strive to be pleasant to our family no matter how rotten we might feel inside. There's no point in making them miserable just because we're down in the dumps for one reason or another. This is especially true at meal times. Do not upset everyone's digestion – including your own – by making the family meal a recitation of troubles, anxieties, fears, warnings, and accusations. Discipline and dinner do not go together. Make every meal a joyful and happy festive occasion. Children are especially cognizant of the kind of family atmosphere they are raised in, no matter how young they are. It's a known fact that abused children group up to be child abusers themselves. And children with mean and grouchy parents will grow up to be mean and grouchy themselves. So, if you want your children to grow up and be the kind of adults whose company other people will enjoy, raise them in a cheerful and pleasant family atmosphere. You and your wife should not allow everyone to eat in different parts of the home. No child should take their plate and go into their room. Dinner time is family time. Dinner time is a special time of the day. You should have a special plate and the corresponding silverware at every meal. You should never eat off of paper plates and out of a Styrofoam boxes if you can help it. A man deserves to be respected in his own home. This is not slavery for your family to show you respect as the man of the house. Your family may think they are doing this for you but they are showing themselves honor and respect by doing this. The whole dinner will go smoother if you would rise to where God wants you to be as a man. When we learn who we really are as men, the wisdom will set us on top of civilization! My teacher shared that the family dining room table is the family conference table. When we sit down to dinner a man is expected to deal with the family issues. A man is expected to have plenty of knowledge, wisdom and understanding for his family when they need it. Whenever our children ask us as men a question we should have an answer or be ready to go to find the answer. Here's a quick tip: If you don't put anything in (Your

Head) then nothing is coming out of you. A powerful and superior man never plays down the intelligence of his children or his wife by stunting and fronting when he really doesn't know the answer. A man should lead the conversation along with his wife. You should not allow anyone at your table to disrespect your wife or for your children to disrespect one another. You should have been preparing for dinner conversation all day long. You don't have to dominate the conversation. As men we must learn how to access information when we need it. It's when we cannot provide answers to our family's questions that they start to look elsewhere. I am so glad that we have a teacher that has so graciously shared thousands and thousands of Audio Tapes, Video Tapes, Cd's and DVD's with us on virtually every topic imaginable so that we can truly be strong and intelligent before our wives and our children. Go and get some now for yourself at: store.finalcall.com. True masculinity is not a matter of exhibiting supposedly masculine characteristics devoid of the context of responsibility. Marriage is unparalleled in its effect on men, as it channels their energies and directs and gives divine purpose to the man. All black men today must aspire to be the kind of man a black woman would gladly marry and that children will trust, respect, and obey.

Gather your entire family in a comfortable setting such as the family room, the den, or the living room. Soft, pleasant background music is permissible if it's turned down low, but no television and no other interruptions are allowed. Each person takes turns being the subject while all the others tell him the good points they see and like about him. There's no end to the good things you can say to each other in a family love feast. And it helps the entire family to get along better, to understand each other, to appreciate each other more, to have fun with each other, and to look for the good qualities instead of the character defects in people. Praise and kind words of love and appreciation for others can make irritable people become warm and outgoing. Sad and despondent persons can become confident and enthusiastic when they are treated to a love feast like this.

A Powerful and Superior man has a Moral Responsibility to his family. Today so many young and older men are heavily marked by their practice of ignorant recklessness, juvenile irresponsibility and unimpressive behavior on virtually any street in North America. As a man grows into manhood, he must develop moral maturity as he aspires to righteousness, learning to think like a decent, honorable and dignified acting black man and showing others how to do the same. A Christian or Muslim man is to be an example to others, teaching by both precept and example. Of course, this requires the exercise of responsible moral reasoning. True moral education begins with a clear understanding of moral standards. These moral standards are found in the Bible and in the Holy Qur'an. We must study both books for they will help us as men to move to the higher level of moral reasoning and then we will learn how the wisdom is translated into godly living and how the moral challenges of his day must be met with the truths revealed in God's inerrant and infallible word. A man simply cannot grow morally strong if he doesn't know God's word. My teacher shares that true education cultivates the person—mind, body and spirit—by bringing us closer to fulfilling our purpose for being. When we are truly educated, we are led out from darkness into light, from ignorance into wisdom, from weakness into strength.

To be a man is to make decisions. One of the most fundamental tasks of leadership is decision-making. The indecisiveness of so many brothers in our community and in our homes is evidence of stunted manhood. A man does not rush to a decision without thought, consideration or care. A man understands that decisions have to be made and is willing to put himself on the line in making a decision in the home and making that decision stick. This requires an extension of moral responsibility into mature ethical decision-making. Our decisions as men should please our Creator for we are acting in His place when we have charge over our families. All of our decisions should be faithful to God's word and should also be open to moral scrutiny. A real man knows how to make a decision and live with its consequences — even if that means that he must later acknowledge that he has learned by making a bad decision, and then by making the appropriate correction. Powerful and Superior men are expected to be the moral force in the life of his family members. A father is expected to settle all disputes between family members by searching for the truth of the situation and not choosing sides. A man is expected to be just, fair, and honest as he delivers justice to his family. My teacher shares that the need for justice at all levels of development is that which helps to make the human being secure. Each child looks to the parents to settle their disputes with justice. When disputes arise in the family, it gives the mother and the father a chance to teach and instill family values, moral values and also to build good character in the children. Some of us think that disciplining our children is abuse, but, everything in creation has its affair regulated by law. Our children will not voice their opinions or share their perspectives in a home that it is ruled by fear, and they will never say to the parents what they really feel. If our homes are ruled by love, and governed by the principle of justice, then, we will encourage our children to speak to us so that we may know how they think and what they see and feel. We then have the task to either help them to see better, or in listening we may find ourselves at fault and we correct ourselves.

There is a scripture in the Bible that teaches that God is Love. The creative force out of which He created the heavens and the earth is the awesome power of His Love. In that great display of love, Allah (God) regulates the affair of His Creatures by means of law. The Honorable Elijah Muhammad taught us that the first law is motion and the second law is order. Out of Allah's (God's) Love, He puts all things in motion, and, out of His Love, He gives order to that motion by means of law. In the home there is a need for rules, regulations or laws. Rules and regulations are a human need, and to deny our children the discipline of rules is to deny them that which ultimately will make them secure. There must be rules in the home. There must be rules that teach us how to relate to one another properly in the home. There must be rules of respect for parents, children, self and one another that are taught in the home because everywhere we go we will find existing rules and regulations. Where there are no rules, there will be no order. Chaos will be the result. Where there is chaos it will bring an end to the activity or the life of the home, school, community, nation and the world.

My teacher shared that having discipline in our homes is not abuse of our children. We learn to respect rules in our home s that when we go to school and meet with the children in the neighborhood, rules of social behavior if taught, accepted and practiced in the home means that our children will be more apt to accept and obey the rules of society, then, jail or prison win not be an end for us. *The respect of rules and regulations starting in the home could mean the end of prisons.*

Children have a need for attention. **"Look at me." "Listen to me."** These are not words coming from the lips of the children, this is written in the nature of the child. We must be careful in disciplining our children. There is a line, which if crossed in disciplining our children could be labeled as abuse. In a world that is prophesied to come to an end; where human beings are suffering loss and enduring great levels of stress, as parents, as teachers, as leaders, as preachers, as foremen, and as authority figures, we must be careful not to take out our stress on those under our authority, thus violating their rights. More and more there are children killing their parents, killing their teachers; workers killing their foremen, or bosses; spouses killing each other because of abuse and violation of rights. Corporal punishment is not abuse if it is done with moderation, with the thought in mind of correction and not the thought of afflicting pain, but, to bring about change in the behavior to make a better child and a better human being. Punishment must always be in accord with the violation, and devoid of anger. The love that we have for our children is the reason why we punish them because our desire is to make the child better.

In today's society the rights of parents are gradually being taken away and although this is supposed to be a Judaeo-Christian society, the Bible's teaching of how to rear the children is being ignored and uprooted. The Bible says, **"He that spares his rod hates his son; but he that loves him chastens him early."** (Proverbs 13:24) **"Withhold not correction from the child; for if thou beat him with the rod, he shall not die."** (Proverbs 23: 13) It also teaches, **"Train up a child in the way he should go and, when he is old, he will not depart from it."** Children are growing up in homes where there is no discipline because there are no rules. Children today do what they please and their parents, mothers in particular, allow this license not realizing that their unwillingness to train the children up in the way they should go will bring great pain to the parents in the future. A train that is on a track is disciplined by the track. The engine pulls the train. Likewise the parents should be the example of what the parent hopes for in the children. The parents are the engine that pulls the child along the track. Whenever a train jumps the track, we have what is called a wreck or disaster. The lives of our children are being wrecked, and disaster is in their future if we do not love them enough to lay down rules that we encourage our children to live by.

Men are expected to settle all the major disputes in the home that arise. We are expected to set down the laws of the family. You are expected to clearly define for the family, this is who we are, this is where we are going, this is how we are going to get there and then solicit the necessary help he needs from his family and others to make his idea or strategy real. A powerful and superior man is not expected to not bring drama home to his family. In today's time a man is expected to guide his family through more filth and indecency than ever before. This places a great responsibility on the shoulders of every man. Your stance to your family against filth and indecency will be compromised if you are a weak man morally. If you love pornography, as many brothers do, how can you truly take a principled stand? Many men talk the talk of morality to their family but very few of us can walk the walk.

A powerful and superior man has an Educational Responsibility to his family. I am going to spend some time on this one. Did you know that our women expect for us to well educated? Many of our sisters have shared with us over the years that the average black man can't even hold a conversation with them. That is sad brother. Since the fall of Adam, man is only a caricature of himself. I have already shared with you what the Scripture says, **"Ye are all Gods, children of the Most High God."** My teacher shares that Satan and his devils have so reversed what Allah (God) intended for us to be that that word would now be, **"Ye are all dogs, children of the most low Satan."** It is this state that the man is in that has driven the female away from him and even made her in some instances hate the very presence of a man. The women who meet with men, who may be desirous of an elevated conversation, usually find the words and actions of the men demonstrating that their minds are below their waists or navels. This is very disheartening to a good female. Men are expected to go out in the world and bring the finest information and knowledge back to our family members. We are expected to constantly bring books and magazines home so that our family can have access to the latest information that is out there. How can a black man have a black family and not have one Ebony Magazine in his home, or one Jet magazine, or one Essence Magazine in his home? Every black household should have the Final Call Newspaper on their table on a regular weekly basis. There is so much information in every Final Call Newspaper. I love the paper so much that for the last 20 years every issue the paper has come out I have pulled two copies off the top for my personal collection. A powerful and superior man is expected to insure that all of his family members can read at a high reading level. How much of a reader are you? So many men don't read at all. A powerful and superior man leads a balanced life. Brother you have to read the best literature and magazines and keep up with current affairs and events. A well read brother is an interesting brother. **Did you know that the person that can read and does not has no advantage over the person who cannot read at all?** Did you know that readers are leaders and that leaders are readers? What are you reading right now? My teacher shared that everything that we want to know is in a book. How often do we read books in the field in which we work? Is your answer once a month, once every six months, once a year or once every five years? Are you a learner? Do you know your learning style? Learning styles are simply different approaches or ways of learning. How do you prefer to learn new things? Knowing your learning style will help you develop coping strategies to compensate for your weaknesses and capitalize on your strengths. The scientists say that there are three Personal Learning Styles for most people. They fall into three categories, Visual, Auditory and Kinesthetic.

When you are a Visual Learner, you learn through seeing. A Visual learner needs to see the speaker's body language and facial expression to fully understand the content of a lesson. They tend to prefer sitting at the front of the room to avoid visual obstructions (e.g. people's heads). A visual learner may think in terms of pictures and learn best from visual displays including: diagrams, illustrated text-books, overhead transparencies, videos, flipcharts and hand-outs. During a lecture or discussion, visual learners often prefer to take detailed notes to absorb the information. Are you a visual learner?

Maybe you are an Auditory Learner, Auditory learners learn through listening. They learn best through verbal lectures, discussions, talking things through and listening to what others have to say. Auditory learners interpret the underlying meanings of speech through listening to tone of voice, pitch, speed and other nuances. Written information may have little meaning until it is heard. These learners often benefit from reading text aloud and using a tape recorder. Are you and auditory learner?

Maybe you are what is called a Tactile/Kinesthetic Learner. These kinds of learners learn through, moving, doing and touching. Tactile/Kinesthetic persons learn best through a hands-on approach, actively exploring the physical world around them. They may find it hard to sit still for long periods and may become distracted by their need for activity and exploration. Are you a tactile / kinesthetic learner? How important is knowing this information to your success? How about your wife? What kind of learner is she? What about your children? What kind of learning style do they have? Is your home set up to support their particular learning style?

It is expected that we will learn at least two languages well enough to converse in. A man must be able to speak, to be understood and to communicate in a way that will attract and edify others. Beyond the context of conversation, a man must learn how to speak before larger groups, overcoming the natural intimidation and fear that comes from looking at a crowd, opening one's mouth, and projecting words. Though not all men will become public speakers, every man should have the ability to take his ground, frame his words, and make his case when truth is under fire and when belief and conviction must be translated into argument. Men are expected to be cultured and refined. We are expected to teach our family how to be civilized. A man is expected to travel. My teacher shared that all wise men are travelers. Since we may already be traveling men, where are we traveling from and where are we going? What are we seeking that causes us to travel? Many men think that to travel means that we can get on a plane and move about the earth. Of course that is traveling but that's traveling on a lower level. My teacher shared that the traveling that we are talking about is man's journey from the darkness of his mother's womb to the light and the presence of Almighty God. When one makes that kind of travel he can never stop his journey. Traveling expands our minds and traveling expands our world view. You meet different kinds of people when you travel and get to have new experiences when you travel. Do you like to travel? Traveling makes you bust out of your comfort zone. When you travel you will sometimes have the privilege of meeting and observing at close range people from amazingly different backgrounds. Some will be well educated in the academic sense; some will have almost no formal education. Some will come from wealthy families, *while others will be the products of poverty.* Some of the people that you will meet will represent many occupations, nationalities and a variety of personal philosophies. Very few people that you meet in this world will ever be highly successful at earning money, rearing families and winning respect.

When was the last time you got away from the city in which you lived? Why did you leave the city in which you live? Since we are talking about traveling on a lower level right now, where have you ever traveled in North America? Could you name five states in which you have been for more than two days? Have you ever been to Europe, have you been to Africa, to Asia, to Australia, to Antarctica? Have you been to South America yet? Do you have plans to go? Have you ever traveled by airplane? Do you believe you can fly? Do you believe that you can touch the sky? Have you ever traveled by boat? Have you ever been on a yacht before? Have you ever been in a helicopter before? Have you ever met any famous people before? If so, who? Did you meet them in your city or did you have to travel to have that experience? May I ask a few more questions about your education? Have you eaten in at least two fine restaurants before? What were the restaurants? Do you consider yourself to be a sophisticated black man? What is your level of sophistication? What about your family members? All of these questions have everything to do with our education as men. Most of the time when we haven't experienced much in this life, it is because we hasn't done much. But despite the fact that we as men may not have traveled much or experienced much in our lives we are still expected to make a contribution. My teacher's master, the Most Honorable Elijah Muhammad said, **"The sign that a person has truly been educated is that person can make a contribution."** Who really cares what walk of life you come from as a black man? Who really cares where you have been educated? The question is can you make a contribution to the onward march of your family and your Nation?

A superior man comes to his Church, Mosque or Temple meetings and sees every lecture or sermon in the light of a classroom. Too many brothers are so concerned with officiating and being impotent in their respective faiths but they are not concerned with getting the teaching into their own ears or into the minds of their wives and into the hearts of their children. As men we have to come to our respective houses of worship to learn. A superior man is always thinking five to ten years down the line. You never know where you will end up. Just because things are rolling along great and beautifully for you doesn't mean that tomorrow it will not change. Tomorrow isn't promised to any of us. I recommend that you always bring a pen and pad with you everywhere you go for learning can take place at anytime and from anyone. You could get a flash of inspiration at any moment. How many good ideas popped into your head only to be lost a few moments later because you didn't have a pen and a paper?

We are still dealing with education. A brother that is striving to be a powerful and superior man needs the following tools at his disposal to help him to make his contribution to his family and to his Nation. You need to teach your children, especially your male sons this information as soon as possible. Every brother needs to have an identification card on his person at all times. Brothers need to have their social security card or at least know their social security number by heart. Every black man needs to have a driver's license if he is going to be driving a vehicle and then he should also know his driver's license number by heart. Every brother should have a working car. It doesn't have to be flashy or fancy but it must work. He should think about purchasing at least two vehicles for him and a larger vehicle for his wife. You will need to learn how to fix the minor problems that come up with vehicles from time to time. Every brother should have car insurance on his car if he is going to operate a vehicle in his state. You don't need the fanciest car out here on the market. You don't need spinners and rims on the car. You need a car that will drive and get you to point A and point B starting off. Down the road you may be in a better position to get the fancy car. It's no crime to have a very basic car. It is considered uncivilized to ride through the neighborhood with your system blasting the filthiest and most profane rap songs.

Many brothers jump into business with no knowledge of how a business works. Many times brothers will start a business up with just an idea. The longer you are committed to staying with your idea the more likely that idea will expand beyond your expectations. You should have a sign for your business and a wonderful location that is easy to get to. My teacher shared that a business with no sign is a sign that you have no business! If you are in business you should have a business card. How can someone take you seriously if you are handing out your contact information on toilet tissue or paper towel? Once you get your business established you should purchase post cards to put out all over the city in which you live to promote your business. Make sure that the card is professionally done. First impressions are lasting impressions. You should also obtain a business license. A powerful and superior man does the necessary and pre – requisite research on business principles before he goes out and tells people that he is in business. Many brothers are in business this week and out next week. Does your business have any literature? Are you representing your ideas by giving people a copy of a copy of a copy? You don't have to open up a store initially to do your business. Many black people are thriving with in home businesses. Here's another thought for your consideration. Many of the brothers don't have anything to involve their wives in besides having another baby. Why don't you help her get into business with you? You can find some businesses that let you buy in to the business. You can get in it and if your wife agrees to run it she can take it and build it up while you are out working on something else. If you don't have any ideas on what to do in terms of a business then just call me at 404-542-3808. I will strive to give you some of the best ideas to help you and your family to come up! We are in this thing together. You should teach your children how to hustle and get their entrepreneurship skills on. They need to be educated very early that the black man and woman must do for self or die a slave. No-one should let you do all the work when it comes to caring for your family. A powerful and superior man assigns his family members tasks to do to help him with his goals and objectives that they are directly benefitting from. This is critical brother for you to do. Place some of the pressure on you on their shoulders. They can help you do something in your efforts to help them even if it's helping you to keep the car clean.

It has been said that most black men don't have a clear knowledge of who they are and they don't have a clear picture of where they want to go. My teacher shared from the Scriptures, **"If the blind leads the blind then both fall in the ditch."** Is this statement true of you? Why or Why Not? How can your family follow you if you haven't done your part? Your part is to come up with a vision that is inspired by God. My teacher shared that vision is the faculty of sight. When a man has vision he has unusual competence in discernment or perception. When we have vision we have gone beyond merely looking at a thing. Vision means that we now have the ability to look into a thing so that we have unusual competence in the ability to discern what others miss. Vision has at its root an idea. An idea is a well developed thought. In the comic strips this was depicted by a light bulb turned on above the head of the comic strip character. But it was not really an idea but he or she had a thought. Ideas are different than thoughts. Ideas exist like thoughts in the mind as a product of mental activity. Our minds must be active. Brainwaves can be shown on a screen to indicate that our brain is alive. Electrical energy allows the brain to do what it is designed to do. Once we have a thought, we have a concept. When thought germinates in the mind, if we don't continue to think on the thought then the thought without more thought, only is a thought that comes and goes. And then we get mad at someone who not only had the same thought but actually put more thought into their thought and manifested for the world to see! Many men don't realize how we mess up with women by bringing her our whim for the day, or for the week. Many of us as men don't put enough time into thinking and planning a real agenda for our family to follow. We will hear some other man say something that connects with something in our head and will bring that home as the official agenda of our family. Initially our wives may go along with us on that but after a while they just shake their heads at our lack of leadership. Many women are so frustrated with this aspect of men. They see in us the potential to be great men and great leaders of our families. But we are not well trained in leadership and how to move our families towards a real, well thought out and planned agenda.

Our family can't follow just any old thing or whim that we come up with. We are going to have to eventually sit down and think about where we would like to go. Once we are clear we should sit down with our wife and let her help us to weigh the idea and see if it can stand up to scrutiny. She is not our enemy. **My teacher shares that the woman is born to find weakness in us as men and to destroy it!** She is your principal helper and helpmeet from God. According to the Bible, God *did not desire the man to be alone.* As men we have to learn how to really utilize the woman and the family that has come to us through that woman that God has given us. We have to learn how to really make our wives our partners in everything. As men we have to accept that our wives are not our personal slaves or maids or our mothers! My teacher shared with us from his teacher that a woman is capable of equaling herself up to a man. As high as we can go as a man is as high as she can go, as our wife. As men, we often set the bar. How can a woman equal herself up to a man that is not striving for anything and doesn't seem to want to be anything? Some men are so frustrated with the success that their wife is having in her life that they actually act as saboteurs of their wife's progress. Some men act like they are envious and jealous over her success. Some men will not speak positively nor encourage their wives to continue making progress because their ego is in the way. Brother we have to say that her success is our success and our success is her success. We are in this together. We are a team! We are not in competition with each other when we are living under the same roof and sleeping in the same bed. We won't be able to keep a relationship evolving if we are immature. Psychologists now talk of **"emotional intelligence,"** or EQ, as a major factor in personal development. While the world has given much attention to IQ, EQ is just as important. Individuals who lack the ability to relate to others are destined to fail at some of life's most significant challenges and will not fulfill some of their most important responsibilities and roles. By nature, many men are inwardly directed. While women have learned over the years how to read emotional signals and connect, many men lack the capacity to do so and seemingly fail to understand the absence of these skills. While a man is to demonstrate emotional strength, constancy and steadfastness, he must be able to relate to his wife, his children, his peers, his colleagues and a host of others in a way that demonstrates respect, understanding and appropriate empathy. This will not be learned by just playing video games and staying in the privatized world experienced by many men in today's times.

We have to make sure our wives have their own materials to operate with. She needs pens, pencils, books, and something to put her materials in. She can't be the woman she wants to be stuck under you all the time. She has a wonderful brain and plenty of energy within her to be utilized. A Powerful and Superior man delights in freeing a woman up to be what Almighty God created her to be in the beginning. A good man will support his wife's goals that she has set for herself like he would want her to do for him. As men we should be the example of what we expect our wives to do for us. We are expected to strive hard to purchase computers in our home so that our family can have the benefit of modern technology and equipment. We need several computers in our home that are all networked together for success in today's times. We are expected to buy the computers, buy the desks, buy the computer chairs, and to buy adequate and up-to-date software. We can't protect our children at the public Library. We should teach our family members how to use the computers to access and to research information. We should teach them how to set up and email account for their friends and buddies and also set up a professional and business sounding email address. We have to show them how to purchase goods and services over the internet. We have to show them how they can access newspapers from throughout the world on the internet as well as watch video streaming of the news on the internet. We have to make sure that everyone in the household, including the children, knows how to turn on and fully operate a computer. A man should get a working telephone number for his home. Get a telephone number at your home and then purchase an answering machine for your house. Make sure your message is to the point on your machine. Don't let your children leave the message, don't put a musical interlude on your message and for God's sake, please don't sing or rap on your message. You are trying to be powerful and superior men. We should train our family on how to answer the telephone. They never know who will call, when they will call and why they are calling. When you are dealing with the telephone, it is serious business. If someone called for you at your home would you get the message that you had received a call? Would it be a written message? Would the message include the person's name? Would the message include the business they called from? Would the message include the time of the call? Would the message include a number to call that person back? A powerful and superior man keeps all of his messages in a box so that if he should ever need that person again he has a telephone number. And it is true that you never know when you may need that person's telephone number again. Do you have a working cell phone number? Why did you purchase your cell phone? Remember when you said you were purchasing it just for emergencies and business calls? Are most of the calls that you receive for business or are most of the calls you receive personal calls? Are you wasting a lot of valuable time on your cell phone playing 'Angry birds', or endlessly texting or 'facebooking' or just chatting away with no real purpose in mind?

Did you know that you have a physical responsibility to your family? Unless afflicted by injury or illness, a man should develop the physical maturity that, by stature and strength, marks recognizable manhood. Of course, men come in many sizes and demonstrate different levels of physical strength, but common to all men is a maturity, through which a man demonstrates his masculinity by movement, confidence and strength. A man must be ready to put his physical strength on the line to protect his wife and children and to fulfill his God-assigned tasks. A man must be taught to channel his developing strength and emerging size into a self-consciousness of responsibility, recognizing that adult strength is to be combined with adult responsibility and true maturity. A powerful and superior man is expected to protect his family from all harm and danger. You are expected to lead your family in the pursuit of physical excellence. You are expected to keep your physical health up. You are expected to remain physically attractive. Are you slowly starting to allow yourself to become fat and greasy? It happened to my father. When he met my mother he was an attractive and slim black man at the age of 19. By the time he was 43 years old he had allowed himself to become 450 lbs and dead from a heart attack. You are expected to go to the doctor and get regular checkups. You may not know this but you are expected to cover all healthcare aspects of your family. You are expected to encourage your family to eat healthy because it promotes a long life. You are also expected to be clean in mind and especially your body. You are expected to bath daily and brush your teeth. You are expected to take your family outside to get fresh air. There is nothing wrong with taking your family on a long walk through one of the State Parks or right around your own community. You are expected not to use drugs or to abuse alcohol. You are expected to understand the impact and damage that the constant abuse of these things will have on your body and mind and how it may impact your future seed. A Powerful and Superior man has a psychological and emotional responsibility to his family. You are expected to protect the minds of your family members. You must be mindful of the music, television and overall entertainment that you are allowing your family to view. You are expected to understand that whatever your family is inputting into their minds and hearts is what they are going to output. You are expected to know how to relieve the burdens of your family member's minds by being amusing, clever and funny. We have a responsibility to keep hope alive in our wives and in our other family members in the household. We are the axis upon which nearly everything turns in the household. It is also the duty of every man to make his family feel loved. You are expected to be very careful of your language to all of your family members. You are expected to strive hard to control your temper. You are expected to hug and kiss your family members and tell them how much you love them and how much you appreciate them. This can be very challenging for some brothers but not for a powerful and superior man. It's natural and human nature to love yourself, and to be self – consumed, self – pre – occupied, and self absorbed. But brothers, we must grow beyond ourselves. For as long as we act like that, we can't properly give ourselves to anyone else with real and lasting love. Marriages are successful because each partner dies a little of him / herself to make the marriage successful. Therefore, you are expected to think five times before you speak. You are expected to know the various ways in which human beings receive love. A powerful and superior man is expected to stay home and give his family quality time as much as possible. You are expected to be emotionally involved with your family members and show concern and care for their problems and general life issues.

A powerful and Superior man has a Sexual Responsibility to his family. What do I mean? Brother, we are expected to have control of our sexual appetites. We are expected to find a woman of our choice and settle down with her. We are also expected to remain faithful to the woman we select and to not cheat on her. The institution of marriage allows the lawful sexual union between male and female in the eyes of God and society. Since both, male and female should dedicate their lives to the Will of Allah (God) and the great struggle in the journey of the meeting with Allah (God), and, the great struggle of the union of the two, then the pleasure derived from sex is divinely given to enhance the union as well as to re-charge the electrical energy of the male and the female that they might continue the great journey and struggle of life. These two, properly motivated, allows the sexual union to be a life-giving experience not only in procreation and continuance of the life of the species, but, it is invigorating as well as life giving to the marriage and the struggle of these two to become as one. My teacher shared that for us to look at marriage as only the legalization of the sex act is to put our minds on a level that will not bring the best out of the experience. **To become extreme in our view that the sex act is only for procreation and not meant by God to give pleasure to married couples is a view that is not in accord with the Will, Plan and Purpose of Allah (God).** These pleasure centers in the human being, used properly and in accord with the Will of God, brings comfort, ease, consolation, rest, reward and joy to the souls that are working hard to fulfill their Divine duty and obligation.

My teacher asked the question, **"What is the purpose of sex in marriage?"**

1. Procreation of human species.
2. Reward the struggle of the two to become one with the joy of the pleasure of each other's complimentary nature.
3. To give rest, relaxation and new energy to the male to continue the great mission of being producer of mastering the earth and its laws as he strives to become Khalifah or one who stands in the place of Allah (God) at his level of development. The female in energizing the male and giving him this comfort, consolation; giving him peace and quiet of mind as a rest period between struggle is also satisfied and is pleased because she has given rest to him to work for Allah (God), her and the family. Therefore, she is rested in herself. This is the Divine Purpose of Sex in Marriage.

Satan however, has taken this natural gift of Allah (God) and made mischief with it causing us to go after pleasure without struggle; without the burden or responsibility of being what Allah (God) created us to be. We have become pleasure seekers without responsibility and misusing our pleasure centers thus becoming coming slaves of pleasure. This has given rise to the misuse of women and the misuse of what Allah (God) gave them for the man so that she becomes a prostitute -sex for hire, he becomes a pimp - using her and the need of the male for pleasure as a means of livelihood. The lust for pleasure is causing the abuse of children, male and female, and the misuse of our bodies. As a result, we are living in a morally degenerate world. We are paying the price for this moral degeneracy through the plague of AIDS and sexually transmitted diseases, which produce the destruction of the male and female and the destruction of our future. This is why we must return to Allah (God) and seek to know His purpose for what He created and use everything of creation in accord with purpose for it. Then, and only then, will we find the genuine peace, joy and happiness that we seek.

We are expected to sexually satisfy our women. This is important brother. There is no crime in getting us some good books on the subject of sex. It is very important that the woman be satisfied during the love making process. Maybe we are over developed in this area. Certainly we have the right when we are lawfully wed to enjoy each other when possible. There is a formula to this. I don't know that you can ever really enjoy the act of sexual intercourse if there has been no fulfillment of duty. A man has a duty by a woman and a female has a duty by a man. When that duty has been performed properly then a man and a woman both are in the mood for sexual expression. But when we haven't performed our respective duties to each other then who wants to submit to a partner who is default in duty? Even as the society celebrates sex in every form and at every age, the truly powerful and Superior man practices sexual integrity, avoiding pornography, fornication, all forms of sexual promiscuity and corruption. He understands the danger of lust, but rejoices in the sexual capacity and reproductive power God has put within him, committing himself to find a wife, and to earn her love, trust and admiration — and eventually to win her hand in marriage. Most marriages are made on the basis of sex and therefore, when the sex drive diminishes there is nothing of substance to hold the marriage together, because it was made from a physical, rather than a spiritual desire. It's critical that men respect this incredible gift, and to protect this gift until, within the context of marriage, they are able to fulfill this gift, love their wives, and look to the Creator's divine gift of children. Male sexuality separated from the context and integrity of marriage is an explosive and dangerous reality. A man must understand that he is accountable to God for his stewardship of this great gift. We are expected to abstain from sexual activity at certain points in our relationship with our wives i.e. / their menstrual cycle. Not only are we not expected to physically or sexually abuse any member of your household but we must insure that neither the male nor the female members of your household are abused in any way.

A Powerful and Superior Man has a Financial Responsibility to his family. Advertisers and marketers know where to aim their messages — directly at adolescent boys and young men. This particular segment of the population is inordinately attracted to material goods, popular entertainment, sporting events and other consumer options. The portrait of young manhood made popular in the media and presented as normal through entertainment is characterized by economic carelessness, self-centeredness and laziness. A real man knows how to hold a job, handle money with responsibility and take care of the needs of his wife and family. A failure to develop economic maturity means that a man will often float from job to job, and take years to **"find themselves"** in terms of career and vocation. An extended adolescence marks a huge segment of today's male population. Slothfulness, laziness and economic carelessness are marks of immaturity. Many of us want financial success so bad that we can taste it. Of course, financial success is not a barometer that we are getting closer to God. So many of us as black people don't think we are anything unless our pocket is straight. Then we can come to God. Then we mistakenly reason that God will look at us as being a little better than somebody else. So we give our money in the Church, in the Mosque, and in the Synagogue often times to be seen of men. **"Did you see brother so and so.... Yes he gave a $1000!! Praise god, that's a good brother there."** A real man knows how to earn, manage and respect money. A Powerful and Superior man understands the danger that comes from the love of money, and fulfills his responsibility as a good, righteous steward. It is expected of every man that he will work and work hard for the direct benefit of his family.

Men and women generally derive their self esteem from different places. A woman may be aiming her efforts at the home and family. A man may be aiming his efforts at a promotion possibility on his job. There may be a boom in their business that is causing everyone to work overtime, and he may be aware of all the pressures but he may see them as only temporary bends in the flow of the healthy routine. A man's work, the place where his self – esteem is built, is largely found outside of his home. Men and women generally derive their self esteem from different places. Men and women build their self – esteem in different locations. A man is caught up with what he does in life. His wife is far more concerned with the relationships that make living worthwhile. Even a woman who works will tend to discuss her family. Work to a woman is the means, not the end. A man, on the other hand, seldom introduces himself, saying, **"Hi. I'm the father of two daughters."** He views himself in terms of what he does or what he owns, his hobbies, titles, clubs, church / mosque and his car. In short, a man's significance is found in what he has authority over. His work is the only way he knows of keeping all those items under his control. Bills are a natural part of life and all bills must be paid. You are expected to pay all the bills of the family. When you misspend the wealth of your family it undermines confidence in your authority and rulership in your home. This type of fiscal mis-management also makes the female talk down to the man as if he is one of the children instead of a leader. It is expected that you will save for each of your children's financial future.

Brother as you can see, this is a lot of weight and responsibility. In order to fulfill these things we have to be balanced men. We have to be active socially, having many friends and a few confidants. We have to be active intellectually, having many interests. We have to read, watch, observe and learn. One of the things that we need to learn is how to live our lives as men successfully. When we know how Almighty God thinks, plans, and organizes then we have been clued in to the missing links. So many men today fall into the category of being scatterbrained. If you listen to us as men, sometimes our ideas are all over the place. Be very careful about running behind or putting your money behind every crazy scheme some brother has come up with that he is promising you, you can get paid with. That's how they always come with the promise that you are going to get paid if you do this or that. As an alternative my brother, why don't you sit still by yourself quietly one day and write down all of the options and ideas that you would like to do and then settle down to the best choice and the best use of our time and energy. Choose the idea that you can actually do. It has been said that the most important thing in any great endeavor is to know where to begin. I personally want to grow to be a powerful and superior man. I don't ever want to be superior to my own brothers. I just simply don't want to be an 'Average Joe' anymore as a man. So many brothers just want to remain ordinary brothers who don't know which way to go. We can't lead our families if we don't know what's going on. A higher knowledge is what will enable us to climb above the present circumstances of our lives and do a whole lot better. A powerful and superior man believes in other people. A powerful and superior man doesn't overreact to negative behaviors, criticism, or human weaknesses. They don't feel built up when they discover the weaknesses in others. They are not naïve; they are aware of weakness. As a man, how do you handle the weaknesses of other people? How well do you handle the disappointments, frustrations and headaches that other people bring and place at your doorstep? If we are not handling those things well then maybe we need a higher knowledge. My teacher shared that we should get knowledge to benefit ourselves. Having more knowledge in your head will improve almost any situation that a man can get into. Having a higher knowledge as a man will help you to work as smart as you are working hard. Seeking and finding more knowledge will help you to become amazingly productive, but in new and creative ways. My teacher shares that every human being can be made productive with greater knowledge of self and God.

A powerful and superior man welcomes challenges and is always actively working to defeat all of his self – defeating behaviors. A self – defeating behavior is any behavior that keeps us from living up to our potential or results in self – inflicted pain. It can include such things as procrastination, anger, fear, denial of feelings, inability to express our needs or inability to stand up for ourselves. As men we need to have principle centered lives. If we look closer we would see that there are principles at the base of all the religions that undergird all of the religions. Men that are successful in life simply do what unsuccessful men do not do. Powerful, superior and successful men live by principles. Unsuccessful men live by their feelings and they walk around blind to how to overcome reality because they are always functioning off of their feelings. A powerful and superior man is a good leader because he is a good follower and is seen practicing that of which he is studying. The more one studies, the more one must practice, for it is only the practice that refines our understanding of the principles. How quick would you compromise your principles for money? How quick would you compromise your principles for advantage, fame, fortune or the spotlight? Are your principles unchanging principles? Are you spending too much time majoring in minor things? Those who study oft-times become separated from those who do not study. The more you practice principles you soon become their master. Then one day we come to the point of graduation and get promoted to practice even higher principles.

Men and even boys used to be able to find literature everywhere that shared stories about true manhood, courage, bravery and audacity. At least, that's the way it used to be. But that was yesterday. Today, men are both minimalized and marginalized everywhere we look. Turn on your television and look at the images of men in general and black men specifically. Over the last few years in nearly every action movie we have see out of Hollywood there are female leads that are kicking plenty of masculine behind throughout the movie. As men we have to define ourselves in God. We have to be men of character and conviction. Powerful and Superior men look for ways to demonstrate their courage. They risk their own lives in defense of others, especially their wife and children, but also anyone who is in need of rescue. Sometimes they show their courage by taking a stand against a woman being beaten or even refusing to succumb to the temptation of silence. They try to stand as a model and example to others, who will then be encouraged to stand their own ground. In these days and times to even want to be a man is a sign that you have great courage. So many men are trying hard to be women today. So many are out here trying to 'out woman' the real and natural woman! I am not throwing off on any one because one sin is no more a sin than any other in the eyes of God. We have to accept our nature as a man. I don't care how much surgery a man has. You can lift it up and tuck it in but brother; you still a man on the inside!

There are some very negative characteristics that we may have picked up as men that interfere with principle centered living in this day and time. One of these is for a man to be **intolerant.** When a man is intolerant this means that he is unwilling, unable and has an inability or refusal to accept others opinions, beliefs or behavior. Another negative characteristic is **minimizing.** When a man minimizes he makes excuses for or makes less of his behavior to make himself and others think he is not that bad. Another negative characteristic is **phoniness.** When a man is phony he is deceptive, insincere, not genuine and an emotional phony. Another negative characteristic is **self centeredness.** When a man is saddled with this one he is overly concerned with his own welfare or interests and has little or no concern for others. He mistakenly believes that what he wants is always the most important thing. We are not going to have a lot of success with our marriages and relationships if we don't learn to compromise! Another negative characteristic is **anger.** So many men today are excessively and uncontrollably angry. My teacher shares that each of us, as human beings can occasionally become angry. When we are angry, we are capable of doing that which, under normal emotional circumstances, we would not do. Anger has degrees to it. We can be angry and have our anger under control. People may see a fire in our eyes; they may hear something in our words, but we are keeping ourselves under control. But, there is another kind of anger when we allow it to get to that point where we are unable to control the reaction that comes from our anger. We reach a point, then, of insanity. We have lost the balance. Then what comes from our mouths and hands can be very destructive. Many of us think of a person with anger as someone who yells at his children and kicks his dog. But more often it is the person who suffers in silence who has the problem. Many of us have been taught how to carefully bury our anger. Many of us instead express our anger in a camouflaged form in our relationships as bitterness, cynicism - *distrusting or disparaging the motives or sincerity of others*, or envy and we often fail to recognize the indicators of anger in our lives. We don't seem to recognize as anger the little inner twinge when a friend makes an ever so carefully phrased insult in the middle of a conversation. We don't recognize as anger the vague bitterness at our family for not appreciating all that we do for them. Many people who are unable to recognize anger in their lives do sense that they have been hurt many times in the past, and that many of the hurts have not been resolved.

We have many misconceptions about anger. Sometimes we can have a slight feeling of irritation at our spouses that can build into something else. Sometimes because we have been brought up to be sensitive we have been mistakenly led to believe that all anger is wrong. And when we are brought up that way we hide from ourselves our own feelings of irritation and anger. We can repress this powerful source of energy so much that we will literally feel nothing for our spouse. Many of us believe that if we don't look, feel, or seem angry, we don't have an anger problem. We work so hard to bring our emotions under control. As they crop up in our lives we master them in our attempt to look like we are a gracious, calm, rational person. Eventually, we may even have everybody fooled and even to a measure, our own spouses. But it is all a fake. We have a nice looking outward appearance; but inside, there is almost nothing there. Sometimes underneath, beyond the reach of our conscious mind is a mass of feelings bottled up. We may not even know that they are there. We may see them surface every now and then but the time may come when the whole thing may blow up in our face, in an emotional breakdown. Then all the things that had been buried so long will come out into the open. There can be no healing, no recovery, no building a new life for you until all of the feelings that we have had or that we may be unconsciously harboring are sorted out, and you have learned to know them for what they are, accept them, and find some way of expressing them honestly and nondestructively.

Many of us believe that if we ignore our hurts and anger, they will go away and won't cause us any trouble later on. Many of us believe that if we just let all of our feelings and anger hang out – just get them out of our system – we'll solve our anger problems. Some of us come across as people who wouldn't hurt anyone, people who are never angry and who seem to have an ideal temperament. People like this are generally friendly and well liked, **"nice people."** But they often pay a tremendous price for their perpetual niceness. After a few years' physical and emotional illnesses often develop that affect their health, their relations with family members, and their job performance. Most times they believe that it won't cost them too much emotionally to be a nice person who never gets angry at anybody. Many of us try to make it appear as if we are not harboring any bitterness or anger toward anybody that we know. But anyone with any therapeutic skill could detect that we have buried a number of hurts over the years. And maybe we don't see any correlation between old hurts and our current symptoms. Some of us believe that if we express our hurts and anger to the person we are angry at, our relationship will suffer. Some psychologists and psychoanalysts are now estimate that at least 50 percent of all emotional, psychosomatic, and interpersonal problems are the result of poorly handled anger. What is more staggering is that a large percentage of these individuals don't even realize that they have an anger problem. It is precisely the person who thinks they never get angry who often has the most serious problem with anger. They may sulk, whine, or stew; they may be cynical, envious, or catty; they may savor secret injustices, make cutting comments, or develop a martyr complex; but if you ask them if they have a problem with anger, they will smile innocently and say, **"Why, no – I never get angry."**

Some of us don't have any trouble expressing our feelings. We make it quite clear when we are angry – a little too clear. Everyone is quite aware of the fact that we are angry because of how we act when we are angry. Some of us break things when we are angry. Some of us become angry when people are critical of any aspect of our words, actions or behavior. Some of us intentionally do things to hurt other people's feelings that we believe have tried or are trying to hurt us. Some of our spouses become very aware of our anger when we break windows, doors, dishes, and furniture. Here's a brother that often yells at his spouse. And one day in a fit of temper he punched a hole in the wall, threw a color TV set through the window, and punched his wife in the stomach. Squelching our feelings never pays. In fact, it's rather like plugging up a steam vent in a boiler. When the steam is stopped in one place, it will come out of somewhere else. Either that or the whole business will blow up in our face. Bottled up feelings are just the same. If we bite down our anger, for example, it often comes out in another form that is much more difficult to deal with. It often changes into sullenness, self – pity, depression, or snide, cutting remarks. Not only may bottled up emotions come out sideways in various unpleasant forms; they may also build up pressure until they simply have to burst forth. And when they do, someone is almost bound to get hurt. Many of us ignore anger and even deny its very existence until it boils over, at which point we can't avoid it any longer. But by that time it may have caused incalculable damage to you and the people that are around you.

One of the most important abilities and needs a person has is that of being aware of their own feelings. As men, many of us have been robbed of the right to our feelings, especially feelings of anger. It's comparable to a kind of psychological rape, in which a vital part of our humanity is violated, leaving us with irreparable emotional damage. Our feelings are like a valuable guide, a sixth sense. They are an important clue to the unconscious and to issues of which we may not be totally aware. They are an invaluable monitor that alerts us to a side of an issue that is not being fully expressed at that time. However, feelings should never be regarded as mandates to action in themselves. They are incompletely formulated pieces of information – partial but vital bits of information that must be evaluated with knowledge, judgment, and understanding in order to give us a valid and complete picture of the situation. Feelings are an indispensable part of our lives. They are vehicles to help us evaluate our actions. Losing the ability to be in touch with our feelings is tragic, certainly as grave in consequence as losing our sense of touch, taste or smell. When we are in touch with our feelings we are best able to be in control of ourselves and to be responsive to those around us. As a N.O.I. Hubbard Dianetics Auditor I am beginning to understand that helping a person recognize and deal constructively with their hurts and anger is one of the most important things that I can do. I am convinced that if a person is able to handle their anger in their life maturely, they will probably mature in other respects of their life and will be fairly free from emotional difficulty.

So many of us still have temper tantrums and rages against people who don't do what we want. Another negative characteristic is **resentment.** When a man is resentful he sulks around and can be a very vindictive person. He dreams of getting even with others and actually relives past emotional hurts and pain from time to time. Another negative characteristic is **covetousness.** This so called society in which we live is actually encouraging this human weakness in the American people very strongly. A man has a great battle and struggle with himself when he has an unreasonable desire for things he does not have, such as another person's possessions, power, money or relationships. Another negative characteristic is this one called **denial.** When a man is in denial he refuses to think about, hear about or admit things that he knows he did or said. Another negative characteristic is **false pride.** When a man is filled with false pride he acts, boasts or pretends to himself and others that he is better than what he actually is. Another negative characteristic is **procrastination.** As men when we do this we keep putting off to some future date things we could have done sooner to avoid unpleasant or undesirable consequences. Another negative characteristic is **self – pity.** It is sad that so many men feel so sorry for themselves and keep talking about their miserable situation. When we are like this we often blame others for our troubles. Another negative characteristic is **impatience.** Some men get very annoyed when we are delayed or something opposes us. We want what we want when we want it. These negative characteristics that are operating in all of us as men help to redirect our will towards ends that are oft-times destructive. My teacher shares that his teacher, The Honorable Elijah Muhammad, did not want us with any weapons, not because he wanted us to be defenseless in the face of Satan and his devils, but because he knew the tendency in us to settle all our disputes with a gun. He wanted us to build our intelligence to deal with our problems properly and not rely on a weapon to resolve our problems. Most of the people who are in prison today—having killed some friend, neighbor, husband or wife—are living with intense regret because they really didn't want to do it, but in anger they did. If the weapon was not there, they might not have done it. Black people are disproportionately represented in homicide statistics because we are constrained from expressing our will to be in direct control of our destiny. **The Black-on-Black homicide statistics are a barometer of our oppression in America.** Throughout this book are positive principles for a man to adopt into his life to help him to be successful in everything.

A man can't just work all the time. My teacher even shared that a man can't be all for God and not for his own family! How many hours do you put in a day at work? Eight, Nine, Ten, Eleven, Twelve, Thirteen hour days! Satan and his devils will never pay you what you are really worth. On the flip side, are your children and family seeing enough of you? Are you giving too much at the office? What effect is all of this having on you mentally? Physically? Emotionally? Financially? How many people are depending on you to be strong for them? How many people take from you without giving anything back? If you continue the pace that you are currently on, where will you be in five to ten years? Do you know how to say No to people who constantly demand of your time and energy? Are you still effective at what you do? As most men grow and mature as men they gradually realize the importance of good character. Real manhood is not about physical prowess or handsomeness. Real manhood is not about personality, talent, intelligence, performance or profession. Real manhood is about the heart of the man, the inner man, his moral character. A man of cheap character is always trying to associate with, gain identity from, or to control people of great talent or character. Some men hide behind the good name of someone else to shield and to compensate for their own lack of character and integrity. When a man's own name is untrustworthy, he is always a namedropper. When a man's charm wears off he has nothing but character left. Charm is for the instant; character will last. Charm deals with the external, character with the internal. Many men in this world have charming manners that disguise poor character that will one day vanish, revealing the truth underneath. A real man's strength of character can be relied upon. Character is what a man is in the dark, when his wife, family, parents and other assorted folks can't see them. Most men are exactly what they seem to be. The way a man lives his life teaches us who that man really is. We can normally judge a man by the kind of enemies he has. If a man doesn't have any enemies it's usually because they don't have much character and they don't stand for anything. By the way, my teacher shares that nobody can claim to be a champion without a good challenger. When a challenge comes up in our lives we shouldn't shrink from it. If a man doesn't stand for something, he will fall for anything. What a man truly is begins to be revealed when his talents decrease and when he stops showing us what he can do. We should never be surprised when fig trees bear figs. A man's character is like a tree and his reputation is like its shadow. The shadow is what we think of it but the tree is the real thing. A powerful and superior man doesn't defraud others for money, recognition or even the respect of his family. Real men recognize truth and cling to it. Real men recognize truth, submit to truth and allow the truth to help them to discipline their lives. A man is only qualified to lead to the degree that he serves. A man must not just teach his family but he must train them. A man must be a living example of the principles that he enunciates, if he truly wants to produce a change in the thinking of his family. This generation of children and young people do not believe in, **"Do as I say and not as I do"**. This generation believes in, **"I will not only do what you do, I will do it ten times worse than you are presently doing it!"** To train your immediate family a man, a father and a husband must invest his time, give of himself, impart understanding, develop skills in his children, and motivate them to make others into followers, who will, in turn lead will lead others. Powerful and superior men understand that, *"Life and death are in the power of the tongue"*. If someone in or out of their family brought it to their attention that his actions hurt them he would apologize and seek that person's forgiveness. Powerful and superior men are not afraid to apologize and that's one of the reasons they are so powerful and superior to the kind of man that this world offers. A powerful and superior man has learned the skill of how to make his family feel important and to do it sincerely. Did you know that *the deepest principle of human nature is the craving to be appreciated? Did you also know that the exact opposite of being appreciated is to be laughed at? In fact, among the Eskimos, laughter is the only punishment for thieves.*

Here are some final tips for men. Every man needs to make an honest evaluation of himself to determine his strong and weak personal qualities. He will have to strive to overcome his weak ones and further strengthen those in which he is strong. Every man should seek the honest opinions of other men to show you how to improve your leadership ability. Powerful men learn by studying the causes for the success or the failure of other leaders. It would be so helpful to develop a genuine interest in people in order to acquire an understanding of human nature. Master the art of effective writing and speech. Have a definite goal and a definite plan to attain your goals. My teacher shares that we have to accept the challenge to overcome everything that is in our path until we reach your goals. Work on becoming more technically and tactically proficient. Before you can lead, you must be able to do the job. The first principle is to know your job. As a man, you must demonstrate your ability to accomplish the mission, and to do this you must be capable of answering questions and demonstrating competence. Respect is the reward of the man who shows competence. Tactical and technical competence can be learned from books and from on the job training. To develop this leadership principle of being technically and tactically proficient, you should attend a service schools and practice daily independent reading and research. It is no crime to seek out and associate with other capable men and observe and study their actions. Broaden your knowledge through association with members of other Churches, Mosques or Synagogues. Seek opportunities to apply knowledge through the exercise of command. Good leadership is acquired only through practice. Know your family members and look out for their welfare. This is one of the most important of all principles. You should know your family members and how they react to different situations. This knowledge can save lives. A family member who is nervous and lacks self confidence should never be put in a situation where an important, instant decision must be made. Knowledge of your various family members' personalities will enable you, as their leader, to decide how to best handle each one of them and determine when close supervision is needed. To put this principle into practice successfully you should put your family members' welfare before your own. To be an effective husband and father you have to correct grievances and remove discontent from your family. Every member of your family must know that you know them. You have to be approachable to your family. Let them see and know your resolve concerning them. Let them see that you are concerned with their living conditions. Encourage them to get the help that they need when you can't provide it for them. Protect the health of your family unit by active supervision of hygiene and sanitation. You have to make sure that everyone in the house is bathing and that you are running a tight ship. Remember that failing is not the worst thing in the world, quitting is. If something happened to you today or tomorrow and you were no longer here, would those who remained behind be better off for having known you? Are you making a significant contribution to your family? Men need to be inspired to want to live a noble life, a Godly life. Once you have truly been inspired then you can make a proper and necessary commitment to your wife and to your family. Once a man is truly committed to becoming a real man, he sees consistent, dramatic changes in his life from the very moment of his commitment. A real man is constantly evolving, purifying and changing the innermost parts of his being. This is how you can be successful as a husband and a father in this day and time. A woman loves all those little inconsequential, unimportant extras and she'll want to make sure they keep coming. Always pay attention to your wife and how you are treating her! Let her know by your actions that you know she's around. Say "please" and **"thank you"** to your wife. My teacher shares, **"Good manners protect good morals!"** Use them constantly. She should say the same to you. This will build a mutual respect between you and your wife. Always thank her for preparing your meal and be sure that you include a compliment on what you particularly liked about the meal. When we pass each other in the house, reach out and touch her gently. Bring her a glass of water when she's watching TV in the evening or whatever her favorite beverage is. What you are after is to prove positively to your wife that you still love her and that you still appreciate her. So if you want to maintain a harmonious relationship and a pleasant atmosphere in your home, all you need do is give your wholehearted efforts to your wife. A man will be happier in the home if he does. When he does these little things for her, his own benefits will multiply. He'll never want for a clean shirt, he'll never put on a pair of unpressed pants and he'll never sit down to a cold supper.

Be careful of your thoughts,
For your thoughts become your words;
Be careful of your words
For your words become your deeds;
Be careful of your deeds;
For your deeds become your habits;

Be careful of your habits,
For your habits become your character;
Be careful of your character,
For your character becomes your destiny.

"What do Men and Women really need from each Other?" - 98

Chapter 4 – Straight Talk to Women regarding Marriage and Male / Female Relationships

The only way I could even attempt to guide my sisters is with the wisdom that I received from my teacher. Otherwise I wouldn't know anything else to tell you. I have observed my own wife and many other women utilize the wisdom and the council that my teacher has shared over these years with much success. There are so many sisters who have really good black men with them right now but they just don't know it. Many sisters claim that they are waiting for 'Mr. Right Brother' but they fail to recognize him when he shows up. Good black men are indeed all around black women. They pass them on the streets, in the malls, and at the halls at work. Most women can't see them because they don't know what a good man really looks like. He usually isn't flashy enough or rich enough to turn their heads. He might not wear a suit or push a Lexus. He might not have a body like Tyson with a Denzel face. But, as they mature, they realize it's better to find someone who's got your back rather than someone who turns their head.

As we go into this Chapter, I wanted to get you thinking a little about the lives that most men have to live with every day. Most men need so much help from you in order to become what Almighty God intended for a man to be. Unless a good man is made for our women, many of you will feel like you feel now, unloved and unwanted. We see you out here as a single mother with your beautiful children but no father there to look after your children. So many sisters that I know personally out here feel unloved but are called upon to give love to their children. As a woman how can you give what you have not received? It is a fact that many of you have done an excellent job with your children, with hardly anything to go on. Every woman should thank God that she has been blessed by Him with a husband. That is probably one of the greatest blessings that a woman could have in this day and time. But what is a husband? My teacher shares that a husband is another name for a conductor. When a woman has a husband that means that she has a guide for herself, a maintainer for herself. She has a man that takes care of her in every respect. Now if that is true and it is a woman ought to be very careful about whom she selects as her conductor. She had better check the train out thoroughly.

Earlier in the book when we were talking about how a man had the potential to be like God what were you thinking as it related to your man? Do you really believe that the man that is in your life right now has that potential, the potential to become a master? Would you be willing to help him to go all the way through the process; a process that would take him from where he is now to where he would indeed be a master? Certainly your husband may not be a master now, but do you at least believe that he has the potential to become the master over all of the laws that govern the whole of creation? My teacher shares that a man can be above and beyond the creation though he too is creation. He shared that a man is so like to the Creator that the Creator can make your man and make him powerful enough to command the forces of nature. So many wives and girlfriends can believe that for every other man but not necessarily for their own husbands or boyfriends. Some women don't know how deeply their husbands are craving for their wives to really believe in them. So many husbands have shared with me that they rarely ever hear from their wives, **"I'm proud of you"**.

Over the last twenty years I have been blessed to work with hundreds of men in various capacities. What kind of men have they been? Men today are some of the most confused men the world has ever seen. So many women have no idea what they are up against as they try to relate to a man in a relationship today. Women are not prepared to deal with the intense levels of immaturity that plague men today. They are not sure how to handle a secretive man or a man that keeps things that bother him to himself. Or men that deny their past or that unpleasant event have even occurred in their life. Women are not prepared to deal with a man that fears letting people know him and who has difficulty interacting with his parents, his spouse and his children. Many men in today's times have a strong fear of criticism. Many men in today's time are angry and can't express their feelings. Many men fear failing and are obsessively driven to succeed. In the last twenty years I have encountered hundreds of men that desperately want their lives to be better but don't know how to change. And when men don't know how to change for the better they often change for the worst. We call this change for the worst self defeating behaviors. A self – defeating behavior is any behavior that keeps you or your man from living up to your potential or results in self – inflicted pain. As a woman if you are strong enough to acknowledge some of your own self defeating behaviors then it won't come as a surprise that your man has some of them as well. In fact, let's be honest about it, men have never as weak as they presently are in the annals of human history. I have talked with countless women who have expressed so much anger and frustration over the horrible mental, emotional, financial, spiritual, social and even sexual condition that they have found among their partners, their own blood brothers and men and general. And it is almost impossible to ask a woman to believe in a man in this kind of condition. Maybe this is why so many women are now saying to men, **"I can do bad all by myself."** Maybe this is why so many men are singing the, "Lean Back" song. They are letting you know as a woman that they are not strong enough for you to lean on their backs yet. They have a lean back. Many men need someone to come along and help strengthen their backside so that you as a woman and your children can lean on him when times get rough.

Some men are striving to do what has to be done in this day and time. Some men feel a sense of ingratitude coming from their wives and their children. Some men feel as though they are being blamed, mistreated and grouped in with the other men out here who have not done and are not doing their part. You must be able to make a distinction today as a woman. There are really only two kinds of men out here today; those who will do their duty and those who won't do their duty to you and your children. Which do you have? This chapter is to help you focus on the needs and the concerns of the man that is trying to be a respectable husband and a respectable father to you and your wonderful children. This chapter is about what those kinds of men need from their woman. Many of these men have expressed to me in my workshops that in uncertain times like these, the one thing a man should be able to depend on is the love and understanding of his women as he tries to get his act together. But nowadays many men are no longer 100% sure about the love of their woman. Let's start there with a couple of questions. Does your husband or your man believe beyond the shadow of a doubt that you love him? Does he believe that you will be with him all the way through the process? Today, many men have self doubts and anxieties. You may not know this but men have emotions. Men hurt; their heart aches and things bother him. A man gets nervous. Many men suffer because they have very little self assurance. Some men don't know the right things to say and in their relationships it seems as if they never know the right things to do. One way that men keep their sanity is by walking away from their problems. And many men have just retreated into their own world leaving their problems behind. Prophet Solomon is recorded in the Bible as saying, **"A constant dripping on a day of steady rain and a contentious woman are alike."** **"It is better to live in a desert land, then with a *contentious and vexing woman.***" What is a contentious woman? What is a contentious woman? One with a disposition to contend - who argues, criticizes, disagrees, opposes, quarrels, or questions you. She is full of questions, reminders, and suggestions - all to help you, of course! Some sisters lash their husbands daily and their complaints about him read like a shopping list. Are You a Contentious Woman?

Just as some women feel that they are suffering with men in today's times unfortunately some men feel they are now in relationships with women in which they are absolutely suffering. Some of these men believe they are suffering because most of the time they are doing their very best to be the man and live up to the image of the man that their preachers and teachers have told them about, other men have told them about and that their own woman said that she wanted. But there is one major problem. They don't have much support around them from their home base which is the number one place where the support should be coming from. Women don't seem to know how to take care of the man that is trying to be a real man. Let's see if we can help you see what we mean. A few years ago some men were talking one day about male – female relationships. Here is the substance of their conversation. One man asked, **"When did women cease to think that a relationship is a team effort?"** Read his words carefully. He said, **"It's hard enough for a man to understand woman, but men who love their women are trying our hardest. We've worked very hard over the past decades to try not to pass judgment on her based even when she doesn't live up to our standards for the sake of keeping a relationship going. Many men have learned not to be so controlling and demanding and have sought out the opinions of their wives in personal matters. Many women don't seem to understand that just as they have been hurt in relationships, we have too. Some of us are also just beginning to learn how to trust a woman again. Many men have become more expressive of their feelings, which, as you know happens to be a major struggle for some men. As men we are trying to get the knowledge of where we may have gone wrong in loving women. We have watched all of these movies over the last few years and have clearly seen how men dog women out and we don't want to be a dog anymore. We don't want to bring a woman down but we want to build her up. But so many women today don't have any real respect for a man that's trying so hard to respect her."** As a woman, do you hear what that man is saying?

This man continued, **"There are many men out here in this day and time whose hard work and effort on behalf of our marriage or relationship is often not reciprocated by our woman. Men are to this very day still judged by their wallets, even though the overwhelming amount of evidence out here suggests that in this current economic environment doesn't favor a poor man. For many men in America, if we cannot immediately get the same things other men are able to purchase for our wives or girlfriends like the house, the car, the college education, etc.), then we may soon be headed to divorce court or put out in the street. Many men who have accepted to be husbands are subjected to less respect as a person in the eyes of their spouses, regardless of how hard we work, what our ambitions are, or what we want out of life and love."** This man said that women often complained that he was too sensitive. And many men feel that because they are trying to be more sensitive to the needs of women, more and more women are taking advantage of that and are now actively working on controlling a man, rather than loving a man.

Another man asked the other day, **"When did money become the ruling factor in keeping a relationship with women?"** It has been the experience of many divorced men before they got married that his woman was saying to him: **"Money doesn't matter".** But when there was very little money left over after that man had taken care of the bills, the rent or mortgage, and other likewise important priorities, he found that he was being demeaned and even demonized by his woman. Some men in our workshops have expressed that they were even being cheated on by their spouses. It is true; adultery is on the rise among women in today's times. This generation is marked by adultery. We are hearing more and more about women who are now cheating on their spouses in the different cities that we go into just as men have always cheated. Now as a woman you might say, **"Yeah it's about time that the women are finally doing to men what men have been doing to women for the longest time."** But let me remind you of what my teacher shared from his teacher, **"Where there are no decent women there are no decent men."** Of course there are reasons for this. And one of the main reasons that women may be cheating today is that men are just not fulfilling women today. This is true. Many men do not know that it takes so much more to fulfill a woman than his ability to pay the bills. You would think as much as men talk about women that we would know a whole lot more about women, but we don't know. Many men do not know much about women at all. I didn't know either, until I was blessed to find my teacher who has helped open up my blinded eyes.

Even in this modern day and time, men don't know that you are more than money and finances. Or that you are more than breasts, hips, thighs and other assorted areas. Most men don't know how intelligent you really are and how your physical beauty is really only a sign of a much greater beauty within you that the human eyes can't see. Most men don't know how painful it is for you to be tied down with a man that doesn't seem to have any goals or ambitions in his life. That's very frustrating to you because your nature is to help a man be something and be somebody in the world. My teacher shared that Almighty God created you as a consolation for somebody who is a worker and a producer. You don't have the spirit to console somebody that's doing nothing. It doesn't matter how handsome a man may be, after a while, good looks look ugly if the man is not producing. God created you to help the man to do God's Will. That's why you are called, in the Bible, a 'help meet.' It didn't say 'mate: it said 'meet.' Help meet what? God laid on man, in his nature, the responsibility to do what? We've already shared that in the first chapter. But in a nutshell, God gave man power, dominion over the fowl of the air, the fish of the sea, and every creeping thing that crawls. God told man to multiply, replenish the earth, and subdue it. And he put woman there, to help the man, to meet what God had put on man to do. Well, if the man isn't doing anything, then how can you help a man do nothing? So when you meet a man, he's handsome, he's good looking, he's beautiful, he has a good rap, then you ask him, **"What are you doing?" "I'm not doing anything." "Where are you going?" "I'm not going anyplace."** Well what do you want to be bothered with somebody who's going nowhere and doing nothing? That's not who you are. And that's why most of you are unhappy women. And that's why you get married and divorced so quickly! Something is missing in the marriage, and most women don't quite understand what it is. It's not the man's fault. Sisters, don't blame him. It's not your fault either and a man should never blame you! My teacher shared that **a man is not going to be the man that he could be unless you help him to become the man that he should be. In order for him to be that kind of man you have to know who he is, know who you are, and above all know how to move him to the goal that God wants him to be at. You have to know how to do that.**

My teacher shared that when a woman really loves a man she will even study and read books in the particular field that he's in just so that she can have intelligent conversation with him about that subject. Most men know that you are supposed to be his help meet but how can you help him go nowhere? He can go nowhere and do nothing by himself. And this is what leads to the high levels of adultery in the community. Women are always going to be looking over the shoulder of a man who cannot satisfy their soul or their nature. Women want to give men more than their bodies today. Every woman knows that her body is limited but the power of her mind is absolutely unlimited. A woman wants to give a man access to the unlimited power of her mind but he has to bring that out of you. He has to call that part out of you otherwise it will never emerge. Just think for a moment. If you can take a man's sperm and turn it around in your womb for nine months and give him back a human child that is in the image and likeness of himself, then what could you do with his ideas? Until men learn who women are by nature, not from the outside, but who you are from the inside he hasn't yet seen the light. Our physical bodies are just a veil that covers a much deeper reality.

Another factor that encourages adultery is the music that is constantly played on the radio 24 hours a day 7 days a week. I mean just think over the songs that have come out over the last ten years over the air waves. Many of these songs are some of our favorite songs. If we are not careful we will find ourselves not just singing along with the artist but actually agreeing with the principles and the verses of the song. Just the other day I heard a man singing a song that maybe seemed harmless enough at first. But I was thinking about the man or the woman that might be in that actual situation or the person that was going through something similar. I believe his name is Luther Ingram. Some of the verses of the song went like this:

"Am I wrong to fall so deeply in love with you
knowing I got a wife and two little children depending on me too
And am I wrong to hunger for the gentleness of your touch
knowing I got three people at home who need me just as much
And are you wrong to give your love to a married man
And am I wrong trying to hold on to the best thing I ever had
If loving you is wrong I don't want to be right
If loving you is wrong I don't want to be right"

Just consider this man's passion! How do we make sense out of so many songs that women are singing that celebrate taking a man away from a woman? What's going on? One man posed questions like this, **"Is all of this adultery because the 'tables have turned', and now women are getting more chances at better jobs, better education, and more access to beneficial programs than men? Is this because our value as men has decreased? If this is so, why don't women just admit that our only worth in their eyes is our ability to bring in some money?"** The group Destiny's Child did sing a song called, **"Bills, bills, bills"**. Some of the verses went like this:

"Can you pay my bills
Can you pay my telephone bills
Can you pay my automobiles
then maybe we can chill
I don't think you do
so you and me are through"

These are just some of the areas that men are starting to question the love of our sisters. But there are many more issues. Here are a few questions for every married woman to think about. If the marriage or relationship isn't going right is it always the fault of the man in the marriage or the relationship? Is he always to blame? Are you paying enough attention to your man? If your man was going through a depression would you even notice? Can you honestly say that your man has no complaints concerning issues that he feels are important to his marriage to you or relationship? Do you even care whether he has an issue or not anymore? If you do still care, then maybe you should start paying some serious attention to these things and maybe things will change in your relationship.

So many women today are not even trying to hide their disrespect of their husbands or men in general anymore. Some of these women feel like their husbands don't deserve their respect anymore because their man isn't making enough money, or he's gone too much, or he just ain't providing what that woman needs. That disrespect is quickly manifested when their man doesn't do what he is told to do. Some women treat their husband as if he is a little boy that is awaiting his mommy to instruct him. Now there is no doubt that some men are like this and rather enjoy a wife trying to mother him....but for a real man when his wife or girlfriend comes at him with this spirit of, **"I'm fixing to whoop you"**, it creates a real resentment inside of that man.

When a man has accepted that he is a man, he is not waiting on your approval or acceptance of that fact. Many women make this critical mistake with their husbands. Sometimes women act as if they only know how to be loving and nice to their man when he is doing exactly what they desire for him to do. That's when they are pleasant to their man. But God help the man who gets out of line and tries to think according to his nature. And what is his nature? Do you know it? Do you know yours? Who has taught you how to deal with a man? Who has taught you how to care for a man? What does a man expect from you when he decides to commit to you? What does he really want and need from you and equally as importantly is what do you really want and really need from him?

Some women really do believe that they are the cat's meow in the house. They really have already judged their husbands or male companions as mental midgets and have already assigned their man a subordinate role while they have assumed the dominant role. **"This ain't the olden days"**, they say with glee. **"If my man doesn't move out to make progress, I will!" "I ain't gonna be no slave to any man"**. And even when they try to hide their feelings of superiority, their contempt for their husband is manifested through their speech and the actions they sometimes take against their husbands. Some women are quick to let their man know that his replacement is just a phone call away.

Many husbands have shared with us that their wives constantly undermine them to their own children. I encourage you to be careful with a man's children. Please be very careful because children are a man's heart and soul. Some men will absolutely walk through hell- fire for them. A man's children are the reason that he rises early in the morning and heads off to a back-breaking and mind-bending job for eight, ten and sometimes twelve hours each day. At the end of the workday, they are the reason that he races home. When a man sees his children's faces light up with a smile and he hears their gleeful shrieks of **"Daddy's Home, Daddy's Home!"** As his children run to greet him when he arrives home, they make him forget how tired he really is. The memory of the difficult time that he may have had at work quickly fades away. For some men, his children are the reason that he lives. So again I say be careful how you deal with a man's children.

How do women undermine their husband and male companions? Is your husband disappointed in your personal level of development as a woman? How is your husband interpreting your actions as a woman? Nowadays many women hate housework. Some women sit home in jogging pants and flip flops on their couch avoiding housework at all expense. Some sisters' email and text people all day long. Some women are on the telephone all day long. What does your husband come home to every day and night, a sink full of dirty dishes? The husband leaves the house and it's a mess and he comes home and it's still the same way. Some women have become so lazy that they don't even want to get out of bed. All they want to do is eat and sleep. Their idea of activity is driving the remote control through the endless number of cable TV channels with an aggressive thumb. Some women watch television all day. Some women know all about the soap operas. You ought to know as a woman that your husband watches you much more that you know. Some women have presented no plan at all to their husband for their children's advancement. They have a whole summer, June, July and August, but haven't planned one activity for the children. They haven't researched anything to present as an option. Some of us are blessed to be in Cities and in a State full of things to do at a very low cost. But as a woman, you haven't let your fingers do the walking through the phone book or used your mouse to plan any trips to all these libraries, any trips to all these Museums to all these aquariums? A man is watching and a man is listening. Nothing inspires her. Nothing moves her. She comes to the Church or to the Mosque but always goes home saying she isn't getting anything out of it. Something is wrong with that picture.

Women shouldn't disrespect their husbands, like belittling him or mocking him. That's more than just not respecting, it's actively disrespecting, and it's destructive. It can be so subtle how disrespect can happen and I don't think women are always aware of it. In America, there's this kind of subtle culture where it's ok for wives to make fun of their husbands in public, saying how e.g. they can't take care of themselves or just subtly treating them like children. As a woman you need to know the effect this has. It's totally demoralizing and emasculating. It sets up and feeds into a culture where it's ok for everyone to belittle men and treat them like children. And that's a culture in which it's impossible for men to lead. It's obviously ok to joke around. It's just, given how much men need respect, everything, including joking, needs to be in a culture of respect. And better to err on joking too little than joking too much. Remember that the Most Honorable Elijah Muhammad teaches us that too much joking is no good. Some women speak about how much they have sacrificed and given up in a relationship without a word on what that man has also had to put up with and gone through and continues to go through for them. Think about it for a minute. Here's a man that's trying to be the means of support to his wife. Most women constantly tell their husbands how much they have sacrificed to be the mother of his children, and how painful their labor was, and how they were on their way to becoming a doctor, or a neurosurgeon before he messed them up and got them pregnant. There is no doubt that as a woman you sacrifice a great deal when you become pregnant and that sacrifice continues up into this very moment. As men, we probably don't give you enough respect for all that you have given up to mother our children. May I ask you to consider something? Did the man give up anything to support the children that he messed you up with? Did he have to alter his life in any way? Did he have to give up any goals or aspirations that he held dear to man up to his responsibilities? I'm talking about the man that is doing what he is supposed to be doing. I'm talking about the husband that's out there right now as you read this portion of the book, probably at work putting in nine, ten, eleven, twelve, thirteen and fourteen hour days to help make ends meet in that household. How much do you consider that man? How much is that man thought about by you every year, every month, every week and every day? In fact who considers your husband at all in any serious way?

Most men are out here going it alone by themselves. The average man that I meet in my workshops doesn't even have any true friends or buddies by the time he settles down to be your husband. It's not that he doesn't want them. It's the grind of life that's got him. **"Everyday he's hustling. Everyday I'm hustling. Hustle, hustle, hustle... hard. Closed mouths don't get fed on this boulevard..."** It's the contests of will that he has engaged himself in. That man is determined not to be a casualty out here as a man and a father. He doesn't want to be MIA – missing in action and so it's his sense of mission to you and the children that's in front of him. He is not in control of anything in his life. He may be an outcast from his own blood family. He may be estranged from his own father. He may not have good relationships with his brothers and sisters. The one thing that he can possibly be proud of and work for is the family that he is trying to produce with your help.

Most women don't know the pride and joy that a man feels as he tries to take care of you and the children. The man that is dutiful is constantly under pressure to produce for his family. When he comes into his home from wheeling and dealing out there in that world, he is tired. He is frustrated. His mind has been stretched and pulled and turned inside out and upside down. Women may never know or understand what their husbands endure to make progress for them and the children. Satan and his devils are specialists at breaking black men and women. Racism is at an all time high now that we have a, "Black President". Please don't be lulled to sleep sisters and think that everything is all right or in some way easier for your husband to make progress. Because sometimes wives don't know, they don't appreciate or pay homage or give that man the respect that he's do. See a man is a simple creature. All a man really needs is a **'lil bit'** but on an everyday basis. It's not your sex. Lord knows we love that part of you. But it's that nature that we are after. My wonderful Sister and Student Minister, Ava Muhammad shared, **"A man needs to have a good woman who will be his helpmeet; who will be his comfort and consoler so that as he goes out into the world and faces the stress of everyday, especially the Black man, if he comes home and does not have that sort of committed relationship it actually ill-affects his health and that's not really recognized widely among us."** You can read more from my sister by visiting her webpage at: www.avamuhammad.com. What woman doesn't want a man to work for her and her children's direct benefit? A real woman knows how to keep a real man going. What does a man need a 'lil' of everyday? He needs the true nature of the woman. He needs the essence of you as a woman. After a man has worked, he may not want to come home and talk about bills. The surer a man becomes of himself; sometimes he just wants and needs to be obeyed without question. Please listen, once a man has proven himself time and time again to himself, to you and his family, he begins to expect you to obey him more and more. Obedience is not slavery. You are only saying silently through your actions, **"Sweetheart, I trust you now as I have trusted you so many times before. I believe in external God and the internal God that's operating in you."** It doesn't take anything away from you to listen to and obey your husband especially when he is telling you right and guiding your family right. When you deliberately disobey him how can you wonder why your children are so wayward and out of control to your leadership? When you submit to that man and he's telling you nothing but right to submit to, what's the real problem? Here are some questions for you to think about. Has your man proven himself to you? How many years has he been on the battlefield for you and the family? With the help of Almighty God, how many years has he made a way out of no way for you and the family? If he hasn't proven himself yet what more must he do? Will you become more submissive if he does these additional things? Or will you continue to fight him tooth and nail for the leadership of the family? If that man has proven himself to you then you should follow what that man says for you to do to the letter as long as what he is asking you to do doesn't conflict with your religion or your belief system. If you follow him in something and it doesn't work out you don't have to tell him, **"See I knew it was wasn't going to work out all the time."** Look at what actually went wrong and try again differently. As you well know, some women's mouths cause huge problems in their marriage. Some husbands can't take their wives mouth so they try to become your dentist. As we have already shared, Domestic Violence is on the rise all over America. Women all over this country and throughout this wicked and evil world know that they are suffering from great abuse. There's hardly a woman reading this book that hasn't been beaten by some man. Although some women are getting pretty tough and beating up their husbands nowadays! My teacher shared that none of that should be necessary.

While I am on that point let me share this. Some days a man needs for a woman to be quiet. Silence is golden to a highly productive man and a secure woman will do that for him. Yes… let that sink in. Many women talk way too much. When a woman talks too much it causes the man to shut – up and shut down. Our research indicates that most men hate a-know-it-all-woman. So many women position themselves in the relationship to compete with the man on all levels. Certainly as a woman there are some areas where you will have a superior knowledge to the man and vice versa. But part of the message that a woman sends out to her husband when she all ready knows everything is, **"I don't need you"**. And that's the message that some men are receiving loud and clear. I believe that's why there are so many lonely women who are single and who are married. When some men can't teach their wives anything then he will go outside and find plenty of women available to teach. Men need women to listen to them as much as women need men to listen to them. Sometimes men can be so aggravating because that's all we do is talk, talk, talk, talk, and talk some more with very little action behind what we say. Being with a man like this requires skill. Women need great skill to deal with just about every kind of husband out here. Always share with other what your husband shared with you in front of him if possible. This lets him know that you were listening. No one else probably wants to listen to your husband so it's your job and responsibility. Good luck.

Do you think that your husband is not affected by love songs? Let me tell you. He most certainly is. When he hears Whitney Houston singing her song, Run to You" When your husband hears Whitney Houston singing that song do you know what he says to himself quietly? He says, **"That's the kind of woman I need right there"**. It's not that he wants Whitney Houston. It's the loving sentiment that she so beautifully expresses in the song. When was the last time you felt like running to your husband? When was the last time you gave off that vibe? I'll bet you probably haven't made him feel that way in years. Listen to these words from that same song. **"Won't you hold me in your arms and keep me safe from harm."**

Ask yourself this question, **"Have I pushed my husband away from me? Why doesn't he want to hold me close at night?"** Because maybe all day long you've made him feel like you didn't need him at all. Some women never even ask their husband for his opinion on anything. Did you know that when the artist, Alicia Keys, sang about keeping a man's secrets safe in her diary, that song resonated with men? Why? Because every man wonders, "Are my secrets safe with my wife?" Do you know how important it is to a man to have someone to keep his secrets? Men listen to the radio and to music all day long. Men love songs that express the sentiments of a woman who is in love with a man and willing to go through whatever she has to go through in order to be with that man. That's what your husband wants to hear and feel from you. The rappers crudely call this kind of woman, **"A ride or die chick."**

You may be independent as a woman but in a marriage you become interdependent. The more a man is made to feel that you are dependent on him to perform his role as a man in the relationship, the more of the man you bring out of him. The more feminine you become in the relationship it should bring out more of the man and the masculine qualities in the man. A real man needs a real woman. When a man looks at a woman he doesn't want to see himself. He wants to see the exact opposite of himself. Men don't want a woman to be some silly girl with no ambition at all. They want a woman to be sure and secure in herself. They just don't want her to be so sure and secure that she sends the message that I don't need a man at all in my life. When a woman recognizes that the man she has received from God truly loves her and is trying so hard to be the means of support for her then it should cause something to happen within her for that man. Although all men have the same basic nature, all men are not all alike in how we express that nature in us. That's why you should never make comparisons between men. This is actually one of the worse things you can do. Some women do that for spite and cause men to hate and even kill each other. If you are getting remarried to another man never compare one to the other in the slightest sense. That's just a tip for your happiness.

When you and your man, are not relating it's a clash. When you're clashing with your man then that's not a relationship. When you are properly relating to your husband there is a relative proximity of spirit and mind and touching and sensitivity and feeling. You like it when it's like that don't you? However, when there is a break in the relationship; when there is stress and strain in the relationship, then your relationship with your husband doesn't have life in it. My teacher shared that some of us marry but we don't have life in the relationship. If life is defined as the sum total of a man or a woman's relationship and activities then if you are arguing with your husband over money and just about everything else then what kind of life is that you and your husband have together? My teacher also shared that arguing drives the spirit of God away from both you and your husband. As women, you have so much power with your husbands. Unfortunately, many of women still don't know how to access their own power. You could make your husband fall so deeply in love with you that he would kill concrete over you. Every woman possesses a natural beauty and charm. Every woman has an inner bloom that is even more special than any outer beauty she has. Once a woman discovers the inner presence in her and actively works to bring out of herself that freshness, that healthy vigor, that inner beauty that comes from her mind and soul being connected to the source of all life, which is her Creator, then she will be able to enjoy a long lasting and satisfying marriage to a man.

Over the years you have probably heard many women complain that the men today are not what they used to be. That most definitely is true. We have to raise the other side of the equation and ask, **"Are women today what they used to be?"** Would the answer be the same? You wouldn't believe the amount of dissatisfaction that so many men have with their wives over the rearing and the care of their children. Let's be honest. Many mothers have no interest anymore in being mothers. Many mothers are part time mothers at best with no real desire to pour themselves into mothering a child. The most productive part of some mothers days are devoted to their professional pursuits away from home. In fact, many women have devoted themselves to ambitious busyness everywhere but in the home. And whether you know this or not, a man is constantly watching you and the level of care and concern that you manifest for himself, his children and his home. **The nature of you is to console a productive man. The very nature of the female is her ability, desire and will to console. The nature of you is to speak to his mind that which consoles him in his effort to do God's Will.** My teacher shared that when a person needs to be consoled, somebody else has to speak the right word to that person's mind, present the right picture, and create the right atmosphere to bring about consolation. When a woman is consoling a man she is alleviating or lessening the grief, sorrow, or disappointment of that man. When a woman is consoling a man she is giving solace or comfort and cheering up that man. Allah (God) teaches us in the Qur'an that He created the woman that the man might find *peace and quiet of mind in her.* The very nature of the female offers to the man that which enables the man to find that natural relief of the stress or the pain involved in the struggle of man to obey Allah's (God's) instructions.

Any man that is not closely monitoring your desire and zeal for more knowledge is failing as a husband. Any man that is happy to have a woman with him that is not educated is foolish. Every woman should be knowledgeable. Why, because a wise woman makes a wise nation. A foolish woman makes a foolish people. To keep women ignorant, looking at soap operas all day long, feeding their minds filth and ignorance, is to keep you in a state where you will never produce children that will be masters and conquerors. A man watches where your energy is directed. When do you seem to get excited? What turns you on? He listens to you when you are on the telephone at how enthusiastic and energetic you are with other people. He's sitting off to the side watching you laugh and joke and have a good time, and then he will watch you get off the phone and within moments become so sour to your own family as if you resent being a wife and a mother. So sometimes when he argues with you he will begin to pick your friends and your family members apart, especially your male friends, companions, associates or male family members. Be careful about positively referencing men in general until you are sure that your husband has the appropriate level of maturity to handle you stating the good that you have found in another man besides himself. Sometimes he will make snide remarks about them and what he is really saying is, **"I want to be the one to make you happy. I want to be the one to put a smile on your face. I'm jealous that you seem to put them ahead of me."** Some men can't handle it when other men can make you laugh and smile and they can't. Your husband knows the other side of you. The same way you have to take his crap sometimes, he has to do the same for you. You are becoming a better woman because your husband is taking your crap too. He's absorbing it from you to free you from it just as you are providing that unique service for him. The proof that he would go into hell for you is the fact he has already taking so much hell from you. You may have never looked at it like this. You have to understand the nature of the male. Your man is working hard to make you happy. He lives to put a smile on your face. He lives for you happiness. He knows that when momma is not happy then the whole house is upset. But who is concerned when he is not happy? Who even notices if he is not happy?

For some women reading this book there is simply not enough time in the day to show your man the affection he really deserves. I wanted to suggest some tips on how you as a woman can make the most of each day with your husband. Here are some truly valuable ways to let your man know that you care about him. One way is to find out what he likes to read and who his favorite author is. Once you find this out surprise him one day by buying him a book by his favorite author. Don't just give him the book. Dress it up in a nice gift basket for him with some of his favorite candy or snacks with a personal note of your complete love and devotion for him. You want to make your man feel like a king as often as possible. If you won't I promise you that someone else will. Another way for you to let your man know that you care is to have a nice warm bubble bath with rose petals waiting for him when he gets home from especially strenuous days or nights of working. Men should do the same for women as well. A man will begin to hint to you when he is in need of some of that powerful nature of yours. Be sure and keep your ears open for when his body is calling for yours. That's not always sexual either. Sometimes your man just needs you to surround him with candles and incense as you massage your man and let the music do what it do to him and you. A simple touch can relieve stress and heal the body, mind, and spirit. Try giving your mate a massage using sensual oils and lotions. You are helping to set the mood with candles and incense. Make sure there are no distractions like little 'chiren' who want to mess up the flow. A simple 20 - 30 minute massage can be very effective. Don't be afraid to ask for one in return. Let him feel the warmth of your hands by gently massaging his scalp. This will get the sensations going. You might choose to purchase a good book on massaging your husband. If you have the means to afford one, buy a massage table.

Another way to bond and keep the connection going with your husband is to enjoy play time and times of relaxation with him. Does he like the Play Station 3 or playing the X-Box 360 or the Wii? Could you learn how to play and have fun with him? Could you learn a little bit more about football or basketball for the sake of having something in common with your man? Who is his favorite team? What television shows does he like to watch regularly? Are his favorite shows mostly cop shows with a lot of violence? Is he into mobster pictures? Perhaps he's into comedies and romance. Imagine what it would be like to just sit there with him watching a movie, snuggled up in his arms on a weekly basis? What woman wouldn't want to do that? Another thing you can do is tell him how much you absolutely love him every chance you get. Sing it to him if you can sing. When he comes home play some love music and mouth the words in his ear. When he walks through the door make him feel that your personal saviour has arrived! Wear his favorite perfume; you know the one that he told you he liked. Well wear that one all over your body for him. Do your hair before he gets home. Brush your teeth before he gets home. Wash your face before your husband or man comes through the door. Take a bath or shower before he comes through the door. For God's sake change out of those beat up sweat pants and sweatshirt! He's been around beautiful women all day long. Women who took time to do all the things I am telling you to do now. Get your house together before your man walks through the door. Get the children together before your husband walks through the door. Stand up when the man walks through the door. Make the children stand up when your husband walks through the door. It's gonna take some work for you to keep your husband in today's time. Don't ever take it for granted that you have got him and he ain't going anywhere. Pick up on any and all efforts that your man makes to teach you anything. When he is expounding or pontificating on this or that stop what you are doing and listen sincerely. Nod your head in agreement. If you want your husband to be successful in his work, then you can help him by the simple act of praising him for what he does. Praise builds his self – confidence and helps him do a better job. Your praise can send him off each morning filled with the confidence that he can solve any problem that comes his way. Try not to argue with him all the time. Let him be right sometimes even when he's wrong especially if the issue is not a life and death issue. Keep your man happy! He knows when he's wrong. *There is not a man that I know of that doesn't go away from an argument or a disagreement with his wife or his woman and doesn't think about what she said to him in that argument or disagreement. Your man probably thinks about you and what you say to him much more than you know.*

Another thing more women need to do in today's times is learn how to cook. What is this slop you are throwing together for your man and calling it dinner? It's an insult to you for your man to not come home and eat what you have prepared. He shouldn't have a favorite restaurant when he has you in his life. But are you cooking today? If you are what's going into the pot? How will you present this meal to him? You don't present a gourmet meal on a paper plate. Where is the effort? You mean you can take the time to get all dressed up to come to the work, or to church or to the Mosque but you won't take any time to prepare a good and decent meal for your man? When does he not deserve a decent meal? One thing men have said consistently in the workshops we have done is that *when you are upset with your man then you will stop doing the things that only you are supposed to do for him*. You will start withholding. So because you are upset with him, you stop being dutiful. Some women stop cooking. Some completely stop cleaning up the house or the apartment. Some wives stop bathing. A man that is truly dutiful can't stop his duty. If a man is still working and still striving to take care of you, if he's still on the grind for you then you should seriously reconsider keeping up your end of the bargain. Maybe after re-reading this book you will consider cooking your man his favorite meal one night a week by candlelight. I know that you may not be functioning under the best of circumstances right now but that's when you show your man truly whether you are by his side or not. They have a saying out there that says, **"When the going gets tough, the tough get going."** Another way to show your love for your man is when you clean his clothes or put them in the cleaners for him. These are not menial tasks. These are especially critical tasks when you consider the world that he has to go out and operate in on behalf of you and your family. Presentation is highly regarded in a world like this. So help him look and feel his very, very best.

One of the real secrets to complete joy and happiness in your home is accepting your partner exactly as he is. Don't try to change your spouse and make him over. Don't try to change your spouse and make him over into a second edition of yourself. Don't nag or criticize. You'll never change your husband that way. You'll never get your husband to do what you want him to do with criticism. Have you ever been able to change him very much through all your years of marriage by nagging and finding fault with him? I know that you probably thought you had good intentions. You felt that you could make him over into the kind of person you thought he ought to be, but did you ever really succeed? Sister, if you're thinking of making your husband over to fit your own specifications by using criticism, forget it. If you give it a little time you may find that you couldn't improve on your spouse at all. The only person you can ever really change in your life is you, yourself, and you alone – no one else. So accept your partner just as he is. You'll never be able to achieve total joy and happiness in your marriage or relationship until you do. When a couple is first married, they are completely blind to each other's faults. They're too much in love to notice the other person's bad habits. But after the honeymoon is over and they realize there are some adjustments that must be made, there can be a tendency to find fault and criticize each other. Then love goes out the window. But this doesn't have to happen. You have to learn how to solve those small irritating problems with courtesy and kindness instead of nagging and criticism. Do that, and you'll be able to keep the fires of love and romance burning all of your life.

A wife can help her husband become highly successful by the simple act of using words of praise for what he does. If you want your husband to get ahead and be successful in his work, then don't criticize him for not bringing home a bigger paycheck. Instead, praise him for his hard work and for all he does for you. Praise builds his self confidence and helps him get ahead. Big businesses and corporations want to find out more about the wife before a man is promoted to a top – level of responsibility. They want to know whether a wife can give her husband a feeling of confidence in himself more than she is interested in her good looks and social acceptability. If she gives her husband the feeling that she is pleased with him and with his work, and if she praises him in every way possible, it's like getting a shot of adrenalin every time he comes home. A wife's praise sends a man off each morning with the self confidence that he can solve any problem that comes along. That's the kind of person a business, an organization and a Nation needs in their top positions. That kind of wife can help put him there. After your relationship with God and His servant, make your mate the next most important person in your life. Think of the importance of your mate all the time. Pay close attention to everything he/she says and does. Always praise, never criticize especially openly in front of the children. Criticism destroys. Criticism destroys people. It creates enemies. It ruins friendships. It destroys love and marriages. So if you want a harmonious and friendly relationship with your spouse, never criticize. Praise instead. Praise creates energy. It makes a person work harder, more effectively, and with greater enthusiasm, because praise makes the person feel proud of himself and what he has done. Simply say to your spouse, **"I am proud of you."** These are magic words; for he'll do whatever you want him to do when he hears them. You just can't miss when you praise a person for what he has done. That will help you to keep your husband coming back home to you all the time!

Before I close this chapter I wanted to share something else with my dear sisters from my teacher. In the Qur'an to prove the importance and the value of a righteous woman, it is written concerning Mary, the Mother of Jesus, **"And when the angels said: O Mary, surely Allah has chosen thee and purified thee and chosen thee above the women of the world. O Mary, be obedient to thy Lord and humble thyself and bow down with those who bow. This is of the tidings of things unseen which We reveal to thee. And thou was not with them when they cast their pens (to decide) which of them should have Mary in his charge, and thou was not with them when they contended one with another. When the angels said: Oh Mary, surely Allah gives thee good news with a word from Him (of one) whose name is the Messiah, Jesus, son of Mary, worthy of regard in this world and the Hereafter, and of those who are drawn nigh (to**

Allah)." (Sura 3 verses 41-45) These verses of scripture teach us that Mary was chosen by God above all the women of the world to be purified by Him. She was commanded then to be obedient to Allah, humble herself, and bow down with those who bow down. Mary, in being obedient to Allah (God), was purified by Him to bring forth into the world the Messiah that would change the condition of human beings and reconcile a fallen human being once again to our Creator.

This is the value of the female. This is the value of a righteous woman. She is more precious than silver and fine gold. In fact, there is nothing in the earth more valuable than a virtuous woman. This is the value of obedience or coming to the foot of mother for only at the feet of a righteous mother will we learn the heavenly life and bring into existence that which is called the Kingdom of Allah (God). My teacher shares that a woman simply cannot take her proper and rightful place without exposure to that knowledge which will cultivate all aspects of her being. In order for the female to produce a great future for us, she must be filled with the desire for knowledge, specifically the knowledge of Allah (God) and His Word. Any society that deprives the female of the deepest aspect of the study of the Word of Allah (God) is a society that will not approach the potential of its greatness. For, only when we have a highly spiritual and moral woman, educated, cultivated, cultured and refined will she be able to bring into existence a civilization bearing these same fine qualities and characteristics. From this day forward, whenever we look at a female child, you are looking at one who has the potential of bringing into existence a World Saviour. Mary grew up among righteous guardians. The Qur'an teaches us exactly the process by which a righteous child is brought into existence and specifically how Mary was brought into existence.

Chapter 5 – Problems in Relationships

My teacher asks, **"What does it mean when you see a man get down on his knee, get out his ring, and propose to a woman?"** It means that in that act the man recognizes your Supreme Value. For a man to get down on his knee, with *honor* and *respect*, indicates that a woman is so valuable. He wants her to come to him; he wants her to give herself to him, so he will *act* in a way to make her give herself. But my teacher shares that a man should never **"have a woman"** just to have her! He's got to be worthy of her, or he's not worth having her! There is hardly a man out here today that's worthy of a woman giving away herself to him. So many of us mistakenly think in our marriages or relationships should not have any problems.

We all face difficult times. When the storms of life hit, how will they affect our marriage? What can we do to make sure our marriage will survive? One of the greatest problems in marriages and relationships today is that folks already think they are married, past participle. They don't understand that they are still in the process of marriage. Therefore they are no longer striving to unite both the masculine and feminine natures into one. They mistakenly think that they have arrived. Unfortunately many of us do not seem to understand that marriage is a long process. So many of us want a spouse who will instantly understand our every whim, all of our complaints, and our complicated situations and that's just not possible. Marriage calls for adjustment – and readjustment – which is different from work. Two people from different families, with unique combinations of genes and chromosomes, varied social and psychological experiences, join in holy matrimony and adjust to one another's idiosyncrasies. This leads to a basic truth. All good marriages are based on compromise. Marriage requires a partnership, teamwork, common goals, and respectful dealings. A marriage must have love, affection, attraction, caring and understanding, plus some consensus in matters of tastes and interests. Perhaps the idea that you have to work at creating a good marriage stems from the fact that most married couples are incompatible. One of the greatest frustrations in marriages today is to be married to someone who is too immature to handle the complexities of not just the marriage but what it means to be with a man or a woman in this day and time. Immature individuals tend to be funnier and more exciting to be around, but when it comes to the important things - sometimes you can be left disappointed. Of course, he or she is your spouse and you love them - and there are many ways to make it work.

My teacher shared that there is no relationship without communication. Why is it so hard to communicate with each other? One of the things that makes communicating and relating to one another so difficult is because we are so immature. It is generally regarded by most people that women mature faster than men do. Some of us are so immature as men, we can't even handle the truth about ourselves from someone we live with and can actually see us. Brother, our wives are totally fed up with our infantile behavior and has been wanting to say something to us for years, but she wouldn't because the last time she tried to tell us, we went into a ridiculous rage that ruined her entire week. What she's been wanting to say to us for years is, **"Grow up!"** Some wives would phrase it a little differently. They'd say, **"For God's sake, grow up, will ya!"** We are not grown-up men because we are over twenty-one or because our body, biceps, portfolio, or even our penis is big. Size really doesn't matter here. We don't want to have big muscles and be mental and emotional midgets, do we? A good husband is a grown-up. A good wife is a grown up. A good husband is a man who remembers he's married to you and is therefore in an actual relationship with you. He should be striving very hard to not be an immature jackass anymore in your marital relationship. A good husband likes the marital connection he shares with you and he knows how to maintain that connection by communication with you. He should also know how to reconnect with you after there's been a disconnection. Maturity is the recognition of responsibility and then the acceptance of that responsibility as a necessity in one's own life. A woman typically comes to this realization faster than a man does. Often a man sees responsibility as an enemy, something that just gets in his way of living and having fun. One problem that plagues countless people is emotional immaturity. While a person may grow older and may achieve many things, his emotional development may be delayed. This attitude is devastating to those who either depend upon him or who wish him to take an active role in a relationship. Sometimes brothers we act so immaturely in our family that we're like having another kid around the house but worse, because we're bigger, louder, and scarier. Many women have asked us over the years, **"Why is my husband so childish? Why does she say these off-the-wall immature things that hurt us?"** A real man no longer has a need to outmaneuver, outmuscle and scare the wits out of his wife with his anger anymore. He's also not interested in ruthlessly hurling names and insults at you when he can't get his way or sulking in some part of the house and giving you the silent treatment for a week. A strong, self-respecting woman has every right to expect her husband to always treat her with respect and kindness. Prophet Muhammad (PBUH) said the best of you is kindest to his wife. Many men don't mature upon marriage. They still have that single guy's attitude and that single guy's penchant for fun and games.

Marriage often doesn't settle him down. Children might settle a man down because sometimes when a man holds an infant that cannot care for itself the realization of that responsibility sinks in for many men.

Sisters don't worry. We are going to share some wonderful strategies with you because there are a number of things that a wife can do about her husband's immaturity. Brother, I can hear you saying as you reading this, **"But my wife is immature too!"** I'm not worried about her immaturity right now. I am trying to help her out with some strategy so that she won't leave you. Just because a man is older doesn't seem to mean much nowadays. Some husbands are much older and act worse than the average 16 year old! As men some of us are so unclean. Some of us shower twice a week and can wears the same pair of pants for weeks at a time. If our wife tries to correct our behaviors of not taking showers, not picking up after ourselves, and having to remind us about everything we get miffed about this. Our wives didn't marry us to become someone's mother and she didn't marry us to live with a slob. In some marriages some of us as men, are absolutely terrible with the money. Our wives have to handle all the money, or the bills won't get paid! Some household are not in bankruptcy because of this very issue. Many men have gone out and got second mortgages on their houses and then couldn't pay for that either. Many of us don't pick up after ourselves while some of us are very forgetful. In addition to all of the responsibilities that our wives have taking care of themselves and our children we pile more and more on her plate to deal with. Some of us have our wives reminding us about all appointments, and activities we need to attend. One of the number one complaints that women nowadays have against men is that we act so helpless when it comes to cooking for ourselves. Some of us have not prepared a meal for ourselves since we got in the process of marriage. Your wife just checks us out. We come home and want to sit in front of a television and just chill out for a while. She's been dealing with stuff from the time she helped us get ready for work until we came back home. The black woman is worn out! She's tired as hell. Especially if she had to get out here and go to work as well. How in the world can we, as men, expect our wives to cook a delicious dinner, clean up after the dinner, get clothes ready for herself, the children and us, do homework with the children, bath the children, and wash clothes and then want some good loving too? Brothers, we must be crazy! Her job is running her ragged! The children are running her ragged! Her extended family may be running her ragged! The Church, the Mosque or the Synagogue is running her ragged and we, her husband, is running her ragged because we are not helping her do much of anything! Many of us think that once we get home that our work has completely stopped. Many of us don't lift a finger to help our wives out in the home. It's not fair, right or just brothers. We get very upset with our wives when they even suggest that we need to learn how to vacuum, do the laundry, clean the tubs, the toilets or the sinks or maybe mop the floors. We chauvinistically view those things as woman's work but we don't seem to possess that same clarity on what a man's work is! We have got our wives working on these jobs and busting her behind like we are supposed to do for our families. She is working as hard as we are and probably making as much money as we are. We've got our hands out expecting half of her check or better to take care of our responsibilities as men which is the bills! Some of us as men are just righteous pimps who just want to lie on a woman to take care of us. She may give us the money but inside she knows that the bills are our responsibility as men. Yet we still fully expect for her to do 100% of the housework without any assistance from us? My teacher shared that when a woman is working outside of the home that her husband should expect half of the respect he's do. He also shared that one of his principles of manhood is that no woman has ever kept him after he left the home of his mother.

Many of our wives have come to us very independent. Don't we understand as men that when our wives were single they never missed a bill? When we talk all of this big talk about who we are and what we can do and can't back it up with concrete action this is truly frustrating for our wives. Some of them are at their wits end with us and our immaturity as a grown man. They are trying so hard to be nice about it. They are not yelling or fighting us. They don't want the marriage to end but they have some very serious issues with us. They love us and they want to spend their golden years with us. Some of them do not have the spirit to baby their husband. Some of them are coming to us from other marriages. Some of them look at how pitiful we act as men and they shake their heads. Some have never come across men so helpless in their life. Some of them don't know how we survived before they came along. The problem may be that many of us as black man are blessed by God to be so doggone good looking and we are charmers.

There are so many women out here that are so hungry for masculine companionship that they are just buying a man today. Some women will take care of every expense for a man and expect nothing from him except to come and be a sexual companion for her. There are those instances where women are the bread winners of the household and the men may invest little to no time in improving his financial status in the household. Some women literally take care of men only to obtain a false sense of security. My teacher shared that many women today are taking care of men because they oft-times have better paying jobs. Women are better trained and oft-times better qualified. They have nice cars, homes or apartments, nice furniture, but, the thing that is missing in the home or apartment is a responsible man who is a provider and maintainer. Some women go looking for a man and oft-times is taking care of him. There is no woman who could honor and respect a man that she is caring for. To her, he is like her little boy. By the time the man decides to get back into the process of marriage he's so spoiled from what all these other women were doing and perhaps are still willing to do for him that his attitude is always, **"I'm outta here!"**

There are many forms of abuse and financial abuse may be the leading cause of marital discord in a marriage. It is vital that an understanding be established prior to marriage. The key is to be realistic about your financial situation and live within your means. So many of us want what we want when we want regardless to how much it costs. Some of us have champagne tastes on ripple money. Even if you get the high priced items can you really enjoy it when you are going broke to have it? Unrealistic expectations oft times lead to a person over extending their financial limits because the pressure to please is on them. Some men like to **"spoil"** their wives. Some wives feel entitled to have things because she was groomed to believe that a man should give her the **"world"**. Financial abuse is a strain on any relationship. We work day and night to pay everyone else but self. Let us live within our means and start paying self first. Once your savings increase examine how you can properly invest in something that is solid and will enhance your financial status. Do this equally with your spouse. Later you will be able to look back with pride and see all the two of you have accomplished as one.

Wives need to isolate what areas her husband is immature in. More than likely, it is not in every area. She should list all of his responsibilities, those things that he is directly responsible for, and rate them. His wife, his children, his job, perhaps the finances, maybe the maintenance of the house, and whatever else you can think of are things that ought to go on this list. This has the added benefit of helping you to isolate your own frustration. He may be good with the children and be lousy with money. He may be great with money but not very good at providing you with needed security. He might be fantastic with his work ethic, but sloppy with his things at home. Find out what areas are causing you the frustration. Again, praise him for the areas he does well in. It is difficult for a man to deal with a nagging and unhappy wife. Most men deal with emotions in such a different way than their wife does that he doesn't know how to handle hers. But he loves praise. Praise will encourage him and may even help him towards being responsible in those other weak areas.

Most men won't seek help on their own. It is the result of that ego and pride that men have in abundance. But if they actually do get some counseling it's helpful to have them talk to another brother that they respect. Another man will be able to show them from a man's perspective, why they need to take responsibility in certain areas of their life. Often, if a man can see the problem from a man's point of view, it may finally dawn on him that he can no longer run or hide from it. In addition, many men just flat out don't know what to do because no one ever taught them. Their solution up until this point is to ignore the problem. Using a man to point out the problems and solutions from a man's perspective will go a long way to helping your husband grow up and mature. He may resist this, but if you can find the right Pastor, Student Minister, Counselor, or mature advisor to help, it'll go a long way.

Brothers, sometimes our immaturity produces fear and frustration in our wives and our children. How can we want more children and we are handling what we have produced so sloppily? Some couples have no children and are asking whether it would it be a wise decision to get married and conceive children in the time we're living in? My teacher shares that even in the worst of times, children are born to master those times. Sisters, when you express your fears and frustration more often than not, it drives your husband away from accepting responsibility. You need to play off his ego and pride. Most men have fantasies of being that knight in shining armor that wishes to rescue the damsel in distress. This isn't true for all men, but it is typical of male psychology. Instead of flailing at him with your words, show your distress in a way that makes him want to come to your rescue.

Good communication is the key to any relationship. I'm writing about it in this chapter because the importance of this concept is generally misunderstood. Yelling, screaming, nagging, and name calling doesn't really do much to get an immature husband to accept responsibility. You have to learn to communicate your fears better. I'm not suggesting that you appear helpless, but I am suggesting that you be a bit smarter in how you express your concerns to your husband. If you always do his job, then you aren't giving him a reason to do it himself. Why should he do it if you will? Unfortunately, many men think this way without consciously being aware of it. In some cases, you may feel that you have no choice, particularly when it comes to money or the children. But in general if you pick up after him, become his alarm clock, become his character, fulfill his promises to his friends, and so forth, he will come to expect that from you. Most of us as black men are still lazy slaves looking for a shady tree to hide under and sleep. Understand that most people, male or female, have grown up being pandered to. Their parents supplied every need and most wants. This so called society panders to children and their innocence and then cuts it all off when they turn 18. There is very little effort or skill at making smooth transitions into adulthood. For eighteen years it was all about him. Now it is no longer true, but he hasn't really come to grips or true understanding of that. He doesn't realize that responsibility is accepting the needs of others. You may need to help your husband learn that. You may need to ignore his irresponsibility and let him suffer the consequences of his own actions. You may have to do it in complete silence. Don't scold, don't yell, don't lecture, don't be a mother, that'll only push him away. But he may need to learn that there are things that he now has to do on his own.

A Pastor tells of a mother that came to him once about her teenage boy who refused to do anything about his messy and somewhat disastrous room. She told the Pastor that when she couldn't stand it anymore, she would just go in and clean it herself. She wanted to know how to get him to do it on his own. The Pastor inquired about, and found out that he would never let his friends into his room. He suggested bringing over to the house girls his age and showing them his room. That didn't happen but twice before he started keeping his room clean on his own from then on out. Even when your sons are teenagers you should at some appropriate point turn to them and say, **"Son, from now on you have to wash, dry, and fold and iron your own clothes. You need to learn how, and I'm not doing it anymore."** From that point on you should never get onto his case about the laundry, never nag your son, and never scold them about laundry. Once you have given up any of your son's responsibilities don't ever, ever take it back. In this age of 'swag' he isn't about to go to school in smelly clothes. You just have to watch him take responsibility for his own appearance. Be very, very wise in how you do this. You don't want to push him to the point where he just gives up. Make sure you are helping and not making the situation worse.

So many times in our marriage relationship we will find ourselves in conflicted situations. Most times the problem will not be what your husband is or is not doing. Instead, the problem will be that the two of you aren't in agreement about how he is doing this or doing that. People can be married in all sorts of ways but the marriages that work are those where the couples have negotiated out their differences. Many times in marriages nowadays the husband isn't negotiating at all. He is just doing his thing. The wife isn't negotiating either. She is just busy giving in. Brothers, it is so overwhelming for our wives to have to deal with all of our children that we have delighted in making, by herself while we are off having our social time. Sister, you have to take a stronger position on needing to have a meeting of the minds. You have to make some demands to your husband and not back off when we start to accuse you of being controlling. It is not being controlling to want to feel like you have a real partner. If the two of you don't sit down and come to a *real* agreement (meaning that you honestly can support what the two of you come up with – not that you just give in), then there is going to be trouble down the road. Quick fixes appeal to an immature urge to avoid the pain of self-discipline necessary for lasting change and consistency. If you and your spouse haven't figured out how to talk so that both of you are reasonably happy with the result you should find a counselor or mediator who can give you some pointers. Call our Marriage Counseling Services number on the back of this book if you need help with this. A mature man would negotiate with his wife so that she would be happy as well.

Sometimes dealing with someone who is immature is similar to dealing with a child. If you want them to remember something, you have to make sure you're getting through to them. Often times, saying something one time is not going to do the trick. Repeat the thing you're trying to make them understand - in different ways if you must. Of course, you have to try not to 'nag,' but make sure you're communicating. For instance, if you need a bill to be paid on a certain day, tell them, write it on the calendar, remind them a few days later and repeat it in other ways. **"Honey, when you pay that bill on the 3rd, can you make sure you put the receipt in my folder?"** This is a way that you can repeat it without nagging! This will help your immature spouse remember what he or she is supposed to do, and will keep you happy!

There's a place and a time for seriousness and a place and time for joking. When you want your spouse to be serious, let him or her know. Explain how important it is that they take an issue seriously or that they 'behave' themselves at a certain event. Usually, if you stress how important it is, your spouse will realize that it's time to knock off with the jokes. However, make sure you recognize the time and place for kidding around as well. Laugh and have a good time with your spouse. Immaturity has its qualities and usually they lie in the fact that your spouse is a lot of fun and makes you laugh. It's alright to be immature at times and when you make sure there is an outlet for the two of you to have fun together, it will help your spouse be more serious on those times when you really need him or her to pull through. For instance, after your spouse has done something really great, like paid a bill on time, saved money or something else - reward them by doing something they enjoy. Avoid becoming too mature (like a stick in the mud) because you're overcompensating for your spouse. Have a great time and enjoy your spouse for who he or she is.

Although it can be difficult at times to deal with your immature spouse, it's also a blessing at times. Using these tips and tricks, you can effectively deal with your immature spouse and keep conflicts or disputes to a minimum. To do anything less is to show an immature and self-centered attitude. What is emotional abuse or verbal abuse of a spouse or intimate partner? You should know that mental, psychological, or emotional abuse can be verbal or nonverbal. Verbal or nonverbal abuse of a spouse or intimate partner consists of more subtle actions or behaviors than physical abuse. While physical abuse might seem worse, the scars of verbal and emotional abuse are deep. Studies show that verbal or nonverbal abuse can be much more emotionally damaging than physical abuse because verbal abuse is 16 times worse than verbal abuse. These are some of the very real problems in relationships in this day and time? Ask yourself honestly,_does your spouse or partner:

Ignore your feelings?
Disrespect you?
Ridicule or insult you then tell you it's a joke, or that you have no sense of humor?
Ridicule your beliefs, religion, race, heritage or class?
Withhold approval, appreciation or affection?
Give you the silent treatment?
Walk away without answering you?
Criticize you, call you names, and yell at you?
Humiliate you privately or in public?
Roll his or her eyes when you talk?
Give you a hard time about socializing with your friends or family?
Make you socialize (and keep up appearances) even when you don't feel well?
Seem to make sure that what you really want is exactly what you won't get?
Tell you that you are too sensitive?
Hurt you especially when you are down?
Seem energized by fighting, while fighting exhausts you?
Have unpredictable mood swings, alternating from good to bad for no apparent reason?
Present a wonderful face to the world and is well liked by outsiders?
"Twist" your words, somehow turning what you said against you?
Try to control decisions, money, even the way you style your hair or wear your clothes?
Complain about how badly you treat him or her?
Threaten to leave, or threaten to throw you out?

Say things that make you feel good, but do things that make you feel bad?

Ever left you stranded?

Ever threaten to hurt you or your family?

Ever hit or pushed you, even "accidentally"?

Seem to stir up trouble just when you seem to be getting closer to each other?

Abuse something you love: a pet, a child, an object?

Compliment you enough to keep you happy, yet criticize you enough to keep you insecure?

Promise to never do something hurtful again?

Harass you about imagined affairs?

Manipulate you with lies and contradictions?

Destroy furniture, punch holes in walls, break appliances?

Drive like a road-rage junkie?

Act immature and selfish, yet accuse you of those behaviors?

Question your every move and motive, somehow questioning your competence?

Interrupt you; hear but not really listen?

Make you feel like you can't win? Damned if you do, damned if you don't?

Use drugs and/or alcohol involved? Are things worse then?

Incite you to rage, which is "proof" that you are to blame?

Try to convince you he or she is "right," while you are "wrong?"

Frequently say things that are later denied or accuse you of misunderstanding?

Treat you like a sex object, or as though sex should be provided on demand regardless of how you feel?

Your situation is critical if the following applies to you:

You express your opinions less and less freely.

You find yourself walking on eggshells, careful of when and how to say something.

You long for that softer, more vulnerable part of your partner to emerge.

You find yourself making excuses for your partner's behavior.

You feel emotionally unsafe.

You feel it's somehow not OK to talk with others about your relationship.

You hope things will change...especially through your love and understanding.

You find yourself doubting your memory or sense of reality.

You doubt your own judgment.

You doubt your abilities.

You feel vulnerable and insecure.

You are becoming increasingly depressed.

You feel increasingly trapped and powerless.
You have been or are afraid of your partner.
Your partner has physically hurt you, even once.

Some men and women often yell at their spouses and in fits of temper punch holes in the wall, throw various things around the house and through windows and even become physically violent to their spouses. Some of us believe that if a man can't blow off some steam, he's likely to end up with stomach ulcers or have a heart attack. Many abusers believe and express the sentiment that their home is where they can let it all hang out. They believe that if you just get your feelings and anger out in the open, you'll feel better and everything will be fine. The workplace is seldom the proper setting for full self expression. At work, most people find it necessary to be on their best behavior, to display tact and diplomacy, to curb their tempers, and to think twice before reacting. Thus, home becomes a haven for spontaneity, the place to release pent up emotions that accumulate in other settings. This mistaken idea can result in behaviors which have dire consequences. There has to be a sense of good manners and good taste in the home. Marital freedom is not an invitation to attack each other's sense of dignity and self – esteem with emotional bombs. Some of our temper's can reach a frantic pitch within seconds. It doesn't matter where we are, who is present, or what is going on at the time. Have you ever known someone's whole body to tremble when they get really angry? Even as some of us have gotten older our tempers still have not decreased. Our angry words cut deeper than a Ginsu knife. Sometimes we unleash unbridled attacks and often our spouse is the predominant target.

Some of have other issues that manifest over time in our marriage relationships. All of us, husbands and wives are crazy but some are completely bugged out. Much of our married life revolves around the use of money. There was a man who had worked all of his life, had saved all of his money, and was a real miser when it came to his money. Just before he died, he said to his wife, **"When I die, I want you to take all my money and put it in the casket with me. I want to take my money to the afterlife with me."** And so he got his wife to promise him with all of her heart that when he died she would put all of the money in the casket with him. Well, he died. He was stretched out in the casket, his wife was sitting there in black, and her friend was sitting next to her. When they finished the ceremony, just before the undertakers got ready to close the casket, the wife said, **"Wait just a minute!"** She had a box with her; she came over with the box and put it in the casket. Then the undertakers locked the casket down and they rolled it away. So her friend said, **"Girl, I know you weren't fool enough to put all that money in there with your husband."** The loyal wife replied, **"Listen, I'm a righteous person and I can't go back on my word. I promised him that I was going to put that money in that casket with him."** "You mean to tell me you put that money in the casket with him?" "I sure did," said the wife. "I got it all together, put it into my account and wrote him a check. If he can cash it, he can spend it."

All couples run into **"touchy subjects"**. These are topics that stir up frustration and lead to awkward silences. Sex and Money are at the top of the list for many marriages. Everybody knows a cheap person, and probably hates them. Frugal people are often mislabeled as cheap. Some of us are so frugal that we can rub the ink off a dollar bill. Many husbands are not just, fair or righteous as we deal with money and finances with our spouses. We love to spend lavishly on ourselves, our goals and our visions. Some men like to play like we're so frugal and conscious of how money it being spent when it comes to our wife and our children's legitimate needs. Some women have to beg their husbands for anything they need even if what they need is for the house. She is constantly second guessing herself because we are always going off about money. She wonders is she being unreasonable with her request for gas money, money for groceries or something for the children. Some husbands literally see red every time money is mentioned. Some wives know what's coming next from their husbands, **"It's my money! It's my money!"** Many women have complained bitterly about how their husbands love to apply the noblest motives and all of our good financial senses to our wives financial needs but don't have any fiscal discipline to impose on our own lives. As men, many times some of us don't include our wives in any important financial decisions. Some men do not like to spending money on things that the family needs. If the cars break down, even though we may not have any knowledge or certification in car repair, we will get out there and try to fix on the cars to get them back to a running state. That would be fine with our wives if we actually knew what we were doing and if two or three months later our cars didn't remain disassembled there in our front yards. So many men don't think about how their wife is going to be affected by often poor decision making process. Some men in the name of being frugal and saving money will cramp their growing families into a small two or three bedroom apartment. It's always supposed to be temporary but the family ends up living there for 10 years! Some men won't even purchase health benefits from their jobs because it costs too much. Some wives have not been to any kind of doctor's office for a check-up since we've married them. Outside of getting pregnant she doesn't have any medical care for herself. Some of our wives have not been to the dentist since we married them. Some men their family back in either his mother or his wife's mother and the man actually wonders why there is so much tension in the home. How is your wife supposed to feel? My teacher shared that no woman can be a woman in another woman's place. As men we have to make sure that our wife's car has heat in it during the winter. She is most likely transporting our babies around so she needs heat in the car. Our wives strongly resent having to come before us to defend every little purchase and financial decision that they've made. They resent that we as men can spend whatever we thought was necessary with no checks, balances or even an explanation being necessary. Women often resent having to be accountable to her husband but that he does not have to be accountable to her. Many times our posture as men is so arrogant and pompous because we may hold the money bag. Money, like sex, is a powerful barometer of marital health, and withholding it can signal problems.

Our wives cannot to continue suffering with us and have nothing to show for it. She's still connected to people who are watching her closely if we haven't cut her off from that. Her parents are watching their daughter suffer through this relationship with us and it's killing them. Some of our wives are at their whit's end. They are just waiting for the proverbial straw that's going to break their back. Some are saying that they really don't know what they feel towards us anymore. At times, when they look at us, they feel sick to their stomachs. If a woman has a fear of asking her husband for money then she most likely is not in a healthy relationship. Withholding money is a form of domestic abuse. Many spouses come from backgrounds where there was not a lot of money to go around. Now that we are older and we are making a little money we may have adopted a miserly spending style toward both self and others. In many homes money is viewed as something to be hoarded for future catastrophes.

Stubbornness is another problem in many marriages today. Has stubbornness gotten you into a lot of trouble over the years with your husband / wife? Let's look at a definition of this word. According to the dictionary we are being stubborn when we refuse to move or to change our opinions. Many of the marriage problems in our homes originate from fear, ego or stubbornness. Some of us purposely refuse to do something because our spouse asked us to do it. Our spouse could be telling us the whole truth and nothing but the truth but we will act like they haven't said anything to us. Then later on, someone else will say the very same thing our spouse was saying, only in a different way, and we will come back to our spouse like we just received a revelation from God! Most of our lack of personal discipline is due to our stubbornness. How many our homes are in constant and total disarray? How many of us have clean, unfolded clothes piled on top of our dressers and stuff that we use every day scattered about the room? What is our attitude about cleanliness? Has your husband given up on the idea of asking you to clean your home? Have you become openly defiant to any and all instructions and guidance that comes through your husband or wife? Or do you eventually get around to doing the things they ask you to do in your own good time and not before? Do you do everything in your marriage on 'your terms'? Be honest with yourself. Are you a defiant, stubborn, and rather childlike or are you a mature adult?

Many of our relationships falter on stubbornness. Graves have been dug with the words, **"I'm right."** Some of us have spent our short, insecure lives trying to prove every nit-picking point. I have watched this tendency in us all my life. Some of us may not truly be as committed to our spouses because we disagree with them on some minor point. For some of us it would be the end of our world to be proven wrong on anything. Animals are used to display the attitude of stubbornness in human beings. We all have seen mules and goats used and the donkey that pushes all of his legs forward which represent he's digging his heels in. We have also seen the notorious bull that snorts steam from his nose as well. There is the picture of the woman with her arms crossed, eyes closed and nose up in the air to consider and two groups of children having a tug-of-war. Two men arm wrestling is a sign of stubbornness, especially if they have been going for a while and are pretty red in the face. You've probably seen scenes like that before, where they keep going back and forth and no one wins for a long time. I am just trying to create a picture for you of how we look in the eyes of our children stubbornly contending with each other over every little detail as their parents. There is an African metaphor that says, **"When the elephants fight, it is the grass that suffers."** The stubborn husband and the stubborn wife! Some spouses resist, whether his or her reasons are valid or not. The adamant person can't stand to lose face; ergo, he/she is always right, which is ludicrous, for who can be always absolutely right? We are stubborn because most times we are too proud to back down. This relates to our self esteem. Stubborn people have a lack of self esteem and this causes them to worry about damaging their pride. If they back down, it's like accepting defeat and recognising the other person's superiority. This is why they will continue to be stubborn, holding their ground often even when they know they are actually wrong. On the other hand, the healthy positive spouse is willing to listen to reason and change his/her mind. This person is willing to change thoughts and feelings if, upon reanalysis of the situation, basic convictions are not compromised. The really confident spouse will concede a point to common sense, whereas the obstinate person concedes nothing. This person does not possess an opinion – it possesses him/her! Unfortunately the "always-right" person dies by degrees from loneliness. After all, who wants to be proven wrong all the time? Stubbornness and stupidity are twins.

Another reason for stubbornness may be the mental or psychological disorders of the husband / wife. Some brothers and sisters are pathologically jealous and possessive. This may create problems for a marriage. How many husbands or wives are creating havoc in their marriages because of their suspicions and self centered attitudes? Sometimes what appears as stubbornness may also be caused by psychological problems that are affecting the husband or the wife. If you are not a doctor you may not know how to properly diagnose what is going on within your husband or wife. Let us strive to remember that our husbands and wives have certain good qualities and some intolerable qualities. We should try to be tolerant of the negative aspects of the spouse and appreciate the positive ones. Are you stubborn about your mental health? Do you have a diagnosed or undiagnosed mental condition that is now spilling out into your relationship with your spouse? Are you already on medication? Are you taking your meds like you have been instructed to take? Are you a stubborn spouse about getting your blood pressure checked? Are you near a stroke and don't know it? Have you as a man got your prostate checked? Was it recently or 10 years ago? You know you need one with all the meat you are eating every day. Why does your wife have to beg you to take better care of yourself? Don't you want to be around to see your grandchildren one day? Are you a stubborn spouse about the need to make a move in your life or your family's life? How long will you keep putting up road blocks and excuses to move forward? Why are you always holding back? Is it because at the root of us, we are just plain ole stubborn?

Stubbornness is the uncompromising insistence on having our own way. As such, **stubbornness is negative**. It involves a kind of blindness, along with a willful rejection of evidence and the perspectives of others. A stubborn husband or wife is someone who is unreasonable and often refuses to change their mind about an idea or an action. Stubborn husbands or wives often refuse to give a clear explanation or reason for their resistance. Stubbornness is particularly evident when the compromise required is easy. If the evidence you need to convince you to change your mind is readily available, or if accepting your spouse's perspective would mean giving up little of importance, then your refusal to yield is not reasonable, but is motivated by stubbornness. There is little to lose except your desire to be in control. *Such rigid clinging to your own will* **hurts you and your own family** *because you refuse to cooperate with others, and it also prevents you from becoming successful and virtuous.* We have to accept responsibility for the damage we have done to our families by our stubbornness. How much is your family suffering today because of your stubbornness? In our homes some of us are very stubborn about the state of our finances. Some men are stubbornly clinging to the same old ideas about how to make money in this modern day and time. We can be stubborn about our gradually declining health condition. Sometimes a husband or wife begins to slide into becoming fat and greasy due to their lack of dietary discipline and their spouse is definitely against that idea! Here are some of the reasons and situations that might cause your spouse to be stubborn. One reason is that they might be defending an idea. Some stubborn spouses believe that if their ideas are abandoned, then they are unimportant. What about if they got those ideas from their mother or father? Spouses strongly identify themselves with their ideas and sometimes with the sources of those ideas. They often feel that their identity will be threatened if their spouses aren't convinced by what they are saying. Sometimes the reason is that our spouses have a reason that they can't reveal to us. Sometimes a stubborn person may have a strong reason for refusing to change their mind but will not tell why.

What are you and your wife stubbornly arguing and holding so firm to? Many husbands believe they are married to a stubborn wife and vice versa. Women appear to be stubborn for many different reasons. For example, a woman may be stubborn because her husband has already developed a wrong conception about how a good wife should be. Is that true of you my brother? Are you saying your wife is stubborn and rebellious because she won't fit into this nice little picture you have in your mind about her? Have you formulated some idealistic picture of what a woman should be and can be and will be if she is going to be married to you? To hell with your picture, deal with the reality of the sister! It's only when you get in the process of marriage that you will get to see a full picture of what being married to her really looks like and is like. Some men have a twisted and skewed perception about how a wife should act and they expect total obedience from their wives without any resistance or thinking on her part. What planet are you living on? These sisters aren't having that today! Because we both have these false pictures of perfection in our minds eye about some of us are not even speaking to each other in our marriages. Some of us are not even sleeping in the same rooms with our spouses anymore and have not slept with our spouse for years. Indeed we are quite stubborn! Why would you deny yourself access to heaven over some minor, trivial, misunderstanding. The Holy Qur'an shares, **"O you who believe, obey Allah and obey the Messenger and those in authority from among you; then if you quarrel about anything, refer it to Allah and the Messenger, if you believe in Allah and the Last Day. This is best and more suitable to (achieve) the end."** This is such good advice for Muslims, Christians and Jews. Every couple should have someone who they can call when things start getting bad in the marriage. This person should be impartial to both sides and only be interested in hearing the truth. This is why we have developed the, **"Wali Counseling Services"**. Please see our flyer on the back of this book. Sometimes a third party can be so helpful. In some of our homes we argue with each other incessantly.

Here are some tips on how to deal with a stubborn husband or wife. You should pray to Almighty God first before you do anything and remember that God is sufficient for you in all of your needs." Also, remember that you probably have a great deal of stubbornness in you as well. Examine your interests and prioritize the interests that are most important to you. For example, perhaps you are more concerned about decisions dealing with children, money, or issues relating to your personal independence. The issues that are most important to you deserve the greatest effort from you. Remember they also have issues as well so be balanced and just. Who is representing the interests of the children? Listen carefully when you talk with your stubborn husband or wife. Listen closely to what they are saying. If what they say is not clear, keep asking questions to find out what underlies their approach. When they finish talking you can say, **"I want to make sure I understood you properly. Did you say 'x, y. & z'?"** Let them know you are listening; make it clear that you expect them to listen to you. You can say, **"I listened to you, now please listen to me."** Try to understand their reasons and encourage them to speak honestly (in a non-confrontational manner). Remember that resolution is possible as long as one partner wishes to keep trying.

We have so many problems in marriages and relationships today that it is really a wonder that everyone is not divorced. You have to know that Satan and his devils have that as their main goal. One of the Satan's, Jerry Springer, has gone out his way to make wickedness fair seeming to us all. As we watch his show we see couples quickly escalate on each other. Every night we can stomach it in America we are fed at the slop trough. After an hour of grueling ridicule from the host and his audience members and brutal fighting on the show Mr. Springer reemerges and casts himself as having a guiding light for his guests and for America. I am surprised that they haven't run Jerry Springer for President of the United Snakes of America! A couple escalates when they are negatively responding back and forth to each other. Some couples continually up the ante so the conversation gets more and more hostile. When we are in these situations with our spouses it is hard not to repay evil with evil or insult with insult. But this is exactly what happens when we are arguing and escalating. Each negative comment increases the level of anger and frustration, and soon a small disagreement blows up into a major fight.

When things are going right in the marriage and we have peace then we are less prone to escalate. When the argument starts to escalate, we are less able to stop the negative process before it erupts into a full-blown fight. When our arguments escalate so many damaging things are said that they may even threaten the lifeblood of the marriage. Escalation can develop in two different ways. The first is a major shouting fight that may erupt over a conflict as small as putting the cap back on the toothpaste. As the battle heats up the partners get more and more angry, saying mean things about each other. Frequently there are threats to end the relationship. Over time those angry words damage oneness, and angry threats to leave begin to seem like prophecy. Once negative comments are made, they are hard to take back and drive a knife into the partner's heart. Reckless words can do great damage to a marriage because when an argument escalates, every comment and vulnerability becomes fair game. Concerns, failings, and past mistakes can now be used by the attacking partner. Oneness and intimacy can be shattered quickly by a few reckless words. You may be thinking, **"We don't fight like cats and dogs."** And while that may be true, your marriage may still have this risk factor. Damaging escalation is not always dramatic. Voices do not have to be raised for couples to get into a cycle of returning negative for negative. Conflict over paying the rent or the mortgage, taking out the garbage, running errands that result in muttering to oneself, rolling your eyes, or throwing up your hands can also be examples of escalation. Couples who escalate arguments must control their emotions and control their tongues. The word control is great misunderstood in the black community. My teacher shares that so many women say, **"Nobody need to control me honey. I control myself."** But sisters, you are out of control. You are like a automobile that doesn't have a driver. Going down a highway 90 miles per hour and there's a turn up ahead and don't nobody see it and you don't see it and you just going. **"Don't nobody control me".** Look at the effect of being out of control; you are tearing up your life, tearing up your children's lives, tearing up the Nations life because you refuse to come under some kind of control. Don't you know that God when He set up things He set up controls for whatever He has created. And He has not created a man or a woman without control. Everything needs to be under some kind of control. **Anything a man doesn't control he cannot protect.**

My teacher shares just look at your children. If we don't exercise control over our children we can't protect them. If we tell our child, **"Go outside, play in front of the door. I do not want you going over in the next block. Do you understand that?"** **"Yes maam."** And you peep out the window to see how your control is. Gone! Now once the child is out from under your control the child is out from under your protection. **Because you cannot protect it beyond your ability to control it! Now if you cannot protect your children beyond your ability to control them, then there is no man that can protect the black woman beyond his ability to control her and there is no God that can protect you black man beyond the ability of God to control your affairs.** All things have to have control. My teacher shares this is why the enemy's world is steadily going to hell because he lost control of his woman. His woman is out in front of him and anytime that which should be led by you starts leading you, you cannot go up, you have got to go down. A woman is not made by nature to control a man. You are created by nature to control a child. But there are some things that grow beyond your control, and when that male child gets thirteen and fourteen he will tell his mother straight up what he is or is not going to do. Many mothers are running around like crazy women because they don't know what's going on with their sons. They can't seem to tell him to do nothing. When you have no man by your side to speak to your son at that stage with the authority of God then you will surely have problems! Sometimes the man that's living with you, he's under your control. A grown man tipping around your house! You ask as his wife, **"Where have you been?"** "I, I I..." You tell him to, **"Shut up! Did you bring the money!"** And the little boy see that. And at thirteen he's a man. He look at that chump that's living with you and say, **"That's a faggot. And I ain't going to be that. Naw momma I ain't going to let you dictate to me."** You got gray hairs. The boy driving you crazy because he already know what your men folk don't know, you can't control him. He's looking for his control. And his control is not a woman. His control is a man. And man is out of control and need control and his control is the wisdom of God. **Only with the wisdom of God will a woman submit to your control.** It is not that a husband should grab his wife and say, "Look here baby..." That's not where it's at. A man can whip her..sometimes. Sometimes she will whip you too. My teacher shares that this is not the way brothers. A man who beats a woman is ugly as hell in the sight of God. If this is the only way that a man can bring a woman under control this says, **"I've run out of the stuff up top. My top is blown and I'm hurt now because the woman showed up a vacuum in my knowledge. Now I've got to resort to the only thing that I've got left. And if she don't move with that, I'm through. If I hit her and she hit me back what I'm going to do then?"** You will probably turn to homosexuality then.

We have to stop escalating conflict in the home because we lack wisdom as men. Couples who want a strong marriage must learn to counteract the tendency to escalate as a couple. The key to a strong and stable marriage is learning to control your emotions and learning how to keep a rein on your tongue.

Since we are discussing problems in relationships we also have to discuss the problem of invalidation. Invalidation is a pattern in which one partner subtly or directly puts down the thoughts, feelings, or character of the other. My teacher shares that even children desire validation from their parents. *"How do I look mommy?" "How did I do daddy?"* No matter what the child does, it desires to be approved by those who mean the most to it: (1) Mother (2) Father (3) Siblings (4) Friends and Playmates. Children need encouragement when they falter that they may do better. The misuse of language and/or the harshness of language in rebuke can hurt the emotional and psychological development of the child. Remember, the need to be made secure is with us throughout our lives. So, as we grow, what it takes to secure us mentally, spiritually, morally, economically, and politically is always at work, even in the home. The child wants to know that we are aware of its presence. Even though consciously the child may not be aware, subconsciously it wants to know that its rights even as a child are respected and protected in the family environment when dealing with parents, guardians and when disputes arise among the siblings. When we do not get sufficient attention as a child, we act in a manner to get attention and sometimes this results in anti-social conduct or behavior. When the need for attention and validation is not supplied in the home or in the school, and we find that we have a gift or talent, that sets us apart and gives us attention, we have a tendency to focus on that talent and give all of our time to that talent, gift, or profession because it has given us the attention, acceptance and validation that we missed coming up as children. **Some of us do not have a great deal of respect for our children.**

In marriage, invalidation can take many forms. Sometimes it can be cutting, in which one partner (or both) attacks the other person verbally. You can hear, and even feel, the contempt one partner has for another. Sarcastic phrases like **"Well, I'm sorry I'm not perfect like you"** or **"I forgot how lucky I am to be married to you"** can cut like a knife. These are attacks on the person's character and personality that easily destroy a marriage. Research has found that invalidation is one of the best predictors of future problems and divorce. Calling our spouses worthless or empty-headed is not what we should do. Invalidation can also be much more subtle. It may involve an argument where contempt for the other partner is not so obvious. One partner may merely be putting the other partner down for his or her feelings. The message conveyed is that your feelings do not matter. A husband may put his wife down because she is more emotional or because she is more easily hurt by comments. A husband may invalidate a wife's fears about the children's safety. A wife may invalidate a husband's desire to succeed in the company, saying that it really doesn't matter if he becomes district manager. Ultimately the partner receiving these comments begins to share less and less so that the intimate level of sharing evaporates. When this happens, oneness is lost. Sometimes invalidation may be nothing more than commonplace clichés like **"It's not so bad"** or **"Just trust in the Lord."** While the sayings may be true, they invalidate the pain or concern of the other partner. They make the other partner feel like their fears or frustrations are inappropriate. When one partner is hurting, the other partner should find words of encouragement that do not invalidate their spouse's pain or concerns. My teacher shares that as Black people growing up in a society where we feel rejected by the larger society, and, are mistreated by the larger society, we grow up with a mentality desiring attention and validation from the members of the larger society. When we discover a gift or talent that sets us apart from the rest of our un-validated people that gives us attention from our former slave masters and their children, we give all of our time to that talent, gift or profession because it has given us the attention and acceptance that we have not experienced growing up Black in White America. Most times we invalidate our spouse because we feel invalidated in everything we are doing. The antidote to invalidation is validation. Couples must work at validating and accepting the feelings of their spouse. That does not mean you have to agree with your spouse on the issue at hand, but it does mean that you listen to and respect the other person's perspective. Providing care, concern, and comfort will build intimacy. Invalidating fears and feelings will build barriers in a marriage. Discipline yourself to encourage your spouse without invalidating his or her feelings.

Another problem is negative interpretations. Negative interpretations occur when one partner consistently believes that the motives of the other are more negative than is really the case. Such behavior can be a very destructive pattern in a relationship, and quickly erode intimacy and oneness in a marriage. A wife may believe that her husband does not like her parents. As a result, she may attack him anytime he is not overly enthusiastic about visiting them. He may be concerned with the financial cost of going home for the holidays or about whether he has enough vacation time. She, in turn, considers his behavior as disliking her parents. When a relationship becomes more distressed, the negative interpretations mount and help create an environment of hopelessness. The attacked partner gives up trying to make themselves clear and becomes demoralized. Another kind of negative interpretation is mind reading. Mind reading occurs when you assume you know what your partner is thinking or why he or she did something. Nearly everyone is guilty of mind reading at some time or other. And when you mind read positively, it does not tend to do much harm. But when you mind read on the negative side, it can spell trouble for a marriage. Negative interpretations are hard to detect and counteract. Research shows that in distressed marriages there is a tendency for partners to discount the positive things they see, attributing them to causes such as chance rather than to positive characteristics of the partner. That is why negative interpretations do not change easily. The key to battling negative interpretations is to reconsider what you think about your partner's motives. Perhaps your partner is more positive than you think. Maybe we need to reassess all of the negative assumptions we may have brought into our marriage. Many couples have made a lifelong pattern of assuming certain things about each other. We have such little understanding of each other's true motivations. Sometimes we marry so young and we're so full of hopes but soon end up in a marriage of disappointment. The man sees a woman that does not appreciate him, does not respond to him sexually, and who does not try to understand his needs. He feels constantly nagged. The woman sees an insensitive man who thinks only of himself and who is growing colder and more distant by the day. The woman says she understands her man all right and that's the problem. What she understands, she doesn't like. We move from delighting in our spouses to demanding that they think, talk, and act as we do. We forget to focus on their obvious strengths and, instead, highlight the irritation of their differences. The factors that push marriage into an emotional drift are largely issues of maleness and femaleness. We misunderstand each other and can, over a period of time, lazily assume the wrong things about how to relate to each other. Refocusing our attention from the negative to the positive is the first basic step in stopping the hurts and misunderstandings that eat away at a marriage. Along with a renewed attitude, husbands and wives can make other positive steps toward the rebuilding of their relationship in to a strong, healthy marriage. These steps must be based on a clear understanding, not only of sexual differences, but of how the different sexes prefer to be treated when it comes to building self – esteem, the different meanings we assign to the same words, and the different goals each is trying to achieve.

Another two problems we have to focus on are withdrawal and avoidance. Sometimes our partner is unwilling to get in or stay in a discussion that is too threatening. Withdrawal can be as obvious as getting up and leaving the room or as subtle as 'turning off' or 'shutting down' during an argument. The withdrawer often tends to get quiet during an argument, look away, or agree quickly to a partner's suggestion just to end the conversation, with no real intention of following through. Avoidance reflects the same reluctance to get into certain discussions, with more emphasis on the attempt to not let the conversation happen in the first place. A person prone to avoidance would prefer that the topic not come up and, if it does, may manifest the signs of withdrawal just described. In a typical marriage, one partner is the pursuer and the other is the withdrawer. Studies show that it is usually the man who wants to avoid these discussions and is more likely in the withdrawing role. However, sometimes the roles reverse. But, for the sake of this discussion, we will assume that the husband is the one who withdraws. Men often withdraw because he does not feel emotionally safe to stay in the argument. Sometimes he may even be afraid that if he stays in the discussion or argument that he might turn violent, so he retreats. When the husband withdraws, the wife feels shut out and believes that he does not care about the marriage. **In other words, lack of talking equals lack of caring.** But that is often a negative interpretation about the withdrawer. Men, on the other hand, may believe that his wife gets upset too much of the time, nagging and picking fights. This is also a negative interpretation because most pursuers really want to stay connected and resolve the issue he does not want to talk about. Couples who want to have a good marriage must learn to stay engaged. No couple should allow avoidance to become a corrosive pattern in their marriage. Couples should build oneness and intimacy by speaking openly and honestly about important issues in their marriage. All of these problems we have identified can build barriers in a marriage leading ultimately to loneliness, isolation and divorce. Couples that want a good marriage need to eliminate these risk factors from their marriage, or else the negative factors will overwhelm the positive aspects of the marriage. It is never too late to put your marriage back on track.

All of the problems listed in this Chapter can lead to divorce. My teacher again reminds us that one of the signs of the decline of any nation or civilization is its rate of divorce. Statistics teach us that many, many thousands of couples are predicted to divorce every year in America. Some spouses don't have the slightest idea how strong their partner's desire is for the marriage to be over so that they can once again taste, **"Sweet freedom"**. If such a thing as a quality relationship or marriage actually exists, it's rare enough to be listed as an endangered species. Even as some of us read this book, the die may have already been cast to end the marriage. Some spouses have already packed their spouse's bags while other spouses have just agreed to hate the sight of each other and just live separately under the same roof. An appalling number of husbands and wives are not really married but simply un-divorced and living in a sort of purgatory. I am totally convinced that we don't have to get divorced if we don't want to. But divorce is so easy in this culture. Many of us no longer believe, if we ever really did, that marriage is a divine and sacred institution. Many divorces could be prevented in our community if couples learned how to communicate and apply the methods that are being shared and have already been shared with us. If our marriages are struggling, are unhappy or on the verge of divorce, we need to have the best information available. This is why this chapter is important to us. We need to know what factors could be working against our marriage right now, even if we see nothing wrong. Many people believe that their marriage is working fine until their spouse gives them the wake-up call. Marriages either **grow** or **weaken**: they don't stay static. That means that a secure marriage isn't one where things are always the same. A solid marriage is one in which you never stop putting in effort to make it better and better. Many divorces in our community could be prevented if couples would stop being so selfish, self centered, arrogant and egotistical. Is your marriage headed for divorce court right now? What are six predictors of divorce and six predictors that our spouses and we will enjoy a long, happy, marriage?

I really want to talk over with you the effects that an impending divorce may indeed have on your children. Here in America, a lot of marriages sadly end up in divorce, and it wrecks a lot of lives, especially if there are children are involved. Some marriages can actually be saved, if the spouses are committed to saving their marriage. There are things that spouses can do to try and salvage their marriage, so that it does not end up in divorce, but they have to want to make it work. Well at least one of them has to. Saving a marriage really boils down to the two of you, and how badly you want to save it. I think it is possible to damage a marriage so bad that it cannot be saved, and even counseling will fail, but those circumstances are the exception. My teacher shared with me that it is written in the Holy Qur'an, which is the Book of Scripture for the Muslims, that Allah created man to face difficulties. God has brought us all onto the Earth to face one difficulty after another and it is the facing of these difficulties and the overcoming of these difficulties that helps us to improve our character and improve ourselves. Now, the key word is 'to face' a difficulty. 'To face' a difficulty means to look at it; to assess it; to summon the total strength or our being to oppose it; to overcome it; to have a determined, persevering, courageous spirit to overcome the difficulty. There is no difficulty that man is faced with that man does not have the ability to overcome, if he will summon the strength of his being against that obstacle in the pathway of his progress. But, how many of us turn our backs on difficulties? Whenever the difficulty comes, we turn away from it; try to find an easy road out of a difficult situation. I am talking to all of us. How many of us, when a difficult situation arises in our lives, summon the strength of our being to stand resolutely and firmly in the face of that difficulty to overcome it? Or, do we turn away? Maybe our marriage is presenting us with a difficulty. Will we fight for our marriage and overcome the difficulties or will we turn away? If we proceed and in fact turn away then what effect will that have on us, our spouse but even more importantly, what effects will that have on our children? And let me add this from my teacher who reminded me that each time we turn away from the struggle to overcome difficulty, there then is deterioration of character and there is destruction of the Will --- and the Will that is within you is God's gift. It is His Essence that He gives to man and anything that deteriorates your Will destroys your ability to cope with the problems of life. Struggle is ordained.

If the nuclear family can be likened to a small, quiet pond, its waters unruffled and at peace, then divorce is a large boulder hurled violently into its middle. The shock waves surge across the entire surface, leaving no edge untouched. Virtually every American's life is touched by divorce from the upper echelons of society to the homeless on the streets. Watching the rich and famous divorce has practically become a spectator sport in America. Unfortunately, unlike most sports, in divorce neither side wins. And worse yet, the biggest losers are the children. Divorce legally severs a marriage, but it also frequently severs the parental relationship, making the children feel that their parents not only divorced each other, but also divorced them. Although adults experience a significant amount of trauma while going through a divorce, children not only suffer during the process but continue to suffer long after the final papers have been signed. Children of divorce battle fear and humiliation for many years, their perception of themselves drastically altered by the loss of their family. This stigma follows these children throughout their lives, making them feel like **"divorced kids."** Struggling to find their own way to cope with the trauma, some children strike out with behavior problems while others succumb to cripplingly low self-esteem. In their weakened emotional condition, divorced kids often blame themselves for the divorce.

No one escapes the trauma of a fragmenting family - parents, children, grandparents, and extended families are all affected. Unfortunately, kids are often the forgotten element in a divorce. Parents are truly in the driver's seat, with access to friends, divorce recovery groups, support groups, church groups, lawyers, and counselors. Children are all too often left to fend for themselves. To an adult, a marriage - even with children - may be a relatively recent event in life's time line. To children, however, the family unit is all they have ever known. It is their world, containing their earliest and most profound memories. The split in the marriage cracks the deepest foundations of their lives, and suddenly everything is unstable. What can they depend on? Can anything be trusted?

Children are very, very devalued in this so called society. The Pew Research Center did a survey and found that Americans of all ages, acknowledge that there has been a distinct weakening of the link between marriage and parenthood. In perhaps the single most striking finding from the survey, just 41% of Americans now say that children are **"very important"** to a successful marriage, down sharply from the 65% who said this in a 1990 survey. Indeed, children have fallen to eighth out of nine on a list of items that people associate with successful marriages – well behind **"sharing household chores," "good housing," "adequate income," "happy sexual relationship,"** and **"faithfulness."** Back in 1990, when the American public was given this same list on a World Values Survey, children ranked third in importance. The new Pew survey also found that, by a margin of nearly three-to-one, Americans say that the main purpose of marriage is the **"mutual happiness and fulfillment"** of adults rather than the **"bearing and raising of children."** In downgrading the importance of children to marriage, public opinion both reflects and facilitates the upheavals in marital and parenting patterns that have taken place over the past several decades.

Divorce is hard on everyone. The damage divorce causes to children is usually worse than the damage caused by living in a two-parent home with marital difficulties. This is contrary to the popular belief that children are better off if their parents' divorce rather than live together. Some children are never told by their mothers or fathers that they are even having problems until they get divorced, but children can feel the tension. At best, marriage is now seen as a fragile promise. I have been blessed to speak with young people across this country over the last 20 years. The young people I talk to are afraid of **"commitment"** because they have seen so little of it from their parents and peers. How can we expect young people to give their hearts and be willing to trust and love, when their own lives have been traumatized, sometimes by multiple losses of family cohesion and stability as their parents marry, divorce, shack-up, move on, again and again? Consequently, these frightened but lonely, needy, and somewhat hopeful young adults are shacking-up. Contrary to their hope of finding the right one through this trial period, the statistics show elevated depression and anxiety, infidelity, violence, and a greater rate of breakup inside or out of a marital relationship. Unfortunately, too many children are born into these even more fragile relationships, only to suffer the loss and hurt along with their parents. This generation is the product of rampant selfishness and devaluation of vows, obligations, and sacrifice for some greater good. They are the generation who watched their parents' infidelities, divorces, drug and alcohol abuse, selfish pursuits, materialism, and basic immaturity. For many, this kind of thinking is the norm, not the anomaly as it should be. One young person shares, *"I have talked to many of my friends whose parents are divorced. They* *tell me they feel personally flawed because the legacy of their parents' divorce scars them in some way that says they are part of a lineage of people who can't follow through, are capable of making huge mistakes, and who walk out when things get tough. They all doubt their ability to spot and maintain love, because they see that their parents thought they were in love, and it didn't 'work out' for them."*

My teacher shared this with every man and woman in the process of marriage; we don't realize the pain in our children when we contemplate divorce. When children love a mother and love a father, one of the most traumatic things in a child's life is to have to choose between two people whom they love. If the child goes on one side it's like they have betrayed the other and if you take moms side against dads, dad doesn't like it. You take dads side against mom, mom don't like it. It's a heck of a thing.

How Divorce has affected other children and how it will affect yours if you get divorced...

"I was real young. I didn't know what was going on. I knew Dad was missing, but I didn't know why."
Eight-year-old girl

"I was very mad at my father and I wanted him to die so I could remember him the way he was before he left us, not what he had turned into."
Nine-year-old boy

"My dad didn't leave us. My mom took me while I was sleeping and she left him. I didn't even know about it."
Five-year-old girl

"I currently reside with my grandparents. I have lived with them since I was nine. My mom and dad have both divorced three times. I went through the first divorce and my mom's second divorce. My grandparents sheltered me from the other divorces."
Eighteen-year-old boy

My teacher shared that there are certain things that a man needs and there are certain things that a woman needs. And if these needs are not met in the education and training of the male and the female when they mature they will not relate to one another as they should and as a result you'll have the madness that we have today between male and female and a high divorce rate and the breakup of the family because we do not know how to relate one to the other. We don't know how to relate to our own natures and most of us don't even know what our nature is. He shared that there was a time in America where in all of the schools from the fourth grade through the twelfth, the female learned academics but she also learned the art of home-making. Whether we like it or not the female is the cornerstone of family and home and family is the cornerstone of community and nature.

Young girls used to have to learn how to cook but if we look in our communities today, many don't know how to cook. So Sara Lee is cooking for us. We don't know what Sara Lee's kitchen looks like but she's cooking for us. Many of us simply don't take the time to prepare a decent meal for our family, like Grandma used to do. So we just pop it in the nuclear blast or the microwave and in three minutes we can get it out and feed it to our family. We are eating all of this trash and actually wondering why cancer is proliferating in the community. The merchants of death are feeding us because we don't know how to cook anymore. We don't know how to shop anymore. We don't know how to sew anymore. When there was a time in America when a young girl knew the art of homemaking. So the clothing merchants have us at their mercy. They give our women dresses up by their thighs and charge our women five hundred dollars for it. Please don't dress to tempt men. Be mindful of the way you walk out of your home. Ask yourself, **"Will this tempt men to see me in a sexual way?"** This is an extremely sick society we live in -- A society where little young girls and boys are being molested every day. It used to be a time when a woman would dress up to go outside and take off her clothes when she came inside. Now the exact opposite seems to be true. Women take off their clothes to come outside and put on clothes when they go inside. A woman closes her window at night and locks it, closes the blinds and the curtains, then closes her bedroom door, puts on a full set of pajamas, and then gets under the covers to go to bed and then wakes up in the morning and puts on a mini – skirt to come out in public. One of the reasons that our grandmothers used to wear those long dresses was to say to grandpapa that all that was under that long dress or skirt was just for him. If our women had a sewing machine with that skimpy little material they could probably make one of those for $3.98. It seems as though it was economically feasible to keep black people away from the knowledge of home-making. Then a lot of people could make money off of us.

Here's how it works. *"We stopped learning how to cook and they, Satan and his devils, now cook for us. We stopped learning how to sew and they, Satan and his devils, now sew and manufacture our clothes for us. We stopped learning how to make a peaceful and loving home for ourselves! Satan and his devils now are the divorce lawyers for both the husband and the wife! We stopped learning how to create jobs and to do for ourselves, Satan and his devils, now become the sheriffs, the jailers and the wardens! Why can't we plainly see that Satan and his devils are making a living off of our ignorance, and our incompetence?"* My teacher shared that it's really sad to see people of intelligence train seals and elephants and whales and ants but can't train children. It's really sad to see that foxes have holes and birds have nests but the children of men, the greatest of God's creation don't know how to make a home for themselves and their children. What creature do we know that looks to another creature to provide for it? There are no **"worm welfare lines!"** Worms looking for a handout to get something to eat. God already provided it for them, isn't that something? Something wrong with that Son of Man, because if a bird can build a nest and a fox can dig a hole, but we as Sons of Men have no place to lay our head, then something has happened to us! We have to be reformed! People come to church to listen to the preaching; listen to good singing, give their tithes and offerings and then they go back to the lifestyle that they are living. Very few pastors, ministers and Imams will rebuke their parishioners to make them better Christians better Muslims, or better Jews.

My teacher shares that his teacher, the Most Honorable Elijah Muhammad strived mightily to make something of the Black woman. He taught her how to sew and cook, how to rear her children, how to take care of her husband, how to keep a clean home, and in general He taught her how to act at home and abroad. His desire was to produce a very high level of civilization coming through a reformed female. He took great joy in seeing our women come from a low state or condition constantly improving themselves. My teacher shared that the Honorable Elijah Muhammad also taught women about loud raucous behavior and laughter. He loved to hear the refined speech of the female. He wanted her highly educated, cultivated, and refined. He taught the female how to walk, sit and stand. He showed her, her mother's dressing room that she had not seen in 400 years; meaning He showed her the styles of the righteous women of the East from whom she is a descendant. He loved to see her speaking with firmness to men and never being forward in the presence of men. He hated sisters to speak to men with soft, sultry speech. He taught her, as well as the male, according to the Qur'an that both should lower their gaze when they are in each other's company. He dressed the female in such a way that men could not know the beauty of their form, but, would only become acquainted with the beauty of their faces and their expressions so that the male would not be physically attracted to her alone, but, spiritually attracted to her as well.

My teacher shared that there is a certain kind of training that a man must have. A home that lacks comfort will cause strain in our marriage and may lead to divorce. This is not something unknown. Nowadays many men refuse to get decent jobs and insist on being self-employed selling trinkets or doing side-work and barely making a profit. They expect their wives to be happy while living in the basement of someone else's house with all the children. Under these circumstances, this woman is forced to cook elaborate meals on a hot-pot with no stove. She is constrained to bathing the children in the bathroom sink. Children will be miserable in a home that they cannot flip and tumble in without bumping their head or being scolded by their flustered parents. This will give them incentive to leave as soon as they reach the age of puberty and they may find friends that indeed have very nice homes but also in which every type of evil is being committed. Ultimately a wife is pushed into an abrasive attitude and a disrespectful tone towards her husband. This is due to the wife being unhappy with the way she is forced to live. She may hate her kitchen even though she must spend plenty of time cooking in it. She may be ashamed of her sitting area and in turn, she will not invite her sisters over to entertain them. Rightfully so, she will complain to her husband who will already be frustrated because he is unable to change the condition of his family. Because he does not have a spacious home to leave her and cool down in another room, he will leave the house at any hour of the night. This creates an even bigger danger because he may meet some people in the heat of his resentment that he might not be open to dealing with. As men we have to work to solve our problem of not having a comfortable place for our family to live. All of us have to pray that our God will protect us from that kind of death style that is so easy to fall into in this day and time.

All of us should be deeply concerned by the growing number of unnecessary and unwarranted relationship breakups based on **"modern"** notions of rights and happiness. Contrary to popular belief, it's not men who seek divorce. Its women, by an overwhelming majority and the reasons for this are varied. Part of it is the nature of divorce laws; you do not even need the other person's agreement to get divorced in some states. Another part is the fact that men tend to have more problems with marriage-destroying behaviors like alcoholism, affairs, and substance abuse that cause their wives to seek separation. About two-thirds of divorces currently are sought by women, and many wives are leaving their husbands because the following assortment of reasons: **Some say that their husbands and they simply are "growing apart," "not happy," "feeling underappreciated," "needs not being met," "differences in changing goals or lifestyle," "boredom," and the old favorite, "find myself."** I'm always amused by this expression, **"I have to find myself."** First, there is the notion of being somewhere other than where you are (some kind of lost-and-found), then there is the idea that you can't find yourself under the present circumstances of marriage and children, and finally there is the epiphany that you can't simply find yourself in the bed of someone new. Truly, you find yourself in your commitments; you find yourself in the eyes of people who depend on you; you find yourself in your dignified responses to life's challenges; you find yourself in your actions and decisions; you find ' yourself right where you are now. This notion of **"finding oneself"** is an intellectually dishonest approach to frustration, a pouty reaction to obligations and routine, and a bratty manipulation of another's compassion and understanding. Why does finding oneself as an individual seem to imply that you must unload significant people from your life like your spouse, and/or parents? The answer is that the most immature part of yourself has reverted back to infanthood-wanting to be the center of the universe without obligations: You get to have, you don't have to give. With that attitude, you will either end up alone, or with superficial escapades, and regrets for a Stupid Breakup. Don't lie to yourself or anyone else. When you feel like it's time to get going, stay put and face whatever it is that worries or frightens you.

What must you be thinking when you put a fantasy aside, your reality and believe that the fantasy will have more depth, longevity, satisfaction, respect, promise, and meaning? The answer is that you don't think-you just imagine; one of the newest and most destructive forces on marriage today is the Internet. Cyber-affairs are costing too many children and innocent spouses the warmth and comfort of an intact home. Both men and women are carrying on in chat-rooms and developing feelings that are sufficient enough to propel them out of their homes and families to be with someone they **"know"** will be everything that's missing in their lives." One husband shared his painful story: He said... **"My wife and I have been married for twenty-seven years. I thought we had a good relationship. We have had our problems, but we always seemed to work them out. To make a long story short, I bought my wife a computer two years ago, and it seemed to make her happy, because she always said she was bored. She had fun in the chat rooms, flirting and having a good time. I thought it was harmless. But, as time went on she spent more and more time on the computer. Well, seven months ago I found out that she is in love with a man that lives eleven hours away from her, whom she's never met. She lies in her bed and cries for him. She still talks to him every day and tells him she really loves him and is going to marry him"**. A study carried out for a divorce website claims Facebook was named in at least 20 percent of divorce petitions in the US last year. And the most common reason is spouses engaging in saucy sex chat with their online **"friends"**. Other social networking sites, including MySpace, Bebo and Twitter, also featured heavily in the sample of

5,000 divorce papers studied. It appears many people are having inappropriate chats with people they were not supposed to. There are many in America who are now saying that Facebook and other social networking sites can be **"hazardous to marriages and relationships."** Some are simply stating that, **"Facebook is the devil."** Whatever we are thinking about it, Facebook is so popular that it now boasts that it has 200 million unique worldwide visitors!

How insensitive and cruel can one be to someone she once thought she couldn't live without! Why is anyone bored in a world like this? The answer is, only because he or she is boring. Bored people rarely think of anything or anyone besides themselves and being entertained, thrilled, titillated, excited, distracted, or being the center of attention. The wise men and women have shared with me that when people say that they're bored in their lives, or bored in their marriage, that you should make them admit that they don't do anything to add to the well-being of themselves or their family - they just want to feel a certain feeling and, in that laziness, think that there is just some other brother or sister who'll just make it happen.

It used to be here in America that women wanted love, attachment, family, and children. But it seems that this wicked and degenerate so called society has diminished the value of motherhood and fatherhood so thoroughly that they have completely beat out of both men and women the desire in a man to provide and protect and for a woman to bond and nurture. Nowadays, many women just find the very idea of marriage itself to be subservient, second-class citizenry and much rather would have a career. When women become "enlightened," they leave the marriage and typically pour themselves more strongly into the rat race. But as one woman shared, **"Even if you win the rat race, you are still a rat!"** How many of us secretly and silently believe that having to provide for your family, or having to raise children, falls into the category of **"being used."**

After a divorce, a woman's standard of living can be expected to drop while a man's standard of living may actually improve. Yet men suffer in other ways. Divorced and separated men are two and a half times more likely to commit suicide than married men. This is partially due to the fact that men, unlike women, are less likely to have a strong support network to share their feelings. Whether due to this need for companionship or not, divorced men are more likely to remarry than divorced women, and they're more likely to remarry sooner. Once a husband or a wife lets the word divorce into their vocabulary, it becomes a part of them and suddenly it consumes them. That couple starts to move closer and closer to divorce, and they become sure that they no longer love each other. All that they can think of is their spouse and what they deserved, and everything that they gave to their spouse freely now becomes attached to the condition that they get something in return. With some of us today, every moment at home with our spouses, all we do is complain that we don't have enough. We spend so much time wondering what's in it for us, that we can't see how much we already have! If only we would lose ourselves in service, then we would indeed find ourselves. It's a fact that we cannot have in life, or from another person, all that we imagine we should, could, or would have. Real life simply has more texture than that. Additionally, can we really imagine being all of what another person imagines they should, could, or would have? No, of course not. Spending one's time in coveting is to lose the moment of appreciation of what we do have which generally includes many blessings and advantages. For example, a woman's husband can't dance to save his life and that may be something she has always loved to do. Yet, that husband would give his life to save that woman's life or her son's life. Somehow, I think that's a pretty good trade-off. And, I'll bet, you could look at your relationship in the same way once we threw away the notion that God put us here to gratify every desire or fantasy that came into our awareness.

Maybe you and your spouse have developed a catalog of personal differences that have escalated from minor skirmishes to major conflicts. They often feel hurt, angry, and misunderstood by each other. They not only disagree but they explode at one another, even in public. These couples have to pin-point their main areas of disagreement. Do you have faulty tactics for dealing with conflict? Do you have ineffective methods of attempting to resolve your differences? Many spouses have become aware of the fact that they have not been giving their spouses the attention that they deserved and need. The solution is so simple; pay more attention to your family. None of us can change the past. But you can change the future when you take positive corrective action. What is needed in many marriages is not a change of partners but a change in partners. There would be fewer divorces if the husband tried as hard to keep his wife as he did to get her. **Being trifling in your Marriage can cause you to get divorced in this day and time.** Judge Joseph Sabbath of Chicago, who has reviewed 40,000 marital disputes and reconciled 2,000 couples, said: **"Trivialities are at the bottom of most marital unhappiness. Such a simple thing as a wife's waving good-bye to her husband when he goes to work in the morning would avert a good many divorces."** My teacher shares that when a husband and a wife have disagreements, if they don't address the reason for the disagreement, the gap between the two continues to widen until the division between them is irreconcilable. Therefore, they have to go before a judge for separation or divorce and then the court must look at the assets that the wife helped the husband to accrue and share it with the woman who is seeking relief. One of the wise men shared that he was in charge of what he calls **"The busiest repair shop in town,"** and added that **"Just around the corner is the busiest wrecking business in town."** He said that the repair shop is the marriage counseling service that he ran as a counselor and that the wrecking business around the corner is the divorce court. That man shared that the major complaints of the over 10,000 people who had passed through his door were listed as follows: sex, money, children, and trouble with in-laws. But that man also shared that he believed that the real problems were selfishness and greed on the part of both of the spouses. How greedy both the husbands and the wives have become in this day and time. My teacher shared from the Holy Qur'an that Allah (God) hates divorce. Before considering the breakup of a marriage, let us look at the biblical perspective concerning this relationship. In speaking of a husband and wife, Malachi says: **"...the Lord is acting as the witness between you and the wife of your youth, because you have broken faith with her, though she is your partner, the wife of your marriage covenant. Has not the Lord made them one? So guard yourself in your spirit, and do not break faith with the wife of your youth. "I hate divorce," says the Lord God of Israel.** Even in the Catholic Church they don't like divorce and if you divorced there was a time when you would be excommunicated from the church and there was a reason for that. Young men and women today and older men and women get into marriage as though it is a joke. Many have taken marriage as a pastime or a plaything. My teacher shares that our word to each other and our word to God is not serious. We have no real commitment. And so when we say for better or worse we mean only for the better. When we say in sickness and in health we really mean and only in health. And when we say for richer or poorer we mean you better have some money honey! When we say till death us do part, we are saying until the death of this marriage then we'll part. We have no commitment to any longevity. We go into marriage with a thought in mind of getting out of it if it doesn't work. We go into marriage with the thought that we will not commit ourselves to fight like hell to make it work. Out in Reno, Nevada the courts grant divorces six days a week, at the rate of one every ten marriages. How many of these marriages do you suppose were wrecked upon the reef of real tragedy? If we could sit there day in, day out, listening to the testimony of those unhappy husbands and wives, we'd know love **"went in little ways."** We walk away so easily from what we promised to stay with forever before the presence of God. My teacher has shared that our women are suffering because of the absence of men. Our women are suffering because we as men have become their older children and that's why we call her momma. And our favorite slang word is you m – f. You understand. And we say that so much because we are really not looking for a wife, because we don't know how to husband. We're looking for another mother. We are in trouble. We've got all kinds of degrees but we have lost the art of simple things to make each other happy in a simple way we have lost that art. Grandma didn't have a television. She hardly had a radio but she knew how to make grandpa happy. And grandpa went out and worked hard and he was trying to be the man of his house even if he was just up from slavery. We've lost something brothers and sisters and I don't think it's by accident. I think it's by the design of Satan and his devils.

In most cases, couples don't try hard enough to stay together. They don't talk about the problems, try to identify the issues, or work them out. And they don't take the time to remember what made them fall in love with each other. Some of these divorces nowadays are caused by materialism. The so called society we live in has been corrupted by materialism. There is competition about having the best car, the biggest house, the nicest clothes - but no one seems to care about having the closest family; the most dinners together as a family, and ongoing friendships with family members. It's true that factors beyond our control can affect how likely we are to divorce, including whether or not you're from a broken family, our age at marriage, and whether or not we lived together before marriage. While these factors can make us statistically more or less likely to divorce, they're not determining factors. We personally have an enormous power to influence and control the course of our marriage. By acting the way we want to feel rather than reacting to the situation, we can stop the deterioration of our marriage in its tracks and set it on the path to healing and recovery. Sound impossible? It's not, but it is extremely difficult. Most people are highly resistant to change. By now, we've built up patterns of negative behavior in your marriage (even if you thought you were doing nothing wrong), and it will take effort, determination, and absolute commitment to change yourself. **Changing yourself is the only way to save your marriage. We don't need any more techniques in how to** manipulate or change our partners or to continue to blame our partners for everything that's gone wrong in the relationship up to this point. Playing the victim will not save our marriages. We cannot abdicate responsibility for marital conflict—even if we don't think we're the one "with the problem." Every marital conflict has two components: the behavior and the response. For something to cause problems in a marriage, **the response to a behavior is more important than the behavior.** In other words, even if we think our partner's actions are causing problems in our marriage, our response to those actions are actually more important to our marriage than the actions themselves. This can be difficult to grasp fully, so let's look at an example. Patina's husband always promises to bring home the groceries that she needs but always forgets to do so. For Patina, this is inexcusable. His broken promises erode the trust in their marriage. She is sorely tempted to react emotionally to the situation and lash out at her husband every time he comes home empty-handed. But she knows that this response will drive her husband away further. Instead, she decides to respond proactively and develops a plan of action. The next time her husband forgets to bring home the groceries she needs for dinner, she doesn't blame or criticize him. Instead, she sets her husband to watching the children, gets in the car, and drives to the store to get the groceries she needs. She enjoys her small outing without feeling bitter. Although they have a late dinner that night, her husband sees that she's not angry with him.

After a few more times like this, Patina realizes that the most important goal in the situation is to have what she needs to make her family dinner—no matter who gets the groceries. Her husband realizes that not having the groceries does indeed inconvenience Patina. As a result, her husband eventually asks her what they could do so that one of them doesn't have to get the groceries during the week. He confesses that he doesn't get the groceries because he is tired after work and hates having to make a detour to the store. Sound familiar? As a result, Patina and her husband decide to plan better and spend a bit more time on their weekend shopping trip so that they don't run out of food mid-week. Patina's response transformed a high-tension situation into a manageable one—even though her husband's behavior didn't change. Was Patina's response an easy one to make? No. She wanted to react emotionally, and it took an enormous amount of self-control not to give into the temptation to blame him or feel resentful. It took time and creativity to decide the best plan of action in the situation. Patina knew that it would have been so much easier just to give in to her anger and expect her husband to change, but she made the effort because she valued her marriage. Similarly, saving our marriages will take effort, dedication, and absolute commitment. It's not easy, but an easy solution is like a band-aid. It will hide the wounds but won't keep our marriage from getting injured again and again. To measure our commitment to saving our marriage, consider this story. One woman often asked people how much effort they put into losing weight. One woman told her that she'd bought dozens of books, tried a hundred and one diets, and even pumped money into a professional weight-loss program. Yet this very same woman had an unfulfilling marriage with a husband who could do no right. **"If you put that much money into weight loss,"** this woman told her, **"why do you put less effort into saving your marriage?"** She was stunned. She'd expected her husband to change to save their marriage; she didn't think that she had to do anything. The real marriage killer is not conflict and it's not even arguing. It's not sniping at each other all the time. It's the loss of love and intimacy. A man and his wife had a fight and because that man was very angry with his wife, he started giving her the cold shoulder and the silent treatment. But before he went to bed, the man realized that he would need his wife to wake him at 5:00 a.m. for a business flight. Since this man did not want to break his silence, he wrote on a piece of paper, **"Wake me at 5:00 a.m."** The next morning the man woke up, only to discover it was 9:00 a.m. and he had completely missed his flight. Furious, he went to see why his wife didn't wake him and that was when he noticed a piece of paper by the bed, which read: **"It's 5:00 a.m. Wake up."** When we stop respecting our partner, we've set our marriages on the path to divorce. Let's look at exactly how it happens and how to prevent it. When we don't put effort into our relationships, love dies. Remember that a marriage either grows or weakens. We should think of our marriages like a plant: if we fertilize it, water it, and notice when it is unhealthy, it will thrive. If we leave it to grow on its own, without any attention, it will wither.

One of the most common marital complaints is that, **"We're not in love anymore."** There are numerous people who file for divorce with the explanation, **"I don't love my spouse anymore."** Where does love go and how can you get it back? Let me address the second question first. If we're the partner who's lost those loving feelings, there's a simple and effective answer to our question. We can get it back by loving our partners. One of the reasons we don't love our partner is probably because we don't really love God who created our partner. We have to learn to love God the way Jesus commanded us, **"To love God with all our heart, our soul and our mind."** Remember, love isn't a feeling; it's an action. If we don't feel warm and affectionate towards our partners, we should ask ourselves a simple question: are we acting warmly and affectionately towards our partner? If not, there's our solution. We cannot maintain feelings of love and affection unless we consistently act in a loving way towards our partners. This means that we listen to our partner. We compliment and verbally appreciate our partner. The best way to compliment our spouse's is frequently! No one should lay a compliment on our spouse like we do because we know them. We should think of a million and one ways to show our partner how much we respect, admire, trust, and believe in him or her. Maybe we should give our partners a card on obscure holidays; maybe we should surprise our partners by washing his or her car, or by initiating a back rub on a quiet weekday night. We may not be able to change our feelings by pure force of will, but we can change our behavior. Luckily, changing our behavior is often all it takes to change our feelings. If we don't love our partner anymore we should love our partners even more. It's not a contradiction. Act out the love that we want to feel.

If we don't want to be divorced then it's going to have to be about **commitment** and **companionship**. Commitment means that we have powerful personal, moral, and structural reasons to stay in the relationship. Companionship means that we and our partner form a unified team against whatever challenges life hands us. Team members may fight, disagree, and encounter stalemates, but they know that their happiness and satisfaction in life depends on the success of the team—not on their individual success. Commitment and respect for vows, promises, obligations, and tradition are much more worthy and predictable building blocks for a good relationship.

What are six predictors of divorce and six predictors that you and your spouse will enjoy a long, happy, marriage in this day and time?

Top Six Predictors of Divorce
Let's start out with the things that you can't change. Some marriages start off with a number of challenges arrayed against them; other marriages have factors in their favor. If any of the following situations apply to you and your partner, don't despair. These are risk factors—not determining factors. It may just mean that you need extra help (such as professional counseling) to work through the issues that you and your partner are facing.

1. You married in your teens.
Study after study shows that age at marriage is one of the most powerful and consistent predictors of marital stability. If you marry before you turn twenty, you are much likely to divorce.

2. You lived together before marriage.
Many people today believe that living together before marrying will test their compatibility and keep them from making a mistake by marrying someone they don't know fully. Despite the widespread prevalence of this belief, the evidence just doesn't back it up. Even though over half of all first marriages are preceded by a period of living together, we shouldn't do it just because everyone else is doing it. Living together before marriage considerably increases your chances of eventually divorcing.

3. Your parents or your partner's parents were divorced.
Children of divorced parents are more likely to divorce themselves (as well as less likely to marry in the first place). This risk can be mitigated if one of you comes from a happy, intact family. If both you and your partner come from broken homes, the divorce risk soars.

4. You have a child together before marriage.
On a positive note, couples with children have a slightly lower risk of divorce than childless couples, if their first child is born seven months or more after they marry. Having a child together before that period will increases your risk of divorce.

5. You haven't been married long.
The first two years of a marriage are critical, and half of all divorces occur by the seventh year of a marriage. The longer you've been married, the more likely you are to stay married.

6. Your annual income is under $25,000.
Money matters. Financial strains often break up marriages, as when money is tight, arguments and marital tensions increase. In fact, the American Academy of Matrimonial Lawyers considers financial problems to be one of the five most common reasons for divorce (along with poor communication, lack of marital commitment, infidelity, and a dramatic change in priorities.)

Top Six Predictors of a Long-Lasting Marriage
If you're facing challenges in your marriage, it may be comforting to know that you have some factors in your favor. These predictors are limited to factors that were set in place when you married and don't include aspects like good communication and conflict resolution skills.

1. You were both older when you married.
Getting married over the age of twenty-five (as opposed to your teens) will decrease your chances of divorce. This is because older individuals tend to be more mature, clearer about what they're looking for in a partner, and have more economic stability.

2. You share the same religion or belief system.
Sharing a religion is a powerful bond, because it brings you and your partner together on a spiritual level and gives your marriage a sense of a higher purpose. When you are both active in a religion, you have counseling and a strong support network available to foster you through difficult times in your marriage. Too, your shared values and life goals sustain your marriage and keep you growing together rather than apart.

3. You have some higher education.
A college degree isn't necessary to increase your chances of a long-lasting marriage, but some higher education will decrease your chances of divorce considerably with comparison to a high-school dropout.

4. Your parents are still together.

If you grew up in an intact family, your chances of divorce are less in comparison to someone who grew up with divorced parents. This is because so much of what we learn about marriage and marital behavior comes from watching our parents. If our parents developed strategies for staying together, we'll absorb those strategies in childhood and be able to use them ourselves in our adult relationships.

5. Your income is above $50,000.

Couples with medium to high incomes tend to experience less strife over money management. They have the financial security to worry less about making a living and more about making a life.

6. You have a child together.

Couples with children have a lower risk of divorce compared to childless couples. However, be warned: the most stressful time in a marriage is after the birth of the first child. That's why it's so important that the first child is born only after the marriage has developed a strong foundation.

You're also wrong if you think there is some one person out there with whom you certainly would sustain a perpetual happy, fulfilled state. You're also wrong if you think that the best of relationships don't go through stages, and phases, and problems, some seemingly insurmountable:

The five Stages of Marriages

Stage 1: *Falling in love.*
Stage 2: *Discovering the foibles, faults, etc.*
Stage 3: *Deciding what to do about this new knowledge.*
Stage 4: *(If you reach it) is the hard work involved in getting through the realities of Stage 2.*
Stage 5: *Is the glorious falling in love at a whole new level of intimacy and commitment.*

Twenty-five Relationship Killers

If your partner is the one who doesn't love you anymore, don't go looking for blame. You cannot make your partner love you again by arguing, tears, manipulation, or threats. The only way you can recapture your partner's love for you is by being a more lovable person yourself. Most of us think that we're easy people to love. Some people mistakenly think that love is an emotion that can be turned on or off. But that's very wrong! Love is an action, and unless it is acted out it will die. As a result, you may be resisting being loved without even knowing it. If you are uncomfortable giving and receiving loving acts, you may be a hard person to love. If you find it more comfortable to criticize than to compliment, you may be a hard person to love. If you shrink away from hugs and avoid kissing in public, you may be a hard person to love. If you show your affection towards your partner by teasing or making fun of him or her, you may be a hard person to love. If you always have to be right and don't listen to your partner, you may be a hard person to love. Lovable people love others. They are positive people. They enjoy physical intimacy and often initiate it. They trust and believe in their partner. They're proud of their partner, and they make sure their partner knows this. Because they are open and uncritical, their partners know that they can come to them with anything. Does this sound like you? Do you want it to sound like you? You may be thinking, **"Those types of people are easily taken for the fool."** It's true. Lovable people can be taken advantage of. But the one place where no walls should exist is in a marriage. Your partner is not like other people. For intimacy to grow, both of you must be comfortable loving one another—both giving love and receiving it. The following relationship killers nip love in the bud. They'll make it impossible for your partner to love you and, as a result, will cause your partner's loving feelings to die. If any of them apply to you, it's up to you to change yourself. You cannot get your partner's love back until you make it easy for him or her to love you.

1. **You're <u>disappointed </u>in your partner.** Your partner can sense when you are disappointed in him or her, even if you try to hide it. Respecting your partner is a must. You cannot have a healthy marriage if you are disappointed in your partner, period.

2. **You're <u>disillusioned </u>with your marriage.** Disillusionment is another marriage killer. You may feel as if your marriage hasn't lived up to your expectations. If so, take responsibility for your feelings. Don't blame your partner or your marriage. If your marriage isn't what you want it to be, change it. If you're disillusioned, examine your expectations. Maybe they weren't realistic in the first place. You are responsible for your own happiness, and blaming your partner for not giving you the marriage you want is a cop-out.

3. **You <u>don't respect </u>your partner.** In some ways, respect for your partner is even more important than love for your

partner. Have you ever noticed how you find it easy to like people who look up to you? When you respect and admire your partner, your partner will feel more loving feelings towards you. If your partner feels as if he or she has to live up to your expectations, constantly disappoints you, or can never get it right, you've failed to show your partner the respect that he or she deserves.

4. You don't like or respect yourself.
5. You don't do what you say you are going to.
6. You let pride get in the way.
7. You always have to be right.
8. You don't listen to your partner.
9. You do things because they annoy your partner.
10. You're dishonest.
11. You have temper tantrums and/or are unable to control your emotions.
12. You are hurtful and put down your partner.
13. You criticize your partner in front of others.
14. You take pride in being difficult to live with.
15. You're unwilling to meet your spouse's requests or compromise.
16. You want your spouse to change who he or she is.
17. You let others get between you and your spouse.
18. You don't fight fair.
19. You want to stay exactly how you are and resist growth.
20. You can't handle stress and take it out on your spouse.
21. You take everything your partner does or says personally.
22. You always see the negative side of things.
23. You refuse to admit there is a problem or seek professional help.
24. You engage in alcohol or substance abuse.
25. You are physically or verbally abusive to your spouse.

Chapter 6 - Secrets of Success on our journey to become married

My teacher shared, **"United we can solve our problems and divided we have nothing."** This is true for a Nation of people and certainly for a marriage. The Bible says, **"A house divided against itself cannot stand."** As we start this last chapter that will share some of the secrets of success that couples have used, I wanted you to consider this story. A man and woman had been married for more than 60 years. They had shared everything. They had talked about everything. They had kept no secrets from each other except that the little old woman had a shoe box in the top of her closet that she had cautioned her husband never to open or ask her about. For all of these years, he had never thought about the box, but one day the little old woman got very sick and the doctor said she would not recover. In trying to sort out their affairs, the little old man took down the shoe box and took it to his wife's bedside. She agreed that it was time that he should know what was in the box. When he opened it, he found two crocheted dolls and a stack of money totaling $95,000. He asked her about the contents. **"When we were to be married,"** she said, **"My grandmother told me the secret of a happy marriage was to never argue".** She told me that if I ever got angry with you, I should just keep quiet and crochet a doll." The little old man was so moved; he had to fight back tears. Only two precious dolls were in the box. She had only been angry with him two times in all those years of living and loving. He almost burst with happiness. **"Honey,"** he said, **"that explains the dolls, but what about all of this money? Where did it come from?"** "Oh," she said, "That's the money I made from selling the dolls." "Well, how much did you sell them for?" "Five dollars apiece!"

Most couples may not know how much they are going to have to put up with and to take in order to have a happy marriage in this day and time. My teacher shares that when people get married, that does not mean they have become united immediately because of some ceremony. Rather, it means that the marriage vows are only the statement of their intention to unite. Immediately thereafter, difficulties arise. The difficulties are generated by our desire to unite in that they bring the man and woman together in a trying situation. While Almighty God created man and woman to incline towards one another and to seek unity with one another, he also made it a difficult thing to do. **The process of uniting through marriage is a replication of the process of uniting with God. If we run away from the difficulties of marriage, we diminish our ability to face the difficulties of seeking to become one with God.** My teacher shares that by our not taking serious our commitment to marriage we don't take serious the commitment to the journey of life. Prophet Muhammad, (Peace and blessings upon him), said **"marriage is one half of faith." Since none comes to Allah (God), except as an honored servant, God has always tried all of His Prophets, Messengers, and people severely in their journey toward Him.** It is these trials and afflictions that are part and parcel of the journey of faith that makes the reward of that journey so soul satisfying. After completing these trials, we become a soul well pleased with Allah (God) and well pleasing in His sight. Since the institution of marriage is one half of faith, then, similar trials that are experienced in the journey of faith are also visited on those two souls that desire to become as one. After completion of many trials, the two become well pleased in the eyes of each other and well pleasing in the eyes of Allah (God). If marriage is one half of faith, marriage is one half of the journey to God. Anything of value presents a difficulty factor. And so the difficulty factor in life itself means that Almighty God had to have created us to face difficulty; not turn our back on difficulty. This is what attending Churches, Mosques and Synagogues are supposed to strengthen for us, our ability to face the great difficulties of life. Not run from the difficulty, but God has brought us into a difficult life and given us the wherewithal with his help to overcome all obstacles that lie in the pathway of our progress towards Him. Marriage is a part of the journey. In marriage, patience is a pervasive virtue. We may indeed have to endure our spouse's immaturity, mockery, and being ridiculed by them for long period of time in the relationship because you truly love them. We have to learn to have the patience of Jesus and Muhammad and to bear patiently what our spouses say. In overcoming the natural force of impatience, we will be rewarded with vision, or the ability to see beyond the present. We will be blessed to **"see"** through our patience that the ends for which we are striving would ultimately come about. God is the greatest. We have to know what we are enduring for in the marriage. Otherwise we will become impatient. Impatience, or the desire for relief or change, may be removed from us, not by yielding to this natural force, but by seeking refuge in Almighty God. My teacher shares that whenever impatience threatens to cause us to turn away from a desired goal we have with our spouse; we must go to our God in prayer. Again, prayer will give us the security and peace of mind that will relieve our irritation. We must keep God between us and our spouse. It is in that frame of mind that we then must re-identify with our desired goal. The desire (and the willingness to be patient in order to obtain it) will then return. Prayer is the re-affirmation of desire. We endure by reaffirming and re-identifying our desires until we reach the goal.

In the happiest marriages, husbands and wives are friends as well as lovers. If you're the husband, you can praise your wife in any number of ways to win her friendship. Just for instance, if your morning coffee is good, then tell her so. (If it isn't, tell her so anyway!) Be generous with your praise. Don't wait until she does something big or unusual to praise her. Praise her for her excellent cooking, her magnificent housekeeping, her beautiful appearance, or her gorgeous new hairstyle. And don't forget to thank her for what she does for you. That's also praise. The two simple words, **"Thank you so much for this or for that,"** can be a real morale booster to a tired and worn – out housewife. Because many of our women are working a job nowadays a husband must be sensitive to this as well. There is nothing wrong with you assuming command of household duties and responsibilities for an evening and letting your wife have the evening off. If you're the wife and you want your husband to be successful in his work, then you can help him by the simple act of praising him for what he does. Praise builds his self – confidence and helps him do a better job. Your praise can send him off each morning filled with the confidence that he can solve any problem that comes his way.

Successful couples are able to spot little advantages that occur every day in their lives. Most folks are about as happy as they make up their minds to be. This principle applies in marriage as well: it is not the responsibility of the partners to make each other happy. People are responsible for their own happiness or unhappiness. Of course it is easier to be happy around a loving, good humored and supportive partner, rather than with one who is aggressive, spiteful and hypercritical. Some spouses believe that their mates are too easily satisfied. They're too content to sit at home, to read a book, and to watch television. What we have to do is attend to our own happiness and allow our spouses to do the same for themselves. And as we stop taking responsibility for our spouse's happiness we will become more relaxed, more outgoing and less anxious. When we take charge of your own gratification and fulfillment it will increase the likelihood that our lives in general and our marriages in particular will be more enjoyable and rewarding. We should not allow anyone including our partners to undermine whatever fun, joviality or buoyant feelings we can inject into our lives. Of course we are talking about all of those things that are keeping with goodness and righteousness. In a happy, successful marriage, people share each other's lives; they don't run each other's lives. It helps to be a good negotiator. Thus, it is no myth to assert that a good marriage requires some effort.

Many times both men and women ask themselves privately, **"Is this all there is to marriage?"** Many times we become angry and resentful at the person or the people who touted the virtues of togetherness and endless compromise. Some couples have to haggle over almost every decision. They disagree about almost everything.

Many couples discover that they have different tastes in clothes, people, art, food, politics and religion even though sexually they have developed a sustained and satisfying relationship. Many couples will admit, **"The only place we really agree is in bed."** They have sex, but they are not lovers. They have a lot of sex but they do not have companionship or mutual happiness.

Successful couples understand that it is a myth that a couple has to do everything together. It's not right for one or both parties in the marriage to exert undue pressures to remain a twosome, and grant the other person very little freedom of movement. Many people perceive marriage as bondage and remain terrified at the prospect. Some people feel guilty when they do things, or go places without their husbands or wives. One person said, **"I don't think it's right or proper for a husband to go one way and for his wife to go another. If they want to act like single people, why did they get married?"** Many couples use coercion and not compromise in their marriages. It is not a good idea to bring pressure to bear on one's marriage partner. Most people strongly dislike being pushed and pressured into something they'd rather not do. The inevitable resentments that arise tend to create marital strife and tensions. Most of the time an acceptable trade off is not even offered. Compromise will win the day for your marriage. Always be willing to compromise with your spouse especially when they may be compromising with you already. **"It's so important to me that you do this, that I promise to get tickets to the next R & B concert that comes to the city."** The result was a new found freedom for both, fewer conflicts and a closer marriage. I love quietness in my life and I'll bet you do to. Sometimes your partner just needs to be alone and by themselves. Sometimes they just need to go off by themselves to reflect and to think. Sometimes they just want to have some dinner alone, go to their room by themselves, relax, take a hot bath, and watch some TV. I'm willing to bet that your partner is truly interested in solitude, rest, peace and some private emotional and physical space. Don't smother your partner by always being in their face all the time. One man sang in his song, **"Everyone needs a little time away. Even lovers need a holiday far away…"**

The key point to a successful marriage is in opening the communication lines between you and your loved one. Communication may be the most neglected aspect of our relationship because we are too busy with work or something else. We have to establish good communication with our partners but we do not want to force the issue on our relationship immediately. When we begin to talk with our wives confidently and without any pressure whatsoever, we are then blessed and highly favored.

At this point, the next thing to do is to spend time with our spouse. If we have children, then we have to explain to them why we need some time off, just the two of us. We should plan a getaway of some sort and rekindle the spark that we have lost along the way. You might choose to attend a marriage retreat with us! www.blackmarriageretreat.com. We have to enjoy our partner's company once more and reestablish lost times together. Sometimes, getting away from the stress of everyday living can be a very good and relaxing way of flushing out the negative aura that surrounds us. We have to show sincerity and be truly sorry for the faults we have committed towards our partners. The part of admission can sometimes be very hard because of pride. But pride is something that can be dealt with if we really know where we want to see ourselves and our marriage in the future.

We have to listen with everything we've got. Listening is hard work. It requires our complete concentration. We need to use not only your ears, but also our eyes to listen. We need to watch for facial expressions; the frown or the smile that can often tell more than the words our spouses are actually using. If we don't listen intently to the other person, we will insult them and turn them off completely. And we will lose a friend in the process. There is no quicker way to insult a person or hurt their feelings than to brush them off or to turn away when they're trying to tell us something. Listening to listen to the other person with everything we've got means putting aside our own interests, our own pleasures, and our own preoccupations, at least temporarily. For those few moments of time we must concentrate 100 percent on what our spouses' are saying. We should focus all of our attention on them. We should listen to our spouse with all the intensity and awareness that we can command. Many times we can learn more by what our spouses' don't say than by what they do say. So learn to listen between the lines. Just because our spouse says they don't want to do things our way is no sign that they do want to do it. The speaker doesn't put everything they are thinking into words for us. Watch for the changing tone and volume of their voice. Sometimes you'll find a meaning that is in direct contrast to their spoken words. And watch the facial expressions, his mannerisms, her gestures, the movements of his eyes and his body. To be a good listener and listen with everything you've got means you'll have to use more than your ears to listen. Look directly at your spouse while they're speaking. Don't be disturbed by anything else. Your spouse will notice your lack of attention immediately and be upset by it. Show interest in what they are saying. You don't have to say a word. Just nod your head and smile when it's called for. That's usually all you need to do. Lean toward the person. This demonstrates a deep interest on your part in what the person is saying. Use feedback to keep him / her going. We can keep the person talking and show our interest by saying such things as **"Oh yes...I see...that's right."** We should ask questions if necessary. All we need to say is something like, **"And then what did you say?" Or "And then what did you do?"** That's enough to keep the person talking indefinitely. Effective listeners use eye contact appropriately. They are attentive and alert to their partner's verbal and nonverbal behavior. Effective listeners are patient and don't interrupt (they wait for their partner to finish). They are responsive, using verbal and nonverbal expressions. Effective listeners ask questions in a non-threatening tone. They paraphrase, restate or summarize what their partner says. They provide constructive (verbal or nonverbal) feedback. Effective listeners are empathic (works to understand their partner). Effective listeners show interest in their husband / wife as a person. They demonstrate a caring attitude and are willing to listen. Effective listeners strives to not criticize, and are nonjudgmental. We have to remember that people are more interested in what they have to say than in what you have to say. They like to talk about themselves, their successes, their families, their hobbies, and their own interests. Use the 5 techniques I've just given you to encourage our spouse to talk and they will feel that they've met, not only a good listener, but also an excellent conversationalist. This kind of behavior on your part will make a positive favorable impression on them. If we can be a good listener and get our spouse to open up and talk, we'll be well liked and popular wherever we go.

Being a good listener in the marriage takes more than being attentive to our partner when he or she talks with us. Instead, the key to strong communication is knowing the characteristics of a poor listener. The opposite of the good listener is the impatient listener, the distracted listener and the selective listener. The act of not listening is not exclusively a fault of men; women do it just as often. It is hard to practice good listening when a husband or wife is insecure about topics that create defensiveness. Some spouses have feelings of being right and their partner are wrong. Some spouses silently resent their partner. Some spouses silently or verbally criticize what their partner is saying. Some spouses are preoccupied with other issues and just too busy to listen. Some spouses are impatient and just not in the mood to talk. Some spouses rehearse what they will say while their partner is talking. Some spouses jumps to hasty conclusions. Some spouses dismiss what they hear. Some spouses races ahead of what their partner is saying. Some spouses builds up strong emotions during discussions with their partner. Some spouses have a huge dislike for the subject. Some spouses feel misunderstood. Some spouses change the subject. Some spouses are judgmental. Some spouses are closed-minded. Some spouses talk way too much and some spouses give unwanted and unsolicited advice.

Good questioning skills may be the world's most unsung talent. If we ask the right questions in the right way we will engage our wives or husband; do it differently, and you'll put them off. Anyone who's ever been married knows how hard it can be to elicit information or opinions from their partner when they've got a case of the **"I don't knows."** By understanding the art of the question, you'll not only get your partner more actively involved, you'll help them learn this important skill themselves. There are three main types of questions. Some are **factual questions.** These kinds of questions have only one correct answer, like **"What did you have for dinner this evening?"** The answer is not always simple, however; it depends on how broad the question is. Sometimes factual questions can have very complicated answers. Factual questions should always be answerable and have room for exploration. Another type of question is the **interpretive question.** These kinds of questions have more than one answer, but they still must be supported with evidence. For example, depending on their interpretations, our partners can have different, equally valid answers to their questions. The answers are not wrong unless they have no relationship to the general truth that you both have accepted. Interpretive questions are effective for starting a discussion. There is another type of question that is referred to as the **evaluative question.** These kinds of questions ask for some kind of opinion, belief or point of view, so they have no wrong answers. Nonetheless, the answers do depend on prior knowledge and experience, so they are good ways to get a discussion going with our partners.

      In general, start questions with "how," "what," "where," "why" or "when." Think that's obvious? When we ask a question, there's nothing more important than generating a true and honest curiosity about the answer. That's why open-ended questions are best for most situations that come up in the marriage, unless we have a particular reason for leading our partner to a specific conclusion or actually need a fact supplied to us. Try to avoid yes/no questions because they're usually a dead end. In contrast, we should ask open-ended questions. We should ask questions that invite opinions, thoughts and feelings, encourage participation, establishes rapport with our partner, stimulates discussion and maintains balance between us and our partners. Since we'll be spending most of our lives together trying to understand each other, we ought to learn how to communicate with each other right now. That's what English is for,' to learn how to communicate; not just to learn how to conjugate verbs!' And to get our spouses to communicate, we will have to ask them for their own ideas and opinions about just about any number of current topics. Perhaps a useful definition of communication is, **"Communication is the exchange of information by any means possible".** *To want to communicate, people need to have a positive* *relationship with a familiar person. It must be an understanding, warm and supportive relationship.* Who was your best example of how to communicate with a woman? Who was your worst example? What did they teach you to do to communicate with a woman? Who was your example of how to communicate with a man? What did they teach you to do to communicate with a man? What are the hardest issues to communicate to your partner in your marriage? What do you talk about most with your partner? What do you talk about least? What was the worst thing you ever heard a man say to a woman or a woman say to a man? How do you generally communicate to your partner that you want some of their attention? How does your partner communicate to you that they want some of your attention? You want to be intimate with your partner. They do not want the same. How do they reject your unwanted sexual advances? Your partner is in the mood to be intimate with you. You do not want the same. How do you reject their unwanted sexual advances? *Communication is a highly effective way of getting what we want. Have we taken the time to state in one word what we want most from our partners? Have we told our spouse what we really need from them this year? Why or why not?*

We are still talking about communication with our spouses. Our minds don't see the words that a person is speaking unless that person is skilled at painting a picture with words that you know. Because of this problem we may be just be responding to the emotion or the passion of their words more than the actual content of what's being said. That's important to know. It's important to not just move off emotions, to not move off of feelings. We want to understand our partners as deeply as possible. Sometimes when your partner says something that we believe is significant – Write it down. Don't rely on your memory. It can and will fail you from time to time. And when in the heat of discussion it is sometimes better not to respond. A man or woman cannot argue by himself or herself. Sometimes our partner will try to bait us into an argument. Have you experienced this? Have you done this? They may say things to tick us off or to get us all riled up. We have to grow to recognize when we are being set – up. And we don't have to announce that we recognize that it is a set – up. Announcing it just makes the person come at us from a different way. Just be quiet for a few minutes. Watch your partner. Watch the emotions that are being represented. You don't hate this person. You love this person. So listen to the argument that they are trying to draw you into. This is a different strategy that I am sharing with you. You don't have to respond! You don't have to get the last word in. Someone has to be the adult. We don't have to debate our partners. In a debate there are winners and losers. If someone has to win the argument, let it be your partner. No one is keeping score. Again, when we argue the spirit and the peace of

God departs from us. And we all feel so terrible when our peace is broken. So sit there and watch your partner rant and rave. And after a while you will hear their voice gradually come down from being so high up there and their good sense will return. When their good sense returns don't respond. Let them settle down a little more. And then maybe the next day or so you might address them in a very dignified and civilized tone, **"Honey, do you really have to speak to me like you did yesterday to represents your concerns to me? Do I really deserve that?"** They may try to turn that into an argument. Don't accept the challenge. Be committed to a no arguing policy in your marriage and in your relationship. Some of us just like to argue. This is the way we have come up in our lives observing the way our mothers and fathers communicated with each other. Our partner may have accepted that as the only way to communicate with a person – To argue with them. I once heard that whenever you see two people arguing, the one who is the loudest is the one who is wrong. Remember, it takes two to make a quarrel, and the one in the wrong usually is the one who does the most talking. So even if you are engaged in intense conversation remember this from my teacher, **"The truth is still the truth even when it is whispered"**.

Part of the communication process is taking in information – what we hear, see, read, and experience. The other part of communication is putting out information – what we write, show, and explain. Here is an absolute rule for handling information we pass along to others: Emphasize the positive and ignore the negative. In other words, if we can't say something good about another person or place or an experience, maybe we don't need to say it! When we speak – even small talk – we should speak good news, never bad. It has been said that the human consciousness matures from self-interest (Small people talk about other people) to interest in the world (Average people talk about material things) to an interest in comprehension (Great people talk about ideas.) Everybody would like to be a better conversationalist but so often we go about it the wrong way. Before I talk to any audience I try to get a good feel of my audience. I also strive to keep my ears open and my mouth shut. I find that most of the chitchat that is overheard is negative. There is a place for small talk. It serves a purpose in a world where people are often strangers. But small talk need not be negative talk. Small talk doesn't have to bad mouth cities, colleges or former coaches. Don't engage in any negative, dull, destructive conversation that is in poor taste. Small talk always has a highly opinionated, pronounced form. Ask good questions to get a good conversation going: **"What is your opinion about..." "What do you think is good solution to...?" "What do you like best about...?"**

Here are some Communication Questions for every couple to consider:

	Statement	Agree	Disagree
1	My way is the only way to see any issue that comes up in my Marriage / Relationship		
2	My spouse should be seen and not heard		
3	I communicate well enough for my spouse to understand me		
4	My spouse never takes anything seriously		
5	I like speaking with my spouse		
6	My spouse only knows how to talk when we get in a bedroom situation		
7	Women have got the devil in them		
8	My spouse doesn't have a good idea of what I am personally up against		
9	My spouse doesn't satisfy my needs		
10	My spouse talks nice to everyone but me		
11	My spouse rarely has anything significant to say		
12	My spouse treats me like a Christian / Jew / Muslim		
13	My spouse treats me like I'm the enemy sometimes		
14	My spouse has cussed me out at least once this year.		
15	I can talk to my spouse when I can't talk to anyone else.		
16	Talking to my spouse is like talking to a brick wall.		
17	I am sometimes afraid of my spouse in our relationship		
18	My spouse is kind of lazy when I think about it		
19	My spouse dominates me.		
20	I wish my spouse would just shut – up sometimes.		
21	My spouse is immature		
22	I have thought about divorcing my spouse at least once this year.		
23	My spouse thinks they are slick.		
24	My spouse is not as intelligent as I		

"What do Men and Women really need from each Other?" - 170

	originally thought.		
25	My spouse refuses to do what I say do		
26	My spouse / partner has made me a very happy man / woman		
27	My spouse and I are the best of friends.		
28	If my spouse would follow the advice I give, they would be successful.		
29	My spouse can't make decisions on their own		
30	My spouse has a secret life much about.		

Ask any adult and they'll tell you that men and women are different in many ways (beyond the obvious physical differences!). Emotionally, men and women often have different needs. Our challenges in understanding the needs of the opposite sex have made books like **"Men are from Mars, Women are from Venus"** bestsellers. Let's take a look at a few things tips on how to successfully romance our partners.

Compliments are a little like frosting – too slick and they slide right off. Too thick, and they're sickening. But a cake without frosting is a little sad; and a partner without compliments may feel the same way. A good compliment can make a partner feel truly appreciated and loved. What then differentiates a "good" compliment from a bad one? Here are a few factors: *Sincerity* – Your partner would like to know that they can trust you. Your partner likes to hear compliments that are clear and specific, that come from the heart. Your partner would rather receive one sincere compliment rather than ten insincere ones. A single insincere compliment can also serve to discredit you, and devalue your future compliments.

Specific – A vague compliment is like that frosting above, but you forgot to add enough sugar. It's okay, but it is just kind of **"neutral"**. Add a specific detail or two, though, and the compliment takes on new value. Compare the impact of **"That's a pretty dress"** with the more specific *"I love your dress. It really brings out the brown in your eyes, and really shows off your sexy body."* Which one do you think is apt to make your partner feel more appreciated?

Frequent – While some partners toss out compliments like they're business cards at a Rotary convention, we may be so frugal with compliments that our partner's end up feeling unappreciated. If you fall into the first category, check out the two recommendations above. If you're in the latter category, you might want to try praising your partner a little more often. Compliments that come freely and more frequently make our partner's feel appreciated and loved.

Unexpectedly – If you find your partner "fishing" for compliments, it may be that you could improve on your complimenting skills. One tip is to offer compliments and praise when they aren't expecting them – as a sign of your love and appreciation for them and all they do for you. Some of our partners say that the only time they get compliments is when they ask for them, or when their partner's want sex. So they are suspicious of all unsolicited compliments. How sad is that? Let your partner know how much you love and appreciate them, and they'll appreciate your attentiveness.

Intelligently – One of the greatest compliments we can give our partner's is to appreciate their mind/soul/intellect. It's far easier to hand out compliments about physical attributes – their appearance, their clothes, their hairstyles, etc. than it is to compliment their intelligence. Next time you have the chance to tell your partner how much you appreciate them for something non-cosmetic, do so. Tell them how impressed you are with their handling of a difficult situation, or their patience in a stressful area, or their creativity in resolving an issue. Tell them how you appreciate the decisions they have made on specific issues. Let them share their day and their accomplishments with you, and listen to the many choices, decisions and frustrations they faced. Appreciating their intellect, their giving nature, their negotiation skills, etc. can help them recognize that not only are you really listening to them, but that you appreciate them as a person, as well.

We really need to practice giving gifts and sharing thoughtful gestures towards our spouses. A heartfelt gift can be an incredibly romantic thing. For those of us on a budget, romance does not have to mean big budgets. One husband left cards for their spouse every day for a week when they knew their partner was struggling with an issue at work, telling them how much they loved them and appreciated them. His wife shared that this was a real source of strength for them as they dealt with the problems during the day, giving their self-esteem a much-needed boost. Sometimes the presentation of the gift can be as important as the gift itself, too. Flowers grabbed in the grocery store and flung at our partner with a **"These were on sale"** comment may show that we care, but a lot of the potential impact is lost in the process. Even an inexpensive grocery store bouquet can be a romantic gesture if presented correctly. We have to learn how to accompany the good we are striving to do with a kiss. We should present the flowers to our partner with a smile, and a gracious compliment. Something like, **"I saw these and couldn't resist getting them for you to brighten up the kitchen. Can I stick them in some water for you?"** will do just fine, if you aren't the naturally romantic type. One caveat – most of our partners don't appreciate having gifts associated with sex. Even if the sex was stunning, we should strive to make sure our gifts are presented as tokens of our appreciation for our partner's giving nature, or our growing love for them, or a wonderful weekend together. We should strive hard to give sincere compliments. Gifts tied to sex can make a man or a woman feel cheap and used; while a gift for the same weekend presented **"because you're always so fun to be with"** carries a far more positive connotation.

One of the most thoughtful gifts you can give your partner is your time and your attention. Listen to them, what they like and dislike. Ask them to tell you about their day, and then listen. Don't' interrupt or tune them out, and don't try to "fix" their problems for them (unless they ask you to intervene). Just listening to them and offering sympathy and caring, laughter and sharing, will tell them that they are important to you. Take an afternoon off and go have a picnic in the park together. Get a babysitter and go out for a romantic dinner, or ask them for a list of five things they want to do and try to hit two or three of them. The most important thing is not how much money you spend, it's the time you spend with them and the fact that you are making them your priority for that time. Most of our partners would love to have more time, attention and interest from their spouses and mates. Although there are obviously exceptions, the fact is that the "romance" fades from most relationships as time and outside demands wear on the couple.

Do you notice how we keep using the word partner? That's what a marriage is supposed to be a partnership. What is the mutual agenda that you and your partner are working on? Is the only time you are communicating in the bedroom for however long the sexual act lasts? Sex can't solve every problem. In fact it really doesn't solve any problems. And if you are not careful it will compound the problems with more unwanted pregnancies. We may not be best friends with our spouse. A best friend is, by definition, one's most intimate confidant. The relationship includes a high degree of openness and exclusive sharing. There are no **"keep off the grass"** signs, no emotional taboos, no unmentionable subjects. Yet in marriage, the continuously close physical proximity and all shared burdens and responsibilities dictate the need for some degree of emotional privacy. Couples need some degree of emotional seclusion in order for their marriage to survive. Our spouses may indeed know everything that we want them to know about us. We have to be wise in this day and time if we want our marriages to survive. It is not wise to tell our spouse all of our woes. It is not wise for us to expose all the good, the bad and the indifferent parts of us. One man told me that his wife knew everything about him. He shared, **"She** knows my worst doubts, my fears, my quirks, and all of my petty shortcomings." Men and women have to be careful about sharing too many unsavory details of their lives with their partners. Many times we build the contempt and the disrespect in the minds and hearts of our companions. They developed that from information that we willingly shared with them.

Twelve Characteristics of Successful Marriages:

Communication
1. Good communication is one of the most important requirements in successful marriage.
2. Poor communication results in increasing anger, tension, and frustration in getting others to listen and understand.
3. Effective communication involves the ability to exchange ideas, facts, feelings, attitudes, and beliefs so that messages from the sender are accurately heard and interpreted by the receiver, and vice versa.
4. Not all communication is helpful to the relationship; it can be either productive or destructive.
5. Politeness, tact, and consideration are required if communication is to be productive.
How would you grade your marriage on the area of communication?
A. _ B. _ C. _ D. _ NI_ F._

Admiration and Respect
1. One of the most important human needs is for acceptance and appreciation.
2. Partners who like, admire, and support each other, are proud of each other, and build each other's self-esteem are fulfilling their emotional needs in a satisfying relationship.
3. Partners who are able to respect each other are usually emotionally secure people themselves.
4. Their approval of each other is what psychologists call non contingent reinforcement, unconditional positive regard.
How would you grade your marriage on the areas of Admiration and respect? A. _ B. _ C. _ D. _ NI_ F. _

Companionship
1. Successful married couples spend sufficient and quality time together.
2. They enjoy each other's company, share common interests and activities, and laugh together.
3. Most people want some separateness in their togetherness. Some differ on how close they want their companionship to be.

How would you grade your marriage on the areas of companionship?
A. _ B. _ C. _ D. _ NI_ F. _

Spirituality, Values

1. Shared spirituality and values contribute to marital success.
2. Religiosity is the most consistent and strongest predictor of marital adjustment. Religiosity is exaggerated or affected piety and religious zeal.
3. Religion contributes to marriage in a number of ways, including social and emotional support, friends and activities to share, encouragement of marital commitment, and increased intimacy as a result of sharing ones faith.

How would you grade your marriage on the areas of spirituality and values? A. _ B. _ C. _ D. _ NI_ F. _

Commitment

1. Successful marriage requires a high degree of motivation: the desire to make it work and a willingness to expend personal time and effort.
2. Marital success is more attainable if the commitment is mutual.
3. The commitment is threefold: to the self, to each other, and to the relationship the marriage and the family.
4. A distinction needs to be made between personal dedication and constrained commitment.
a. Personal dedication refers to the desire of an individual to maintain or improve the quality of his or her relationship for the joint benefit of the participants.
b. Constrained commitment refers to forces that constrain individuals to maintain relationships regardless of their personal dedication to them.
5. One of the hardest tasks is to balance commitment with personal autonomy and freedom
6. Commitment is enhanced if made with an assumption of permanence.

How would you grade your marriage in the area of commitment?
A. _ B. _ C. _ D. _ NI_ F. _

Affection

1. One important expectation of most married partners is that they will meet each other's need for love and affection. However, needs vary.
2. It is important that partners agree on how to show affection and on how often to do so.
3. Both physical and verbal expressions of affection are important.
4. In successful marriages, love grows, but changes over the years with fewer components of romanticism and stronger bonds of attachment and affection.

5. Emotional bonding and affective expression are important ingredients of marital success.

How would you grade your marriage in the area of affection?
A. _ B. _ C. _ D. _ NI_ F. _

Ability to deal with Crises, Stress
1. All couples experience problems and stress. Successful couples are able to solve their problems and manage stress in a creative way.
2. They also have a greater tolerance for frustration than do unsuccessful couples.

How would you grade your marriage in dealing with crises and stress?
A. _ B. _ C. _ D. _ NI_ F._

Responsibility
1. Responsibility involves being accountable for one's own behavior within the context of the family.
2. Successful marriage depends upon the mutual assumption, sharing, and division of responsibility in the family.
3. In marriages in which couples report a high degree of satisfaction, two conditions exist in relation to the division of responsibility: there is a fairly equal division of labor, and gender-role performance matches gender-role expectations.

How would you grade your marriage in the area of responsibility?
A. _ B. _ C. _ D. _ NI_ F. _

Unselfishness
1. Selfishness in marriage lessens each partner's willingness to assume responsibility for the relationship.
2. the most successful relationships are based on a spirit of mutual helpfulness.
3. Paradoxically, the people who are the most self-centered and self-serving are less likely to feel fulfilled and happy and are less often able to bring happiness to others.

How would you grade your marriage in the area of unselfishness?
A. _ B. _ C. _ D. _ NI_ F. _

Empathy and Sensitivity
1. Empathy means the ability to identify with the feelings, thoughts, and attitudes of another person.
2. Empathy is affective sensitivity to others and is important in a successful marriage.
3. Affective sensitivity develops in five steps: perception, experiencing, awareness, labeling, and stating.

How would you grade your marriage in the areas of empathy and sensitivity? A. _ B. _ C. _ D. _ NI_ F. _

Honesty, Trust, Fidelity

1. These old-fashioned virtues are important ingredients in contemporary successful marriages.
2. Partners need to know that they can accept each other's word, believe in each other, depend on each other to keep promises, and be faithful to commitments that are made. They need to be honest and sincere.
3. Research on trust indicates that it is the degree of confidence people feel in their relationship; it is the feeling that the other person is predictably dependable. People who trust others are more dependable and trustworthy themselves. High trusters are more likable, happier, more ethical, more attractive to the opposite sex, better adjusted, and more desirable as close friends than are low trusters. They are not more gullible or less intelligent. When they have evidence that others cannot be trusted, they are not more trusting. Once trust has been violated, it becomes doubly difficult to reestablish.

How would you grade your marriage in the areas of honesty, trust and fidelity? A. _ B. _ C. _ D. _ NI_ F. _

Adaptability, Flexibility, Tolerance

1. Adaptable, flexible people recognize that people differ in the way they think, in their attitudes, values, habits, and ways of doing things.
2. They don't insist that everyone be a carbon copy of themselves.
3. They recognize that life is not static, that people and circumstances change.
4. Adaptability and flexibility require a high degree of emotional maturity.
5. the most difficult people to deal with are perfectionists, who have only one rigid standard by which they judge everyone, who have impossibly high standards, who fear criticism and rejection and so are always on the defensive, and who inhibit self-disclosure and so are hard to communicate with.

How would you grade your marriage in the areas of adaptability, flexibility, and tolerance? A. _ B. _ C. _ D. _ NI _ F _

Your Marriage Grades	Your Spouses Marriage Grades	Average together
1.	1.	1.
2.	2.	2.
3.	3.	3.
4.	4.	4.
5.	5.	5.
6.	6.	6.
7.	7.	7.
8.	8.	8.
9.	9.	9.
10.	10.	10.
11.	11.	11.
12.	12.	12.

The last thing I wanted to share with you as we close this book out is on atonement and forgiveness. My teacher shares that many of us want forgiveness but we don't want to go through the process that leads to it. When we say we forgive, we forgive from our lips but we have never pardoned in the heart, so the injury still remains. God is always ready to forgive us for our failures. Forgiveness means to grant pardon for or remission of an offense or sin; it is to absolve, to clear, to exonerate and to liberate. We are not liberated from the evil effect of our own sin until we can ask God for forgiveness and then forgive others. This is why in the Lord's Prayer, we say, **"forgive us our trespasses, as we forgive those who trespass against us."** It means to cease to feel offense and resentment against another for the harm done by an offender. It means to wipe the slate clean.

Sometimes when we marry and have our children, we choose our gift and our talent and its ability to create wealth over the needs of and our duty to our wives and children. Oft-times as we become "great" in our profession, getting the attention and validation for our gift, skill, or talent, we may find that somewhere along the line we have lost our balance and neglected our duty to our wives, and our children. While we bask in the adoration of our fans, patients, students, clients, and congregation, we may find that we have lost something more precious than what we gained in the world, because, in our blindness, we did not look at life and the needs of our children and our wives from their perspective, and, therefore, failed in our duty to them. This is why people whom we look up to, that have everything in life that we think we would want are very unsuccessful in marriage, and very unsuccessful in parenting their children. We need to seriously think about asking for forgiveness from our family.

My teacher shares that the wisdom of God is hidden in very simple truths that is true on the surface but profound in the interior if we dig. I am hoping that you can give praise to Almighty God for the light of the Honorable Elijah Muhammad as it came to us in this book from his star student, the Honorable Minister Louis Farrakhan and for all the digging we were able to share in this book. God made Adam and he was lonely. He's was alone and he was by himself. When you are alone, by yourself you feel the spirit of loneliness. Adam felt that need for something. So the God saw that and said, **"Well I will give him some company."** So He puts Adam into a sleep and then He takes the rib. And He makes woman. And her job is to help Him and the woman is called Eve. My teacher shares that the rib is that which encases two powerful organs – the heart and the lungs. The lungs enable us to take in the breath of life, the heart pumps the life blood through the veins. Adam's rib stands for the love that he has for the God who gave him the breath of inspiration and he needs protection for the vital part of Himself. The Holy Qur'an teaches that woman is a covering for man and man is a covering for a woman. A woman protects you brother. When you are a single man you're flanks are unprotected. But when you got a consolation and a covering in a woman then you are protected from the influences that cause us to break the Divine law of God. So it is with a woman. The rib is the protector of the vital inspiration and love of God and when we have got a good woman it can be so beautiful. A woman protects our inspiration! The breath means the word of God when it comes into a man it makes him want to stand upright to God. A man can't be upright without a woman. A woman protects our faith. Without a woman we don't know what we are because a woman is the natural tester of whatever is in the character of a man. She shows a man what he is. As long as a man doesn't have a woman he doesn't know what he is. A man can always look good in a mirror but he doesn't look good until he can look good in the eyes of a woman. After she says a man is good then he's good indeed! We can so that so and so is a bad man! That brother is bad! Or we can blow our own horn. **"I'm the biggest boss that you've seen thus far!"** But all we have to do is go and ask our wife. She say, **"Who that negro?"** Now we're exposed brother because our wives know us. The woman has our protection. She's like that rib, she protects our vital organs, our heart and our lungs which are the breath of life and the very pump of life, the seat of our emotions. When we've got a good woman, we are clothed. When we don't have a good woman, we are naked and ain't no fig leaf going to do the trick. My teacher shares, **"If you want to know what a man is, ask his wife."**

When a man has an obligation and a duty to God the woman is given to him to help him meet his obligation. And in order for her to help him meet his obligation she has got to recognize in him that his duty to God is so great that what she wants to do is not equal to that duty to God. So she rearranges her priorities out of her love for him since she came from him, she inclines to him. And she helps him to meet his obligation. The first relationship that we must establish is a relationship with our Creator, Almighty God. That's our primary relationship. Any relationship outside of that is a secondary relationship. Every relationship is an investment of our time, our energy and our money. Sometimes the problem is we have done all the investing and we are not getting a return on our investment. The value of marriage is not that adults produce children, but that children produce adults. More marriages might survive if the partners realized that sometimes the better comes after the worse. Being in a relationship is like a job. You have to work at it and you have to want it to work. How can we expect success in our relationships if we aren't putting any effort into them? Most of us pray for more things than we are willing to work for. We shouldn't pray for rain if we are going to complain about the mud. Pray for you're the success of your marriage. Pray that you can forgive your spouse for falling victim to Satan and his devils. Pray that your spouse will overcome the Satan of their own life and that you will be able to overcome yours. Prayers can't be answered unless they are prayed. The prayers a man or woman lives on their feet are just as important as those they say on their knees.

If this book has touched you and you feel like pressing on then give Almighty God the glory. You may even choose to recommend this book to a friend. If this book has convicted you to want to do better and you feel that you need to confess anything then my teacher shares that the way to relieve ourselves of the burden of sin is to recognize that confession is good for the soul. Do not go to the preacher to confess. Go to Allah (God). We do not have any intercessor between ourselves and our Creator. We do not need any minister, priest, father or pope. Go to your Creator and talk to Him, because He already knows. When we openly confess, no one has to be there with us. If we are sincere and sorry over what we did, we will start crying as we pray. When we finish our prayers, we will feel clean and when we come out of the private place where we confessed our faults, the burden is lifted. We should not go back to that behavior ever, ever again. When we make up our minds and do not go back to that behavior, we are free of it. Let's make up our minds to be a part of a Strong and Healthy Marriage! Let's practice loving each other! **Allah-u-Akbar! God is the greatest!**

If this book has touched you and you feel like pressing on then give Almighty God the glory. You may even choose to recommend this book to a friend. If this book has convicted you to want to do better and you feel that you need to confess anything then my teacher shares that the way to relieve ourselves of the burden of sin is to recognize that confession is good for the soul. Do not go to the preacher to confess. Go to Allah (God). We do not have any intercessor between ourselves and our Creator. We do not need any minister, priest, father or pope. Go to your Creator and talk to Him, because He already knows. When we openly confess, no one has to be there with us. If we are sincere and sorry over what we did, we will start crying as we pray. When we finish our prayers, we will feel clean and when we come out of the private place where we confessed our faults, the burden is lifted. We should not go back to that behavior ever, ever again. When we make up our minds and do not go back to that behavior, we are free of it. Let's make up our minds to be a part of a Strong and Healthy Marriage! Let's practice loving each other! **Allah-u-Akbar! God is the greatest!**

<u>Contact information for Brother Marcus!</u>:

Student Minister / Hubbard Dianetics Auditor / National Motivational Speaker and Trainer / Author / Counselor / Internet Talk Radio / Television Host and Overall Brother and Servant

Mobile Office: 404-542-3808

Email Address: marcusgirard34@yahoo.com

Please, take advantage of our Health Products and Services: www.immunotec.com/respect4life

Join our Social Network:
http://thebrothermarcusshow.ning.com

Catch Brother Marcus Live every Friday on his Intenet TV Show at 11:00 a.m.: www.wain.tv

Subscribe to our Internet Radio Show:
www.blogtalkradio.com/brothermarcusshow.rss

Connect with Brother Marcus on Facebook:
www.facebook.com/BrotherMarcus

(Every day God's gives us we strive to post new links to interesting stories)

Connect with Brother Marcus on Twitter:
www.twitter.com/brothermarcus

Connect with the Premiere Black Newspaper in America and the World and meet Brother Marcus's teacher: www.finalcall.com

Made in the USA
Charleston, SC
11 February 2012